Century 21

SOUTH-WESTERN
Accounting 9E

Multicolumn Journal
Working Papers, Chs. 1–16

Claudia Bienias Gilbertson, CPA
Teaching Professor
North Hennepin Community College
Brooklyn Park, Minnesota

Mark W. Lehman, CPA
Associate Professor
School of Accountancy
Mississippi State University
Starkville, Mississippi

SOUTH-WESTERN
CENGAGE Learning

Australia · Brazil · Canada · Mexico · Singapore · Spain · United Kingdom · United States

SOUTH-WESTERN
CENGAGE Learning

Working Papers, Chs. 1–16, Multicolumn Journal, Century 21 Accounting, 9E

**Claudia Bienias Gilbertson, CPA;
Mark W. Lehman, CPA**

VP/Editorial Director: Jack W. Calhoun

VP/Editor-in-Chief: Karen Schmohe

VP/Director of Marketing: Bill Hendee

Sr. Marketing Manager: Courtney Schulz

Marketing Coordinator: Gretchen Wildauer

Marketing Communications Manager: Terron Sanders

Production Manager: Patricia Matthews Boies

Content Project Manager: Diane Bowdler

Consulting Editor: Bill Lee

Special Consultants: Sara Wilson, Robert E. First

Manufacturing Buyer: Kevin Kluck

Production Service: LEAP Publishing Services, Inc.

Compositor: GGS Book Services

Cover Designer: Nick & Diane Gliebe, Design Matters

Cover Images: Getty Images, Inc.

For product information and technology assistance, contact us at
Cengage Learning Academic Resource Center, 1-800-423-0563

For permission to use material from this text or product,
submit all requests online at **www.cengage.com/permissions**
Further permissions questions can be emailed to
permissionrequest@cengage.com

ISBN-13: 978-0-538-44708-9
ISBN-10: 0-538-44708-7

South-Western Cengage Learning
5191 Natorp Boulevard
Mason, OH 45040
USA

Cengage Learning products are represented in Canada by Nelson Education, Ltd.

For your course and learning solutions, visit **school.cengage.com**

Printed in the United States of America
4 5 6 13 12 11

TO THE STUDENT

These *Working Papers* are to be used in the study of Chapters 1–16 of CENTURY 21 ACCOUNTING, 9E. Forms are provided for:

1. Study Guides
2. Work Together Exercises
3. On Your Own Exercises
4. Application Problems
5. Mastery Problems
6. Challenge Problems
7. Source Documents Problems
8. Reinforcement Activities 1 and 2

Printed on each page is the number of the problem in the textbook for which the form is to be used. Also shown is a specific instruction number for which the form is to be used.

You may not be required to use every form that is provided. Your teacher will tell you whether to retain or dispose of the unused pages.

The pages are perforated so they may be removed as the work required in each assignment is completed. The pages will be more easily detached if you crease the sheet along the line of perforations and then remove the sheet by pulling sideways rather than upward.

Name	Perfect Score	Your Score
Identifying Accounting Terms	22 Pts.	
Identifying Accounting Concepts and Practices	18 Pts.	
Analyzing How Transactions Change an Accounting Equation	10 Pts.	
Analyzing How Transactions Change Owner's Equity in an Accounting Equation	12 Pts.	
Total	62 Pts.	

Part One—Identifying Accounting Terms

Directions: Select the one term in Column I that best fits each definition in Column II. Print the letter identifying your choice in the Answers column.

Column I	Column II	Answers
A. account	1. Planning, recording, analyzing, and interpreting financial information. (p. 6)	1. _D_
B. account balance	2. A planned process for providing financial information that will be useful to management. (p. 6)	2. _G_
C. account title	3. Organized summaries of a business's financial activities. (p. 6)	3. _F_
D. accounting	4. Financial reports that summarize the financial condition and operations of a business. (p. 6)	4. _N_
E. accounting equation	5. A business that performs an activity for a fee. (p. 6)	5. _T_
F. accounting records	6. A business owned by one person. (p. 6)	6. _Q_
G. accounting system	7. Anything of value that is owned. (p. 8)	7. _H_
H. asset	8. Financial rights to the assets of a business. (p. 8)	8. _K_
I. business ethics	9. An amount owed by a business. (p. 8)	9. _O_
J. capital	10. The amount remaining after the value of all liabilities is subtracted from the value of all assets. (p. 8)	10. _P_
K. equities	11. An equation showing the relationship among assets, liabilities, and owner's equity. (p. 8)	11. _E_
L. ethics	12. The principles of right and wrong that guide an individual in making decisions. (p. 8)	12. _L_
M. expense	13. The use of ethics in making business decisions. (p. 8)	13. _I_
N. financial statements	14. A business activity that changes assets, liabilities, or owner's equity. (p. 10)	14. _U_
O. liability	15. A record summarizing all the information pertaining to a single item in the accounting equation. (p. 10)	15. _A_
P. owner's equity	16. The name given to an account. (p. 10)	16. _C_
Q. proprietorship	17. The amount in an account. (p. 10)	17. _B_
R. revenue	18. The account used to summarize the owner's equity in a business. (p. 10)	18. _J_
S. sale on account	19. An increase in owner's equity resulting from the operation of a business. (p. 14)	19. _R_
T. service business	20. A sale for which cash will be received at a later date. (p. 14)	20. _S_
U. transaction	21. A decrease in owner's equity resulting from the operation of a business. (p. 15)	21. _M_
V. withdrawals	22. Assets taken out of a business for the owner's personal use. (p. 16)	22. _V_

Part Two—Identifying Accounting Concepts and Practices

Directions: Place a *T* for True or an *F* for False in the Answers column to show whether each of the following statements is true or false.

Answers

1. Accounting is the language of business. (p. 6)

    1. _____

2. Keeping personal and business records separate is an application of the business entity concept. (p. 6)

    2. _____

3. Assets such as cash and supplies have value because they can be used to acquire other assets or be used to operate a business. (p. 8)

    3. _____

4. The relationship among assets, liabilities, and owner's equity can be written as an equation. (p. 8)

    4. _____

5. The accounting equation does not have to be in balance to be correct. (p. 8)

    5. _____

6. The sum of the assets and liabilities of a business always equals the investment of the business owner. (p. 10)

    6. _____

7. Recording business costs in terms of hours required to complete projects is an application of the unit of measurement concept. (p. 10)

    7. _____

8. The capital account is an owner's equity account. (p. 10)

    8. _____

9. If two amounts are recorded on the same side of the accounting equation, the equation will no longer be in balance. (p. 11)

    9. _____

10. When a company pays insurance premiums in advance to an insurer, it records the payment as a liability because the insurer owes future coverage. (p. 11)

    10. _____

11. When items are bought and paid for later this is referred to as buying on account. (p. 12)

    11. _____

12. When cash is paid on account, a liability is increased. (p. 12)

    12. _____

13. When cash is received from a sale, the total amount of both assets and owner's equity is increased. (p. 14)

    13. _____

14. A sale for which cash will be received at a later date is called a charge sale. (p. 14)

    14. _____

15. The accounting concept Realization of Revenue is applied when revenue is recorded at the time goods or services are sold. (p. 14)

    15. _____

16. When cash is paid for expenses, the business has more equity. (p. 15)

    16. _____

17. When a company receives cash from a customer for a prior sale, the transaction increases the cash account balance and increases the accounts receivable balance. (p. 16)

    17. _____

18. A withdrawal decreases owner's equity. (p. 16)

    18. _____

Part Three—Analyzing How Transactions Change an Accounting Equation

Directions: For each of the following transactions, select the two accounts in the accounting equation that are changed. Decide if each account is increased or decreased. Place a "+" in the column if the account is increased. Place a "−" in the column if the account is decreased.

Transactions

1–2. Received cash from owner J. Nichols as an investment. (p. 10)
3–4. Paid cash for supplies. (p. 11)
5–6. Paid cash for insurance. (p. 11)
7–8. Bought supplies on account from Suburban Office Supplies. (p. 12)
9–10. Paid cash on account to Suburban Office Supplies. (p. 12)

Trans. No.	Assets			=	Liabilities	+	Owner's Equity
	Cash +	Supplies +	Prepaid Insurance	=	Accts. Pay.—Suburban Office Supplies	+	J. Nichols, Capital
1–2.							
3–4.							
5–6.							
7–8.							
9–10.							

Part Four—Analyzing How Transactions Change Owner's Equity in an Accounting Equation

Directions: For each of the following transactions, select the two accounts in the accounting equation that are changed. Decide if each account is increased or decreased. Place a "+" in the column if the account is increased. Place a "−" in the column if the account is decreased.

Transactions

1–2. Received cash from sales. (p. 14)
3–4. Sold services on account to Imagination Station. (p. 14)
5–6. Paid cash for rent. (p. 15)
7–8. Paid cash for telephone bill. (p. 15)
9–10. Received cash on account from Imagination Station. (p. 16)
11–12. Paid cash to owner J. Nichols for personal use. (p. 16)

Trans. No.	Assets				=	Liabilities	+	Owner's Equity
	Cash +	Accts. Rec.—Imagination Station +	Supplies +	Prepaid Insurance	=	Accts. Pay.—Ling Music Supplies	+	J. Nichols, Capital
1–2.								
3–4.								
5–6.								
7–8.								
9–10.								
11–12.								

Study Skills

Setting Goals

Most of us do not spend much time thinking about the things that will affect us in the years ahead. It is easier just to concentrate on more immediate things, such as the activities we have planned for the day. If we want to control our futures, however, we must set definite goals for ourselves and implement specific plans to meet these goals. Each of us should have personal, educational, and professional goals, as well as a plan to meet the goals.

Some Questions to Think About

To set your goals, you should sit quietly and think about your future. You should determine what you want to do and when you plan to do it. When you know exactly what you want to accomplish, you can begin to make a specific list of things you should do to meet these goals. You need not fear that making plans now will limit your future. It is always possible to modify your plans. However, if you do not set goals for yourself, you will never be able to accomplish them. Your goals should not be the same as those of your friends or classmates. Your goals must fit you individually, and they should lead to a fulfilling future.

Start Now

There is no better time than right now to begin planning for the years ahead. Begin to make plans now concerning your personal life, your education, and your work. It is your future you are planning.

1-1 WORK TOGETHER, p. 9

Completing the accounting equation

Assets	=	Liabilities	+	Owner's Equity
11,000		3,000		8,000
10,000		4,000		6,000
63,000		35,000		28,000

Completing the accounting equation

Assets	=	Liabilities	+	Owner's Equity
30,000				13,000
		60,000		20,000
51,000		25,000		

1-2 WORK TOGETHER, p. 13

Determining how transactions change an accounting equation

Trans. No.	Assets	=	Liabilities	+	Owner's Equity
1.	+		+		
2.	+				+
3.	+, −				
4.	−		−		

Determining how transactions change an accounting equation

Trans. No.	Assets	=	Liabilities	+	Owner's Equity
1.					
2.					
3.					
4.					
5.					

1-3 WORK TOGETHER, p. 17

Determining how transactions change an accounting equation

Trans. No.	Assets				= Liabilities	+ Owner's Equity
	Cash	+ Accts. Rec.—Bowman Co.	+ Supplies	+ Prepaid Insurance	= Accts. Pay.—Maxwell Co.	+ Susan Sanders, Capital
1.						
2.						
3.						
4.						
5.						

Determining how transactions change an accounting equation

Trans. No.	Assets				= Liabilities +	Owner's Equity
	Cash	Accts. Rec.— + Navarro Co. +	Supplies +	Prepaid Insurance =	Accts. Pay.— Barrett Co. +	Vincent Orr, Capital
1.						
2.						
3.						
4.						
5.						

1-5   CHALLENGE PROBLEM, p. 22

Determining how transactions change an accounting equation

1.

Trans. No.	Assets				= Liabilities +	Owner's Equity
	Cash	Accts. Rec.— + Mary Lou Pier +	Supplies +	Prepaid Insurance	Accts. Pay.— = Kollasch Co. +	Zachary Martin, Capital
Beg. Bal. 1.	8,552	1,748	1,485	615	3,145	9,255
New Bal. 2.						
New Bal. 3.						
New Bal. 4.						
New Bal.						

2.

_____
_____
_____
_____
_____
_____
_____
_____
_____
_____
_____
_____
_____
_____
_____
_____

Study Guide 2

Name	Perfect Score	Your Score
Identifying Accounting Terms	5 Pts.	
Analyzing Transactions into Debit and Credit Parts	20 Pts.	
Identifying Changes in Accounts	15 Pts.	
Total	40 Pts.	

Part One—Identifying Accounting Terms

Directions: Select the one term in Column I that best fits each definition in Column II. Print the letter identifying your choice in the Answers column.

Column I	Column II	Answers
A. chart of accounts	1. An accounting device used to analyze transactions. (p. 29)	1. _____
B. credit	2. An amount recorded on the left side of a T account. (p. 29)	2. _____
C. debit	3. An amount recorded on the right side of a T account. (p. 29)	3. _____
D. normal balance	4. The side of the account that is increased. (p. 29)	4. _____
E. T account	5. A list of accounts used by a business. (p. 32)	5. _____

Part Two—Analyzing Transactions into Debit and Credit Parts

Directions: Analyze each of the following transactions into debit and credit parts. Print the letter identifying your choice in the proper Answers columns.

Account Titles

A. Cash
B. Accounts Receivable—Imagination Station
C. Supplies

D. Prepaid Insurance
E. Accounts Payable—Suburban Office Supplies
F. J. Nichols, Capital

G. J. Nichols, Drawing
H. Sales
I. Rent Expense

		Answers	
		Debit	**Credit**
1–2.	Received cash from owner as an investment. (p. 32)	1. _____	2. _____
3–4.	Paid cash for supplies. (p. 33)	3. _____	4. _____
5–6.	Paid cash for insurance. (p. 34)	5. _____	6. _____
7–8.	Bought supplies on account from Suburban Office Supplies. (p. 35)	7. _____	8. _____
9–10.	Paid cash on account to Suburban Office Supplies. (p. 36)	9. _____	10. _____
11–12.	Received cash from sales. (p. 38)	11. _____	12. _____
13–14.	Sold services on account to Imagination Station. (p. 39)	13. _____	14. _____
15–16.	Paid cash for rent. (p. 40)	15. _____	16. _____
17–18.	Received cash on account from Imagination Station. (p. 41)	17. _____	18. _____
19–20.	Paid cash to owner for personal use. (p. 42)	19. _____	20. _____

Part Three—Identifying Changes in Accounts

Directions: For each of the following items, select the choice that best completes the statement. Print the letter identifying your choice in the Answers column.

Answers

1. The values of all things owned (assets) are on the accounting equation's (A) left side (B) right side (C) credit side (D) none of these. (p. 28)

1. _____

2. The values of all equities or claims against the assets (liabilities and owner's equity) are on the accounting equation's (A) left side (B) right side (C) debit side (D) none of these. (p. 28)

2. _____

3. An amount recorded on the left side of a T account is a (A) debit (B) credit (C) normal balance (D) none of these. (p. 29)

3. _____

4. An amount recorded on the right side of a T account is a (A) debit (B) credit (C) normal balance (D) none of these. (p. 29)

4. _____

5. The normal balance side of any asset account is the (A) debit side (B) credit side (C) right side (D) none of these. (p. 29)

5. _____

6. The normal balance side of any liability account is the (A) debit side (B) credit side (C) left side (D) none of these. (p. 29)

6. _____

7. The normal balance side of an owner's capital account is the (A) debit side (B) credit side (C) left side (D) none of these. (p. 29)

7. _____

8. Debits must equal credits (A) in a T account (B) on the equation's left side (C) on the equation's right side (D) for each transaction. (p. 32)

8. _____

9. Decreases in an asset account are shown on a T account's (A) debit side (B) credit side (C) right side (D) none of these. (p. 30)

9. _____

10. Increases in an asset account are shown on a T account's (A) debit side (B) credit side (C) left side (D) none of these. (p. 30)

10. _____

11. Decreases in any liability account are shown on a T account's (A) debit side (B) credit side (C) right side (D) none of these. (p. 30)

11. _____

12. Increases in a revenue account are shown on a T account's (A) debit side (B) credit side (C) left side (D) none of these. (p. 38)

12. _____

13. The normal balance side of any revenue account is the (A) debit side (B) credit side (C) left side (D) none of these. (p. 38)

13. _____

14. The normal balance side of any expense account is the (A) debit side (B) credit side (C) right side (D) none of these. (p. 40)

14. _____

15. The normal balance side of an owner's drawing account is the (A) debit side (B) credit side (C) right side (D) none of these. (p. 42)

15. _____

Attendance and Promptness

Being in the proper place at the proper time is certainly one of the most important things you can do while you are in school. Attendance and promptness affect your grades. If you are not in class, you cannot possibly get all the information that you need to complete all the accounting activities in your lessons. If you are not prompt, you are sure to miss valuable information.

A Good Relationship

Attendance and promptness also affect the teacher-student relationship. When you are in your seat before class begins every day, you are saying to the teacher, "I believe you have something important to say, and I am ready to learn." This is the foundation of a good relationship. When you miss a class, you are in effect saying to the teacher, "I do not believe that the class is worth attending." This is precisely the wrong message to send. You might ask, "How many absences may I have in this class?" When you do, you are telling the teacher that you want to do exactly what is required and no more. This is also the wrong message to send. If you arrive late, you may distract the teacher and all other members of the class. This can result in the wrong kind of attention as well as embarrassment. When some students are a few minutes late, they do not go to the class at all. Even though entering late is not good, it is still better than missing class altogether.

Causes of Absence and Tardiness

There are a number of things that could cause us to miss a class. Serious illness could be our excuse, but it is seldom the actual cause. Family responsibilities often are blamed, but the real problem is usually a lack of planning. Sometimes we are not prepared for class, and we would rather miss the class than admit we have not completed an assignment. This can be corrected easily by preparing for class.

There are also a number of reasons for being late. Car trouble is often the excuse given, but in most cases the actual reason is a lack of proper planning. Not enough time was set aside to allow for any problems that could develop. Preparing properly and allowing enough time to get to class can usually prevent absence and lateness. It makes little sense to miss class or to be late. Getting to class on time every day is the easiest part of making a good grade and a good impression.

The good study skills you develop in your accounting class will be valuable as tools to apply in the workplace. Attendance and promptness are key success drivers for all employees.

Name _Matthew Worns_ Date _____ Class _____

Assets = liabilities + Owner's Equity

Determining the normal balance and increase and decrease sides for accounts

Cash

DR	CR
NB ↑	↓

AP - Miller Supplies

DR	CR
↓	NB ↑

AR - Christine Kelly

DR	CR
NB ↑	↓

AP - Wayne Office Supplies

DR	CR
↓	NB ↑

Supplies

DR	CR
NB ↑	↓

Jeff Dixon, Capital

DR	CR
↓	NB ↑

Prepaid Insurance

DR	CR
NB ↑	↓

Determining the normal balance and increase and decrease sides for accounts

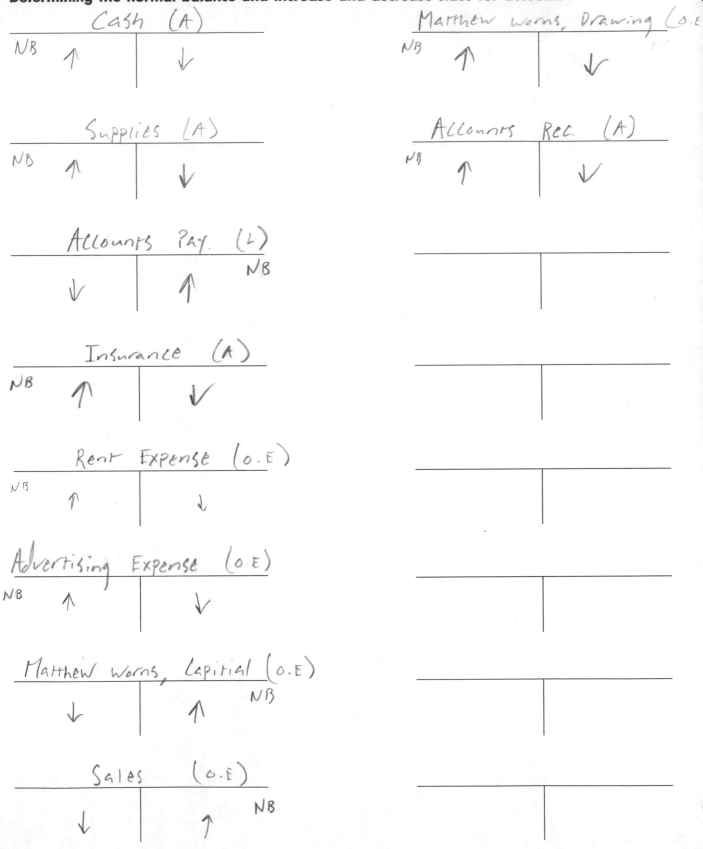

Cash (A)

NB ↑ | ↓

Matthew Worns, Drawing (O.E.)

NB ↑ | ↓

Supplies (A)

NB ↑ | ↓

Accounts Rec. (A)

NB ↑ | ↓

Accounts Pay. (L)

↓ | ↑ NB

Insurance (A)

NB ↑ | ↓

Rent Expense (O.E.)

NB ↑ | ↓

Advertising Expense (O.E.)

NB ↑ | ↓

Matthew Worns, Capital (O.E.)

↓ | ↑ NB

Sales (O.E.)

↓ | ↑ NB

2-2 WORK TOGETHER, p. 37

Analyzing transactions into debit and credit parts

Apr. 1.

Cash

5,000

Kathy Bergam, Capital

5,000

Apr. 2.

Cash

50.00

Supplies

50.00

Apr. 5.

Cash

75.00

Insurance

75.00

Apr. 6.

Supplies

DR   100.00   CR

A.P. & Bales; Supplies

DR   CR 100.00

Apr. 9.

Cash

50.00

AP - Bales Supplies

50.00

Analyzing transactions into debit and credit parts

Sept. 1.

_____|_____
                |
                |
                |
_____|_____
                |
                |
                |
                |

Sept. 4.

_____|_____
                |
                |
                |
                |
_____|_____
                |
                |
                |

Sept. 5.

_____|_____
                |
                |
                |
                |
                |
_____|_____
                |
                |
                |
_____|_____
                |
                |
                |

Sept. 6.

_____|_____
                |
                |
                |
_____|_____
                |
                |
                |
                |

Sept. 11.

_____|_____
                |
                |
                |
_____|_____
                |
                |
                |
_____|_____
                |
                |
                |

2-3 WORK TOGETHER, p. 44

Analyzing revenue, expense, and withdrawal transactions into debit and credit parts

Apr. 10.

Apr. 18.

Apr. 11.

Apr. 20.

Apr. 14.

Analyzing revenue, expense, and withdrawal transactions into debit and credit parts

Sept. 13.

Sept. 18.

Sept. 15.

Sept. 21.

Sept. 16.

Study Guide 3

Part One—Identifying Accounting Terms

Directions: Select the one term in Column I that best fits each definition in Column II. Print the letter identifying your choice in the Answers column.

Column I	Column II	Answers
A. check	1. A form for recording transactions in chronological order. (p. 56)	1. _F_
B. double-entry accounting	2. Recording transactions in a journal. (p. 56)	2. _G_
C. entry	3. A journal amount column headed with an account title. (p. 57)	3. _M_
D. general amount column	4. A journal amount column that is not headed with an account title. (p. 57)	4. _D_
E. invoice	5. Information for each transaction recorded in a journal. (p. 57)	5. _C_
F. journal	6. The recording of debit and credit parts of a transaction. (p. 57)	6. _B_
G. journalizing	7. A business paper from which information is obtained for a journal entry. (p. 57)	7. _L_
H. memorandum	8. A business form ordering a bank to pay cash from a bank account. (p. 58)	8. _A_
I. proving cash	9. A form describing the goods or services sold, the quantity, and the price. (p. 58)	9. _E_
J. receipt	10. An invoice used as a source document for recording a sale on account. (p. 58)	10. _K_
K. sales invoice	11. A business form giving written acknowledgment for cash received. (p. 59)	11. _J_
L. source document	12. A form on which a brief message is written describing a transaction. (p. 59)	12. _H_
M. special amount column	13. Determining that the amount of cash agrees with the accounting records. (p. 76)	13. _I_

Part Two—Identifying Accounting Concepts and Practices

Directions: Place a *T* for True or an *F* for False in the Answers column to show whether each of the following statements is true or false.

Answers

1. Information in a journal includes the debit and credit parts of each transaction recorded in one place. (p. 56)

1. _____

2. The Objective Evidence accounting concept requires that there be proof that a transaction did occur. (p. 57)

2. _____

3. Examples of source documents include checks, sales invoices, memorandums, and letters. (p. 57)

3. _____

4. A check is the source document used when items are paid in cash. (p. 58)

4. _____

5. The source document for all cash payments is a sales invoice. (p. 58)

5. _____

6. A receipt is the source document for cash received from transactions other than sales. (p. 59)

6. _____

7. A calculator tape is the source document for daily sales. (p. 59)

7. _____

8. The source document used when supplies are bought on account is a memorandum. (p. 64)

8. _____

9. The source document used when supplies bought on account are paid for is a check. (p. 65)

9. _____

10. The journal columns used to record receiving cash from sales are cash debit and sales credit. (p. 67)

10. _____

11. The source document *sales invoice* is abbreviated as SI in a journal entry. (p. 68)

11. _____

12. The journal columns used to record paying cash for rent are general debit and cash credit. (p. 69)

12. _____

13. The journal columns used to record paying cash to the owner for personal use are general debit and cash credit. (p. 71)

13. _____

14. To prove a journal page, the total debit amounts are compared with the total credit amounts to be sure they are equal. (p. 73)

14. _____

15. Double lines across column totals mean that the totals have been verified as correct. (p. 74)

15. _____

16. To correct an error in a journal, simply erase the incorrect item and write the correct item in the same place. (p. 77)

16. _____

17. Dollars and cents signs and decimal points should be used when writing amounts on ruled accounting pages. (p. 77)

17. _____

Part Three—Recording Transactions in a Five-Column Journal

Directions: The columns of the journal below are identified with capital letters. For each of the following transactions, decide which debit and credit amount columns will be used. Print the letters identifying your choice in the proper Answers columns.

JOURNAL   PAGE

	DATE	ACCOUNT TITLE	DOC. NO.	POST. REF.	GENERAL DEBIT	GENERAL CREDIT	SALES CREDIT	CASH DEBIT	CASH CREDIT	
1	A	B	C	D	E	F	G	H	I	1
2										2
3										3

Answers

	Debit	**Credit**
1–2. Received cash from owner as an investment. (p. 60)	1. _____	2. _____
3–4. Paid cash for supplies. (p. 61)	3. _____	4. _____
5–6. Paid cash for insurance. (p. 63)	5. _____	6. _____
7–8. Bought supplies on account. (p. 64)	7. _____	8. _____
9–10. Paid cash on account. (p. 65)	9. _____	10. _____
11–12. Received cash from sales. (p. 67)	11. _____	12. _____
13–14. Sold services on account. (p. 68)	13. _____	14. _____
15–16. Paid cash for an expense. (p. 69)	15. _____	16. _____
17–18. Received cash on account. (p. 70)	17. _____	18. _____
19–20. Paid cash to owner for personal use. (p. 71)	19. _____	20. _____

A Place to Study

Every student needs a good place to study. When you come home from school in the afternoon, you need a place where you can concentrate on your schoolwork for an extended period of time.

Your study area should be a pleasant place to work with a comfortable place to sit. This is extremely important for your accounting work where you will be completing many problems. It is a good idea to sit in an upright chair at a desk. Lying in bed or on a sofa tends to put you in a position more conducive to sleep than to study.

Keep It Private

Although you may not have a private room, you can make the most of whatever space you have available. If you share a room with one or more other family members or friends, you should establish study hours and study rules. For example, you can set aside a period from six to nine each evening for study. During that time, the room should not be used for any other purpose.

You will probably wish to keep the door closed, and you might even wish to place a small note on the door alerting others to the fact that you are studying.

Be Neat

It is very important that you keep your study area clean and neat. When you sit down to study, if you are faced with clutter and disorganized papers, you will have difficulty concentrating.

If you have a neat and orderly work area, you will feel more comfortable, and you will enjoy your study more. You will be able to find the things you need quickly, and you can use your time to the greatest benefit.

When you finish studying, you should put all your materials away. This will help others who may use the area, and you will be delighted to find a clean desk when you return to work.

Quiet Please

It is necessary to keep your study area quiet. You should not try to study with a radio or TV on. You might think that you can study better listening to music. Actually, you will very likely use more energy trying to concentrate if you are distracted by a radio or TV. In addition, the quality of your work will suffer.

A Good Lamp

You should have proper lighting in your study area. It is difficult to study if there is insufficient lighting or if the lighting is of poor quality. Try to place a lamp close to your work in such a way that there is no glare on your papers. If light is reflected into your eyes, you will be distracted and possibly end the study period with a headache.

Your Desk

It may be necessary for you to share your desk with others. Just as with a shared room, you can reserve certain hours for private use. If you share a desk with others, try to reserve a drawer or two for your things.

Each person who uses the desk should take responsibility for keeping his or her supplies in good order.

Storage Facilities

You will need to keep your supplies handy, but they may be stored in a dresser drawer or in a cardboard box if there is not sufficient room in the desk. You will likely have personal papers as well as school papers which you will need to keep. You can use a file drawer for this purpose. If a file drawer is not available, you can purchase an expandable cardboard file that you can store in a nearby dresser or closet.

A bookcase is an ideal place to keep your textbooks and notebooks. However, a shelf in a closet will work quite well. You should keep the materials together for each course that you take. For example, you should place your textbook and notebook for your English class together, along with any other items that you use in this particular class. In this way you can find the materials you need easily and quickly.

It's What You Make It

Your study environment is exactly what you make it. With just a little effort, you can have a quiet place to study where you can get your work done quickly with minimum effort. A proper study area can help you make the kind of grades you want.

3-1, 3-2, 3-3, and 3-4 WORK TOGETHER, pp. 62, 66, 72, 78

3-1 Journalizing entries in a five-column journal
3-2 Journalizing entries in a five-column journal
3-3 Journalizing transactions that affect owner's equity in a five-column journal
3-4 Proving and ruling a journal

JOURNAL

PAGE 1

	DATE	ACCOUNT TITLE	DOC. NO.	POST. REF.	GENERAL DEBIT	GENERAL CREDIT	SALES CREDIT	CASH DEBIT	CASH CREDIT
1	2015 Apr. 1	Norm Derner, Capital	R1			1 500 00		1 500 00	
2	2	Supplies	C1		375 00				375 00
3	5	Supplies	M1		500 00				
4		Accts. Pay. - Palm Supply				500 00			
5	7	Prepaid Insurance	C2		300 00				300 00
6	9	Accts. Pay. - Palm Supply	C3		250 00				250 00
7	12	Rent Expense	C4		1 000 00				1 000 00
8	13	✓	T13				2 500 00	2 500 00	
9	14	Accts. Rec. - L. Rohe	S1		510 00		510 00		
10	15	Utilities Expense	C5		148 00				148 00
11	20	Accts. Rec. - L. Rohe	R2			255 00		255 00	
12	21	Norm Derner, Drawing	C6		1 000 00				1 000 00
13	23	Accts. Rec. - L. Rohe	S2		375 00		375 00		
14	27	Norm Derner, Drawing	C7		500 00				500 00
15	27	Carried forward	✓		4 958 00	2 255 00	3 385 00	4 255 00	3 573 00

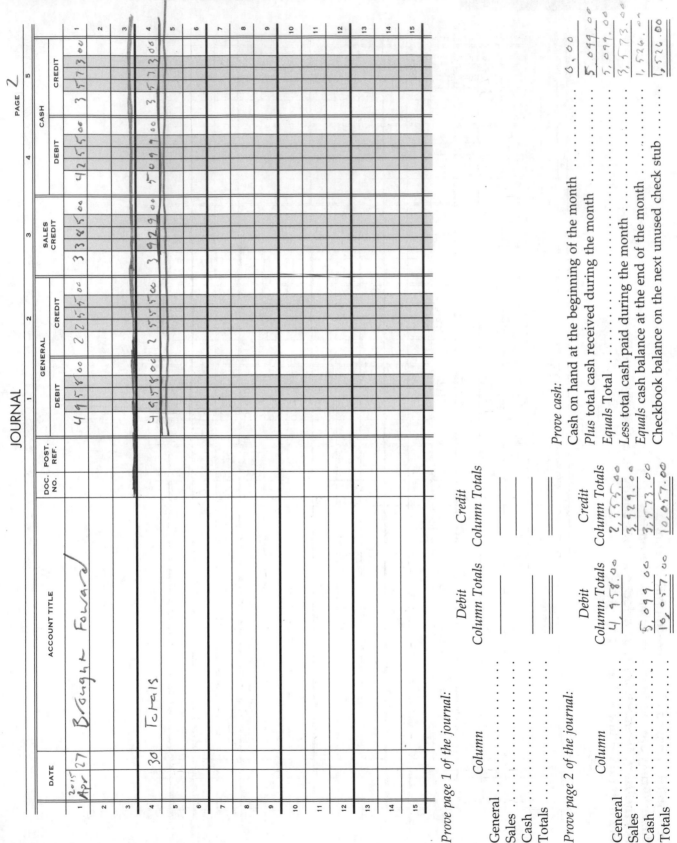

JOURNAL

PAGE 2

DATE	ACCOUNT TITLE	DOC. NO.	POST. REF.	GENERAL DEBIT	GENERAL CREDIT	SALES CREDIT	CASH DEBIT	CASH CREDIT
2015 Apr 27	Brought Foward			4 958 00	2 255 00	3 385 00	4 255 00	3 573 00
30	Totals			4 958 00	2 555 00	3 929 00	7 097 00	3 573 00

Prove page 1 of the journal:

Column	Debit Column Totals	Credit Column Totals
General		
Sales		
Cash		
Totals		

Prove page 2 of the journal:

Column	Debit Column Totals	Credit Column Totals
General	4 958.00	2 555.00
Sales		3 929.00
Cash	5 099.00	3 573.00
Totals	10 057.00	10 057.00

Prove cash:

Cash on hand at the beginning of the month 0.00
Plus total cash received during the month 5 099.00
Equals Total 5 099.00
Less total cash paid during the month 3 573.00
Equals cash balance at the end of the month 1 526.00
Checkbook balance on the next unused check stub 1 526.00

3-1, 3-2, 3-3, and 3-4 ON YOUR OWN, pp. 62, 66, 72, 78

3-1 Journalizing entries in a five-column journal
3-2 Journalizing entries in a five-column journal
3-3 Journalizing transactions that affect owner's equity in a five-column journal
3-4 Proving and ruling a journal

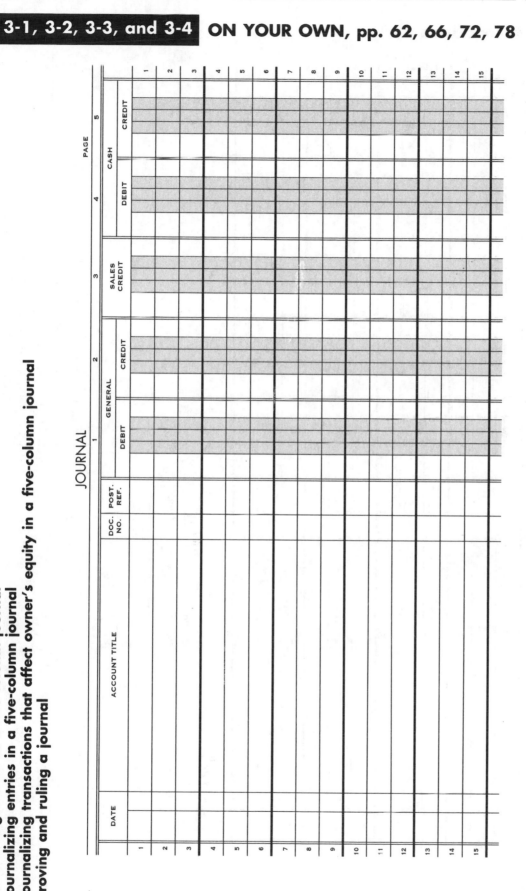

JOURNAL

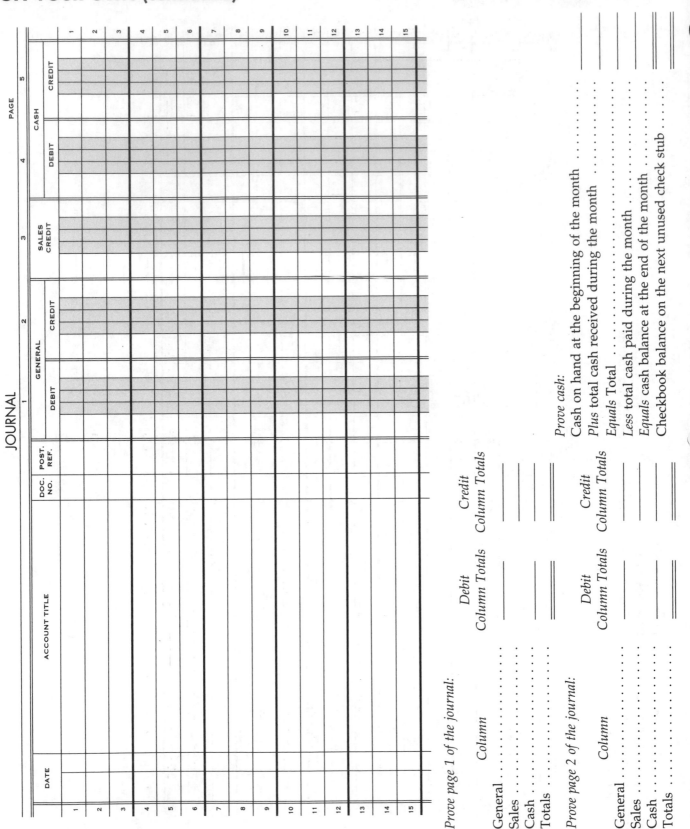

Prove page 1 of the journal:

Column	Debit Column Totals	Credit Column Totals
General		
Sales		
Cash		
Totals		

Prove page 2 of the journal:

Column	Debit Column Totals	Credit Column Totals
General		
Sales		
Cash		
Totals		

Prove cash:

Cash on hand at the beginning of the month ....

Plus total cash received during the month ....

Equals Total ....

Less total cash paid during the month ....

Equals cash balance at the end of the month ....

Checkbook balance on the next unused check stub ....

USING SOURCE DOCUMENTS, p. 85

Journalizing transactions and proving and ruling a journal

Receipt No. __1__	Receipt No. __1__ Form __1__
Date _May 1_ , 20--	Date _May 1_ _____ 20--
From _Cy Sawyer_	Rec'd from _Cy Sawyer_
For _Investment_	For _Investment_
	Five Thousand & ⁿᵒ/100 Dollars
$ 5,000 00	Amount $ 5,000 00
	_CS_
	Received by

NO. _1_		Form _2_
Date: _5/3_ 20 -- $ _200.00_		
To: _National Supply Co._		
For: _Supplies_		
BAL. BRO'T. FOR'D		0 | 00
AMT. DEPOSITED	_5—1_	5000 | 00
SUBTOTAL		5000 | 00
AMT. THIS CHECK		200 | 00
BAL. CAR'D. FOR'D		4800 | 00

NO. _2_		Form _3_
Date: _5/5_ 20 -- $ _500.00_		
To: _SW Management Co._		
For: _May Rent_		
BAL. BRO'T. FOR'D		4800 | 00
AMT. DEPOSITED		
SUBTOTAL		4800 | 00
AMT. THIS CHECK		500 | 00
BAL. CAR'D. FOR'D		4300 | 00

No. _1_	Form _4_
MEMORANDUM	

Bought supplies on account from
Atlas Supplies, $550.00

Signed: _CS_ Date: _5/8/--_

NO. 3	Form 5
Date: 5/9 20-- $ 75.00	
To: City Electric	
For: Electric bill	

BAL. BRO'T. FOR'D	4300	00
AMT. DEPOSITED		
SUBTOTAL	4300	00
AMT. THIS CHECK	75	00
BAL. CAR'D. FOR'D	4225	00

NO. 4	Form 6
Date: 5/11 20-- $ 350.00	
To: Atlas Supplies	
For: Payment on account	

BAL. BRO'T. FOR'D	4225	00
AMT. DEPOSITED		
SUBTOTAL	4225	00
AMT. THIS CHECK	350	00
BAL. CAR'D. FOR'D	3875	00

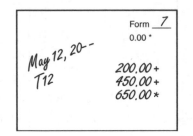

Form 7

0.00 *

May 12, 20--
T12

200.00 +
450.00 +
650.00 *

CRS				
Cy's Repair Service	Sold to:	J. Hutton	Form	8
4814 Central Avenue		199 Park Drive	No.	1
Great Falls, MT 59405-6184		Great Falls, MT 59401-9043	Date	5/15/--
			Terms	2/10, n/30

Description	Amount
Repair condenser unit	500.00
Repair motor	300.00
Repair generator	400.00
Total	1,200.00

USING SOURCE DOCUMENTS (continued)

NO. 5   Form   9
Date: 5/16   20 -- $ 175.00
To: Pineridge
    Insurance Co.
For: Insurance

BAL. BRO'T. FOR'D		3875	00
AMT. DEPOSITED	5—12	650	00
SUBTOTAL		4525	00
AMT. THIS CHECK		175	00
BAL. CAR'D. FOR'D		4350	00

Form 10
0.00 *

May 19, 20--
T19   150.00 +
                 214.00 +
                 294.00 +
                 658.00 *

NO. 6   Form   11
Date: 5/23   20 -- $ 45.00
To: Sunset Delivery Co.

For: Miscellaneous
     Expense

BAL. BRO'T. FOR'D		4350	00
AMT. DEPOSITED	5—19	658	00
SUBTOTAL		5008	00
AMT. THIS CHECK		45	00
BAL. CAR'D. FOR'D		4963	00

Form 12
0.00 *

May 26, 20--
T26   307.00 +
                 323.00 +
                 630.00 *

NO. 7   Form   13
Date: 5/29   20 -- $ 20.00
To: Foothills Cleaning Co.

For: Miscellaneous
     Expense

BAL. BRO'T. FOR'D		4963	00
AMT. DEPOSITED	5—26	630	00
SUBTOTAL		5593	00
AMT. THIS CHECK		20	00
BAL. CAR'D. FOR'D		5573	00

USING SOURCE DOCUMENTS (continued)

Receipt No. _2_

Date _May 29_ , 20--

From _J. Hutton_

For _On Account_

_____

$ | 1,000 | 00

Receipt No. _2_   Form _14_

Date _May 29_ _____ 20--

Rec'd from _J. Hutton_

For _On Account_

One thousand & ⁿᵒ/100 _____ Dollars

Amount $ | 1,000 | 00

_CS_
Received by

NO. _8_   Form _15_

Date: _5/29_   20 -- $ _50.00_ _____

To: _Great Falls Telephone_
_____ _Company_

For: _Telephone_
_____ _bill_

BAL. BRO'T. FOR'D		5573	00
AMT. DEPOSITED	5—29	1000	00
SUBTOTAL		6573	00
AMT. THIS CHECK		50	00
BAL. CAR'D. FOR'D		6523	00

NO. _9_   Form _16_

Date: _5/30_   20 -- $ _1500.00_ _____

To: _____ _Cy Sawyer_ _____

For: _Owner_
_____ _withdrawal_

BAL. BRO'T. FOR'D		6523	00
AMT. DEPOSITED			
SUBTOTAL		6523	00
AMT. THIS CHECK		1500	00
BAL. CAR'D. FOR'D		5023	00

Form _17_

0.00 *

May 31, 20--
_T31_   200.00+

200.00 *

NO. _10_   Form _18_

Date: _____   20 -- $ _____

To: _____

For: _____

_____

BAL. BRO'T. FOR'D		5023	00
AMT. DEPOSITED	5—31	200	00
SUBTOTAL		5223	00
AMT. THIS CHECK			
BAL. CAR'D. FOR'D			

USING SOURCE DOCUMENTS (concluded)

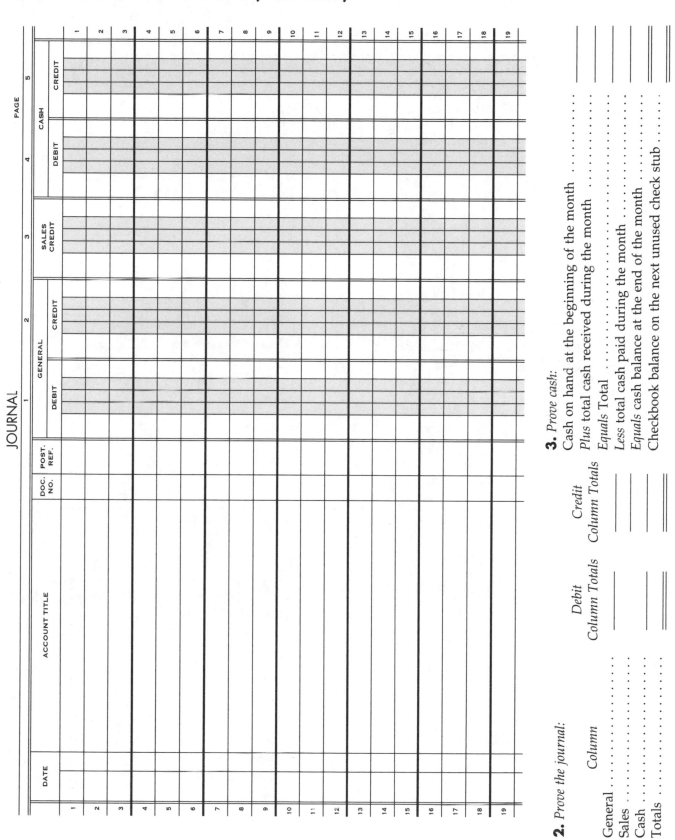

2. *Prove the journal:*

	Debit Column Totals	*Credit* Column Totals
General	____	____
Sales	____	____
Cash	____	____
Totals	____	____

3. *Prove cash:*

Cash on hand at the beginning of the month ....
Plus total cash received during the month ....
Equals Total
Less total cash paid during the month ....
Equals cash balance at the end of the month ....
Checkbook balance on the next unused check stub ....

Name	Perfect Score	Your Score
Identifying Accounting Terms	7 Pts.	
Identifying Accounting Concepts and Practices	15 Pts.	
Analyzing Posting from a Journal to a General Ledger	13 Pts.	
Total	35 Pts.	

Part One—Identifying Accounting Terms

Directions: Select the one term in Column I that best fits each definition in Column II. Print the letter identifying your choice in the Answers column.

Column I	Column II	Answers
A. account number	1. A group of accounts. (p. 92)	1. _____
B. correcting entry	2. A ledger that contains all accounts needed to prepare financial statements. (p. 92)	2. _____
C. file maintenance	3. The number assigned to an account. (p. 92)	3. _____
D. general ledger	4. The procedure for arranging accounts in a general ledger, assigning account numbers, and keeping records current. (p. 93)	4. _____
E. ledger	5. Writing an account title and number on the heading of an account. (p. 94)	5. _____
F. opening an account	6. Transferring information from a journal entry to a ledger account. (p. 96)	6. _____
G. posting	7. A journal entry made to correct an error in a previous journal entry. (p. 108)	7. _____

Part Two—Identifying Accounting Concepts and Practices

Directions: Place a *T* for True or an *F* for False in the Answers column to show whether each of the following statements is true or false.

1. Because an account form has columns for the debit and credit balance of an account, it is often referred to as the balance-ruled account form. (p. 91)

   1. _____

2. The asset division accounts for TechKnow Consulting are numbered in the 100s. (p. 92)

   2. _____

3. The cash account is the first asset account and is numbered 100. (p. 92)

   3. _____

4. The second division of TechKnow Consulting's chart of accounts is the owner's equity division. (p. 92)

   4. _____

5. The first digit of account numbers for accounts in the owner's equity ledger division is 3. (p. 92)

   5. _____

6. The last two digits in a 3-digit account number indicate the general ledger division of the account. (p. 92)

   6. _____

7. When adding a new expense account between accounts numbered 510 and 520, the new account is assigned the account number 515. (p. 93)

   7. _____

8. TechKnow Consulting arranges expense accounts in chronological order in its general ledger. (p. 93)

   8. _____

9. The two steps for opening an account are writing the account title and recording the balance. (p. 94)

   9. _____

10. Separate amounts in special amount columns are posted individually. (p. 96)

    10. _____

11. Separate amounts in general amount columns are not posted individually. (p. 96)

    11. _____

12. The only reason for the Post. Ref. columns of the journal and general ledger is to indicate which entries in the journal still need to be posted if posting is interrupted. (p. 97)

    12. _____

13. A check mark in parentheses below a General Debit column total indicates that the total is not posted. (p. 100)

    13. _____

14. The totals of special amount columns in a journal are not posted. (p. 101)

    14. _____

15. With the exception of the totals lines, the Post. Ref. column is completely filled in with either an account number or a check mark. (p. 105)

    15. _____

Part Three—Analyzing Posting from a Journal to a General Ledger

Directions: In the journal below, some items are identified with capital letters. In the general ledger accounts, locations to which items are posted are identified with numbers. For each number in a general ledger account, select the letter in the journal that will be posted to the account. Print the letter identifying your choice in the Answers column.

JOURNAL   PAGE 1 A

	DATE		ACCOUNT TITLE	DOC. NO.	POST. REF.	GENERAL DEBIT	GENERAL CREDIT	SALES CREDIT	CASH DEBIT	CASH CREDIT	
1	20-- May	2	J. Nichols, Capital	R1		1 0 0 0 00				1 0 0 0 00	1
2		4	Supplies	C1		2 0 0 00 ←B				2 0 0 00	2
3		6	✓	T6	✓			8 0 0 00 ←C	8 0 0 00		3
25		31	Totals			2 0 5 5 00	5 0 0 00	3 4 0 0 00	3 9 0 0 00	2 0 5 5 00	25
26	D	E			F	G	H	I	J	K	26

ACCOUNT Cash   ACCOUNT NO. 110

	DATE		ITEM	POST. REF.	DEBIT	CREDIT	BALANCE DEBIT	BALANCE CREDIT
	1	2		3	4			
						5		

ACCOUNT Supplies   ACCOUNT NO. 120

	DATE		ITEM	POST. REF.	DEBIT	CREDIT	BALANCE DEBIT	BALANCE CREDIT
	6	7		8	9			

ACCOUNT Sales   ACCOUNT NO. 410

	DATE		ITEM	POST. REF.	DEBIT	CREDIT	BALANCE DEBIT	BALANCE CREDIT
	10	11		12		13		

A through F (pp. 96–100)

G through K (pp. 101–103)

Bold Numbers in Ledger Accounts   **Answers**

1. _____

2. _____

3. _____

4. _____

5. _____

6. _____

7. _____

8. _____

9. _____

10. _____

11. _____

12. _____

13. _____

Assets

Cash

Accts. Rec. - Megan Alvarez

Accts. Rec. - Tyler link

Supplies

Prepaid Insurance

Liabilities

Accts. Pay. - Mid City Supplies

Accts. Pay. - Sherer Supplies

O. E

Clara Ross, Capital

Clara Ross - Drawing

Revenue

Sales

Expenses

Auto. Expense

Insurance Expense

Miscell. Expense

Rent Expense

Supplies Expense

4-1　WORK TOGETHER, p. 95

Preparing a chart of accounts and opening an account

1.

Ross Company

Chart of Accounts

Balance Sheet Accounts	Income Statement Accounts
(100) Assets	(400) Revenue
110 Cash	4100 Sales
120 Accounts Receivable · Megan Alvarez	(500) Expenses
130 Accounts Receivable - Tyler Link	510 Automobile Expense
140 Supplies	520 Insurance Expense
150 Prepaid Insurance	530 Miscellaneous Expense
(200) Liabilities	540 Rent Expense
210 Accounts Payable - Mid City Supplies	550 Supplies Expense
220 Accounts Payable - Sherer Supplies	
(300) Owner's Equity	
310 Clara Ross, Capital	
320 Clara Ross, Drawing	

2.　　　New accounts

Account Number	Account Title
535	Postage Expense
560	Utilities Expense

3.

ACCOUNT　Cash　　　　　　　　　　　　　　　ACCOUNT NO.　110

DATE	ITEM	POST. REF.	DEBIT	CREDIT	BALANCE DEBIT	BALANCE CREDIT

Preparing a chart of accounts and opening an account

1.

2.

3.

ACCOUNT								ACCOUNT NO.	
DATE		ITEM	POST. REF.	DEBIT	CREDIT	BALANCE			
						DEBIT		CREDIT	

4-2 and 4-3 WORK TOGETHER, pp. 99, 104

4-2 Posting separate amounts to a general ledger
4-3 Posting column totals to a general ledger

JOURNAL PAGE 1

DATE		ACCOUNT TITLE	DOC. NO.	POST. REF.	GENERAL DEBIT (1)	GENERAL CREDIT (2)	SALES CREDIT (3)	CASH DEBIT (4)	CASH CREDIT (5)	
2015 Mar.	1	Leonard Witkowski, Capital	R1	310		5000 00		5000 00		1
	3	Prepaid Insurance	C1	140	660 00				660 00	2
	4	Supplies	M1	130	78 00					3
		Accts. Payable—Joshua's Supplies		210		78 00				4
	8		T8	✔			675 00	675 00		5
	9	Accts. Receivable—Danielle Braastad	S1	120	163 00		163 00			6
	12	Rent Expense	C2	510	375 00				375 00	7
	15	Accts. Payable—Joshua's Supplies	C3	210	50 00				50 00	8
	16	Accts. Receivable—Danielle Braastad	R2	120		100 00		100 00		9
	25	Leonard Witkowski, Drawing	C4	320	1000 00				1000 00	10
	31	Totals			2326 00	5178 00	838 00	5775 00	2085 00	11
					(✓)	(✓)	(410)	(110)	(110)	12

GENERAL LEDGER

ACCOUNT Cash   ACCOUNT NO. 110

DATE	ITEM	POST. REF.	DEBIT	CREDIT	BALANCE DEBIT	BALANCE CREDIT
2015 Mar 31		1	5 7 7 5 00		5 7 7 5 00	
31		1		2 0 8 5 00	3 6 9 0 00	

ACCOUNT Accounts Receivable—Danielle Braastad   ACCOUNT NO. 120

DATE	ITEM	POST. REF.	DEBIT	CREDIT	BALANCE DEBIT	BALANCE CREDIT
2015 Mar 9		1	1 6 3 00		1 6 3 00	
16		1		1 0 0 00	6 3 00	

ACCOUNT Supplies   ACCOUNT NO. 130

DATE	ITEM	POST. REF.	DEBIT	CREDIT	BALANCE DEBIT	BALANCE CREDIT
2015 Mar 4		1	7 8 00		7 8 00	

ACCOUNT Prepaid Insurance   ACCOUNT NO. 140

DATE	ITEM	POST. REF.	DEBIT	CREDIT	BALANCE DEBIT	BALANCE CREDIT
2015 Mar 3		1	6 6 0 00		6 6 0 00	

ACCOUNT Accounts Payable—Joshua's Supplies   ACCOUNT NO. 210

DATE	ITEM	POST. REF.	DEBIT	CREDIT	BALANCE DEBIT	BALANCE CREDIT
2015 Mar 4		1		7 8 00		7 8 00
15		1	5 0 00			2 8 00

4-2 and 4-3 WORK TOGETHER (concluded)

GENERAL LEDGER

account **Leonard Witkowski, Capital**   account no. 310

DATE	ITEM	POST. REF.	DEBIT	CREDIT	BALANCE DEBIT	BALANCE CREDIT
2015 Mar 1		1		5 0 0 0 00		5 0 0 0 00

account **Leonard Witkowski, Drawing**   account no. 320

DATE	ITEM	POST. REF.	DEBIT	CREDIT	BALANCE DEBIT	BALANCE CREDIT
2015 Mar 25		1	1 0 0 0 00		1 0 0 0 00	

account **Sales**   account no. 410

DATE	ITEM	POST. REF.	DEBIT	CREDIT	BALANCE DEBIT	BALANCE CREDIT
2015 Mar 31		1		8 3 8 00		8 3 8 00

account **Rent Expense**   account no. 510

DATE	ITEM	POST. REF.	DEBIT	CREDIT	BALANCE DEBIT	BALANCE CREDIT
2015 Mar 12		1	3 7 5 00		3 7 5 00	

account _____   account no. _____

DATE	ITEM	POST. REF.	DEBIT	CREDIT	BALANCE DEBIT	BALANCE CREDIT

4-2 Posting separate amounts to a general ledger
4-3 Posting column totals to a general ledger

JOURNAL   PAGE 1

	DATE	ACCOUNT TITLE	DOC. NO.	POST. REF.	GENERAL DEBIT	GENERAL CREDIT	SALES CREDIT	CASH DEBIT	CASH CREDIT
1	20-- Sept. 1	Heather Hasley, Capital	R1			4 5 0 0 00		4 5 0 0 00	
2	4	Supplies	M1		6 7 00				
3		Accounts Payable—Bodden Company				6 7 00			
4	7	Prepaid Insurance	C1		3 0 0 00				3 0 0 00
5	10	Accounts Receivable—Ken Garlie	S1		1 9 5 00		1 9 5 00		
6	13	✓	T13	✓			1 2 0 0 00	1 2 0 0 00	
7	18	Advertising Expense	C2		4 9 00				4 9 00
8	21	Accounts Payable—Bodden Company	C3		3 5 00				3 5 00
9	27	Accounts Receivable—Ken Garlie	R2			1 0 0 00		1 0 0 00	
10	30	Heather Hasley, Drawing	C4		1 3 0 0 00				1 3 0 0 00
11	30	Totals			1 9 4 6 00	4 6 6 7 00	1 3 9 5 00	5 8 0 0 00	1 6 8 4 00
12					(✓)	(✓)			
13									
14									
15									
16									
17									
18									
19									
20									
21									
22									
23									

4-2 and 4-3 ON YOUR OWN (continued)

GENERAL LEDGER

ACCOUNT **Cash** ACCOUNT NO. 110

DATE	ITEM	POST. REF.	DEBIT	CREDIT	BALANCE DEBIT	BALANCE CREDIT

ACCOUNT **Accounts Receivable—Ken Garlie** ACCOUNT NO. 120

DATE	ITEM	POST. REF.	DEBIT	CREDIT	BALANCE DEBIT	BALANCE CREDIT

ACCOUNT **Supplies** ACCOUNT NO. 130

DATE	ITEM	POST. REF.	DEBIT	CREDIT	BALANCE DEBIT	BALANCE CREDIT

ACCOUNT **Prepaid Insurance** ACCOUNT NO. 140

DATE	ITEM	POST. REF.	DEBIT	CREDIT	BALANCE DEBIT	BALANCE CREDIT

ACCOUNT **Accounts Payable—Bodden Company** ACCOUNT NO. 210

DATE	ITEM	POST. REF.	DEBIT	CREDIT	BALANCE DEBIT	BALANCE CREDIT

GENERAL LEDGER

ACCOUNT Heather Hasley, Capital   ACCOUNT NO. 310

DATE	ITEM	POST. REF.	DEBIT	CREDIT	BALANCE	
					DEBIT	CREDIT

ACCOUNT Heather Hasley, Drawing   ACCOUNT NO. 320

DATE	ITEM	POST. REF.	DEBIT	CREDIT	BALANCE	
					DEBIT	CREDIT

ACCOUNT Sales   ACCOUNT NO. 410

DATE	ITEM	POST. REF.	DEBIT	CREDIT	BALANCE	
					DEBIT	CREDIT

ACCOUNT Advertising Expense   ACCOUNT NO. 510

DATE	ITEM	POST. REF.	DEBIT	CREDIT	BALANCE	
					DEBIT	CREDIT

ACCOUNT   ACCOUNT NO.

DATE	ITEM	POST. REF.	DEBIT	CREDIT	BALANCE	
					DEBIT	CREDIT

4-4 WORK TOGETHER, p. 109

Journalizing correcting entries

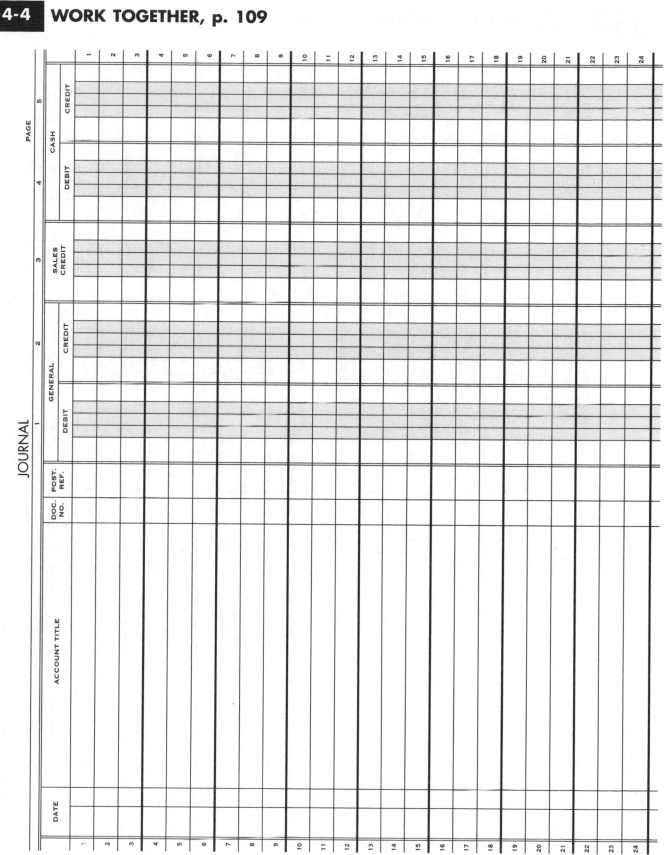

JOURNAL

PAGE

Journalizing correcting entries

JOURNAL

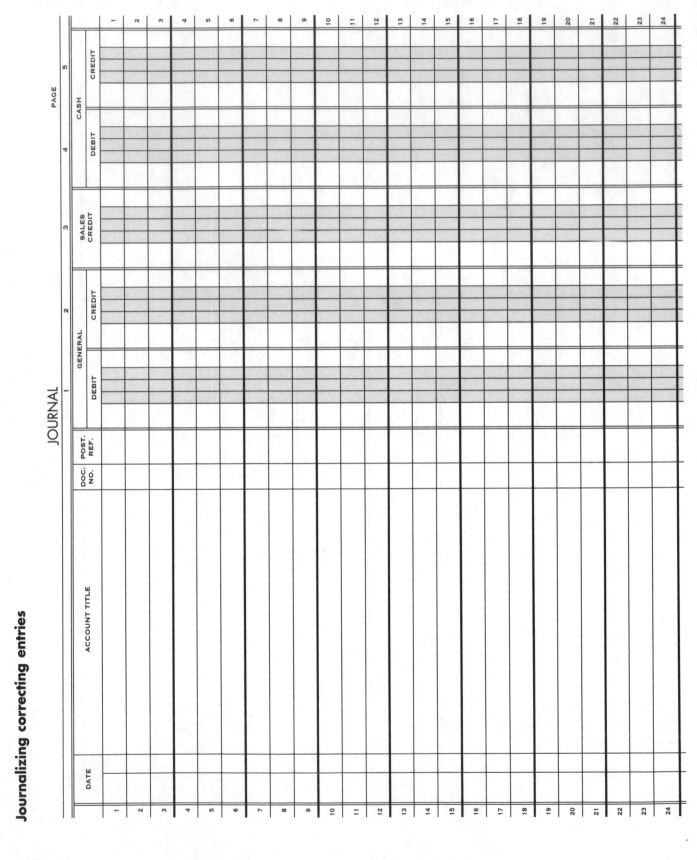

| | | | GENERAL | | SALES | CASH | |
| DATE | ACCOUNT TITLE | DOC. NO. | POST. REF. | DEBIT | CREDIT | CREDIT | DEBIT | CREDIT |

4-6 CHALLENGE PROBLEM (continued)

GENERAL LEDGER

ACCOUNT Cash   ACCOUNT NO. 110

DATE	ITEM	POST. REF.	DEBIT	CREDIT	BALANCE DEBIT	BALANCE CREDIT

ACCOUNT Accounts Receivable—Joelle Chu   ACCOUNT NO. 120

DATE	ITEM	POST. REF.	DEBIT	CREDIT	BALANCE DEBIT	BALANCE CREDIT

ACCOUNT Supplies   ACCOUNT NO. 130

DATE	ITEM	POST. REF.	DEBIT	CREDIT	BALANCE DEBIT	BALANCE CREDIT

ACCOUNT Accounts Payable—Dollar Supplies   ACCOUNT NO. 210

DATE	ITEM	POST. REF.	DEBIT	CREDIT	BALANCE DEBIT	BALANCE CREDIT

ACCOUNT Frances Fessler, Capital   ACCOUNT NO. 310

DATE	ITEM	POST. REF.	DEBIT	CREDIT	BALANCE DEBIT	BALANCE CREDIT

GENERAL LEDGER

ACCOUNT Frances Fessler, Drawing   ACCOUNT NO. 320

DATE	ITEM	POST. REF.	DEBIT	CREDIT	BALANCE DEBIT	BALANCE CREDIT

ACCOUNT Sales   ACCOUNT NO. 410

DATE	ITEM	POST. REF.	DEBIT	CREDIT	BALANCE DEBIT	BALANCE CREDIT

ACCOUNT Advertising Expense   ACCOUNT NO. 510

DATE	ITEM	POST. REF.	DEBIT	CREDIT	BALANCE DEBIT	BALANCE CREDIT

ACCOUNT Miscellaneous Expense   ACCOUNT NO. 520

DATE	ITEM	POST. REF.	DEBIT	CREDIT	BALANCE DEBIT	BALANCE CREDIT

ACCOUNT Rent Expense   ACCOUNT NO. 530

DATE	ITEM	POST. REF.	DEBIT	CREDIT	BALANCE DEBIT	BALANCE CREDIT

ACCOUNT Utilities Expense   ACCOUNT NO. 540

DATE	ITEM	POST. REF.	DEBIT	CREDIT	BALANCE DEBIT	BALANCE CREDIT

USING SOURCE DOCUMENTS, p. 113

Journalizing transactions and posting to a general ledger

Receipt No. _1_

Date _7/2_ , 20--

From _Darcia Tomzak_

For _Investment_

_____

$ 7,000 00

Receipt No. _1_   Form _1_

Date _July 2_   20--

Rec'd from _Darcia Tomzak_

For _Investment_

Seven Thousand & no/100 Dollars

Amount $ 7,000 00

LCB
Received by

NO. _1_   Form _2_

Date: _7/3_   20 -- $ _1,000.00_

To: _Quincy Rental Agency_

For: _July Rent_

BAL. BRO'T. FOR'D		0 00
AMT. DEPOSITED	7—1	7000 00
SUBTOTAL		7000 00
AMT. THIS CHECK		1000 00
BAL. CAR'D. FOR'D		6000 00

No. _1_   Form _3_

MEMORANDUM

_Bought supplies on account
from Music Supply Co., $1,300.00_

Signed: _LCB_   Date: _7/6/--_

USING SOURCE DOCUMENTS (continued)

NO. _2_ Form _4_
Date: _7/7_ 20 - - $ _119.00_

To: _City Telephone_
Company

For: _Telephone_
bill

BAL. BRO'T. FOR'D	6000	00
AMT. DEPOSITED		
SUBTOTAL	6000	00
AMT. THIS CHECK	119	00
BAL. CAR'D. FOR'D	5881	00

Form _5_
0.00 *

July 7, 20--
_T7_

175.00 +
80.00 +
475.00 +
70.00 +
800.00 *

Darcia's
School of Dance
313 King Street
Concord, NH 03303

Sold to: _Kid's Stop_
366 Park Street
Concord, NH 03303

Form _6_
No. _1_
Date _7/10/--_
Terms _2/10, n/30_

Description	Amount
Pre-School Dance class-1 Hr.	300.00
K-3 Dance class-1 Hr.	350.00
Total	650.00

NO. _3_ Form _7_
Date: _7/11_ 20 - - $ _795.00_

To: _Orion Insurance_
Company

For: _Insurance_

BAL. BRO'T. FOR'D		5881	00
AMT. DEPOSITED	7—7	800	00
SUBTOTAL		6681	00
AMT. THIS CHECK		795	00
BAL. CAR'D. FOR'D		5886	00

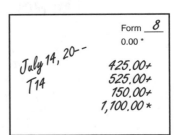

Form _8_
0.00 *

July 14, 20--
_T14_

425.00 +
525.00 +
150.00 +
1,100.00 *

USING SOURCE DOCUMENTS (continued)

NO. **4**   Form **9**
Date: **7/16**   20-- $ **325.00**
To: **Prescott Media**

For: **Advertising**

BAL. BRO'T. FOR'D	5886	00
AMT. DEPOSITED **7–14**	1100	00
SUBTOTAL	6986	00
AMT. THIS CHECK	325	00
BAL. CAR'D. FOR'D	6661	00

Form **10**
0.00 *

July 21, 20--
T21
575.00+
275.00+

850.00 *

NO. **5**   Form **11**
Date: **7/23**   20-- $ **850.00**
To: **Music Supply**
        Company
For: **On account**

BAL. BRO'T. FOR'D	6661	00
AMT. DEPOSITED **7–21**	850	00
SUBTOTAL	7511	00
AMT. THIS CHECK	850	00
BAL. CAR'D. FOR'D	6661	00

Receipt No. **2**
Date **7/24** , 20--
From **Kid's Stop**
For **On account**

$ 425 00

Receipt No. **2**   Form **12**
Date **July 24** 20--
Rec'd from **Kid's Stop**
For **On account**
Four hundred twenty-five & $^{no}/100$ Dollars

Amount $ 425 00

LCB
Received by

NO. 6   Form __13__
Date: _7/26_   20-- $ _600.00_
To: _Columbus Supplies_

For: _Supplies_

BAL. BRO'T. FOR'D		6661	00
AMT. DEPOSITED	7—24	425	00
SUBTOTAL		7086	00
AMT. THIS CHECK		600	00
BAL. CAR'D. FOR'D		6486	00

Form __14__
0.00 *

July 28, 20--
T28   500.00+

500.00 *

NO. 7   Form __15__
Date: _7/30_   20-- $ _110.00_
To: _Concord Electric_
        Company
For: _Electric bill_

BAL. BRO'T. FOR'D		6486	00
AMT. DEPOSITED	7—28	500	00
SUBTOTAL		6986	00
AMT. THIS CHECK		110	00
BAL. CAR'D. FOR'D		6876	00

Darcia's
School of Dance
313 King Street
Concord, NH 03303

Sold to: _Kid's Stop_
366 Park Street
Concord, NH 03303

Form __16__
No. _2_
Date _7/30/--_
Terms _2/10, n/30_

Description	Amount
K-3 Dance class-1 Hr.	350.00
Consultation-1 Hr.	125.00
Total	475.00

USING SOURCE DOCUMENTS (continued)

```
                              Form  17
                              0.00 *

   July 31, 20--             225.00+
   T31                       225.00+
                             250.00+
                             700.00 *
```

```
NO. 8                        Form    18
Date:  7/31      20 -- $ 1000.00
To:    Darcia Tomzak

For:   Withdrawal

BAL. BRO'T. FOR'D              6876  00
AMT. DEPOSITED      7–31        700  00
SUBTOTAL                       7576  00
AMT. THIS CHECK                1000  00
BAL. CAR'D. FOR'D              6576  00
```

```
NO. 9                        Form    19
Date:_____   20 -- $ _____
To:   _____

For:  _____

BAL. BRO'T. FOR'D              6576  00
AMT. DEPOSITED
SUBTOTAL
AMT. THIS CHECK
BAL. CAR'D. FOR'D
```

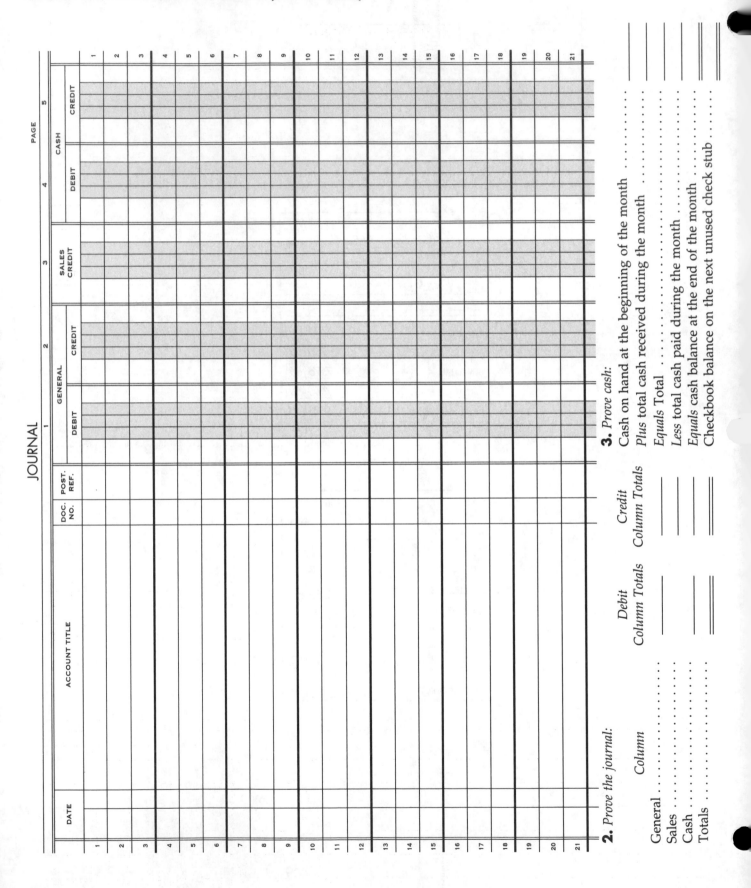

2. *Prove the journal:*

Column	Debit Column Totals	Credit Column Totals
General	_____	_____
Sales	_____	_____
Cash	_____	_____
Totals	_____	_____

3. *Prove cash:*

Cash on hand at the beginning of the month . . . . _____

Plus total cash received during the month . . . . _____

Equals Total . . . . _____

Less total cash paid during the month . . . . _____

Equals cash balance at the end of the month . . . . _____

Checkbook balance on the next unused check stub . . . . _____

USING SOURCE DOCUMENTS (continued)

GENERAL LEDGER

ACCOUNT Cash   ACCOUNT NO. 110

DATE	ITEM	POST. REF.	DEBIT	CREDIT	BALANCE DEBIT	BALANCE CREDIT

ACCOUNT Accounts Receivable—Kid's Stop   ACCOUNT NO. 120

DATE	ITEM	POST. REF.	DEBIT	CREDIT	BALANCE DEBIT	BALANCE CREDIT

ACCOUNT Supplies   ACCOUNT NO. 130

DATE	ITEM	POST. REF.	DEBIT	CREDIT	BALANCE DEBIT	BALANCE CREDIT

ACCOUNT Prepaid Insurance   ACCOUNT NO. 140

DATE	ITEM	POST. REF.	DEBIT	CREDIT	BALANCE DEBIT	BALANCE CREDIT

GENERAL LEDGER

ACCOUNT Accounts Payable—Music Supply Company   ACCOUNT NO. 210

DATE	ITEM	POST. REF.	DEBIT	CREDIT	BALANCE DEBIT	BALANCE CREDIT

ACCOUNT Darcia Tomzak, Capital   ACCOUNT NO. 310

DATE	ITEM	POST. REF.	DEBIT	CREDIT	BALANCE DEBIT	BALANCE CREDIT

ACCOUNT Darcia Tomzak, Drawing   ACCOUNT NO. 320

DATE	ITEM	POST. REF.	DEBIT	CREDIT	BALANCE DEBIT	BALANCE CREDIT

ACCOUNT Sales   ACCOUNT NO. 410

DATE	ITEM	POST. REF.	DEBIT	CREDIT	BALANCE DEBIT	BALANCE CREDIT

USING SOURCE DOCUMENTS (concluded)

GENERAL LEDGER

ACCOUNT Advertising Expense   ACCOUNT NO. 510

DATE	ITEM	POST. REF.	DEBIT	CREDIT	BALANCE DEBIT	BALANCE CREDIT

ACCOUNT Rent Expense   ACCOUNT NO. 520

DATE	ITEM	POST. REF.	DEBIT	CREDIT	BALANCE DEBIT	BALANCE CREDIT

ACCOUNT Utilities Expense   ACCOUNT NO. 530

DATE	ITEM	POST. REF.	DEBIT	CREDIT	BALANCE DEBIT	BALANCE CREDIT

ACCOUNT   ACCOUNT NO.

DATE	ITEM	POST. REF.	DEBIT	CREDIT	BALANCE DEBIT	BALANCE CREDIT

Study Guide 5

Name		Perfect Score	Your Score
	Identifying Accounting Terms	13 Pts.	
	Analyzing Transactions in a Cash Control System	12 Pts.	
	Identifying Accounting Concepts and Practices	20 Pts.	
	Total	45 Pts.	

Part One—Identifying Accounting Terms

Directions: Select the one term in Column I that best fits each definition in Column II. Print the letter identifying your choice in the Answers column.

Column I	Column II	Answers
A. bank statement	**1.** A statement that guides the ethical behavior of a company and its employees. (p. 118)	1. D
B. blank endorsement	**2.** A bank account from which payments can be ordered by a depositor. (p. 119)	2. C
C. checking account	**3.** A signature or stamp on the back of a check, transferring ownership. (p. 120)	3. H
D. code of conduct	**4.** An endorsement consisting only of the endorser's signature. (p. 120)	4. B
E. debit card	**5.** An endorsement indicating a new owner of a check. (p. 120)	5. M
F. dishonored check	**6.** An endorsement restricting further transfer of a check's ownership. (p. 120)	6. L
G. electronic funds transfer	**7.** A check with a future date on it. (p. 121)	7. K
H. endorsement	**8.** A report of deposits, withdrawals, and bank balances sent to a depositor by a bank. (p. 124)	8. A
I. petty cash	**9.** A check that a bank refuses to pay. (p. 129)	9. F
J. petty cash slip	**10.** A computerized cash payments system that transfers funds without the use of checks, currency, or other paper documents. (p. 131)	10. G
K. postdated check	**11.** A bank card that automatically deducts the amount of a purchase from the checking account of the cardholder. (p. 132)	11. E
L. restrictive endorsement	**12.** An amount of cash kept on hand and used for making small payments. (p. 134)	12. I
M. special endorsement	**13.** A form showing proof of a petty cash payment. (p. 135)	13. J

Part Two—Analyzing Transactions in a Cash Control System

Directions: Analyze each of the following transactions into debit and credit parts. Print the letters identifying your choices in the proper Answers columns.

Account Titles

A. Cash
B. Petty Cash
C. Accounts Receivable—R. Sandell

D. Supplies
E. Accounts Payable—Suburban Office Supplies
F. Miscellaneous Expense

Transactions	Answers Debit	Credit
1–2. Received bank statement showing bank service charge. (p. 127)	1. _____	2. _____
3–4. Received notice from a bank of a dishonored check from R. Sandell. (p. 130)	3. _____	4. _____
5–6. Paid cash on account to Suburban Office Supplies using EFT. (p. 131)	5. _____	6. _____
7–8. Purchased supplies using a debit card. (p. 132)	7. _____	8. _____
9–10. Paid cash to establish a petty cash fund. (p. 134)	9. _____	10. _____
11–12. Paid cash to replenish a petty cash fund: $12.00; supplies, $3.50; miscellaneous expense, $8.50. (p. 136)	11. _____	12. _____

Part Three—Identifying Accounting Concepts and Practices

Directions: Place a *T* for True or an *F* for False in the Answers column to show whether each of the following statements is true or false.

Answers

1. Because cash transactions occur more frequently than other transactions, the chances for making recording errors affecting cash are less. (p. 118)

1. _____

2. When a deposit is made in a bank account, the bank issues a receipt. (p. 119)

2. _____

3. There are four types of endorsements commonly used: blank, special, original, and restrictive. (p. 120)

3. _____

4. A check with a blank endorsement can be cashed by anyone who has possession of the check. (p. 120)

4. _____

5. When writing a check, the first step is to prepare the check stub. (p. 121)

5. _____

6. Most banks do not look at the date the check is written and will withdraw money from the depositor's account anytime. (p. 121)

6. _____

7. The amount of a check is written twice on each check. (p. 121)

7. _____

8. A check that contains errors must be marked with the word VOID and another check must be written. (p. 122)

8. _____

9. An important aspect of cash control is verifying that the information on a bank statement and a checkbook are in agreement. (p. 125)

9. _____

10. An outstanding check is one that has been issued but not yet reported on a bank statement by the bank. (p. 125)

10. _____

11. Banks deduct service charges from customers' checking accounts without requiring customers to write a check for the amount. (p. 126)

11. _____

12. Not only do banks charge a fee for handling a dishonored check, but they also deduct the amount of the check from the account as well. (p. 129)

12. _____

13. The journal entry for a payment on account using electronic funds transfer is exactly the same as when the payment is made by check. (p. 131)

13. _____

14. The source document for an electronic funds transfer is a memorandum. (p. 131)

14. _____

15. The source document for a debit card purchase is a memorandum. (p. 132)

15. _____

16. TechKnow Consulting maintains a petty cash fund for making large cash payments without writing checks. (p. 134)

16. _____

17. Businesses use petty cash when writing a check is not time or cost effective. (p. 134)

17. _____

18. A memorandum is the source document for the entry to record establishing a petty cash fund. (p. 134)

18. _____

19. Anytime a payment is made from the petty cash fund, a petty cash slip is prepared showing proof of a petty cash payment. (p. 135)

19. _____

20. When the petty cash fund is replenished, the balance of the petty cash account increases. (p. 136)

20. _____

Budgeting Your Time

There is an old saying that time flies. And indeed it does. We all have a limited amount of time available for all the things we want to do every day. One of the most important things you do while in school is to prepare your lessons for class. Your study time is one of the most valuable assets that you have. It must be used to the greatest benefit.

What Happens to Your Time?

You might plan to spend a certain amount of time studying, but for one reason or another, you do not get the studying done. The telephone may ring, a friend might drop by, or a family member might ask you to run an errand. Soon the time that you intended to use for studying is gone, and you hardly realize what happened to the time.

Make a Schedule and Keep It

The only way to be sure that you do not lose your valuable study time is to make a schedule and stick with it. Let's suppose you are taking four major subjects this term, and you need to spend from 30 minutes to an hour on each of them every evening. You may wish to set aside two hours before dinner and one hour after dinner for study. Your schedule might look like this.

4:30–6:30	study
6:30–7:30	dinner
7:30–8:30	study

On those days when you have less homework to do, you may be able to forego the study period after dinner. This will leave you an hour and a half or so before you go to bed to talk with friends or to watch a television program. Or you may wish to use that time for reading.

Your study schedule may be entirely different from this plan, but it is vital that you budget the time that you have available.

Studying Before Class

You may like to study before class in the morning. You may feel fresher in the morning and believe that you can get more work done then. This may be true, but it is usually unwise to leave assignments to complete just before class. It is very easy for an unavoidable interruption to occur, and you will not complete your work on time.

If you like to study early in the morning, it is suggested that you use this time for organizing your work for the day, rereading assignments, or for reviewing for an examination.

Working Students

Many students are employed a few hours a day while they are in school. Those who work often budget their time better than those who do not work. Because they have a more rigid schedule, they often feel they must use their study time to better advantage. If you work, be assured that you will still be able to get all your assignments prepared properly.

Stick To It

Time does indeed fly. If we do not budget our time, we will not get all we should from school. The only way to be sure that you get your studying done on time is to set a study schedule and stick to it.

Name _Matthew Worns_   Date _____   Class _M3_

5-1   WORK TOGETHER, p. 123

Endorsing and writing checks

1.   **a.**

ENDORSE HERE
X   *Matthew Worns*
DO NOT WRITE, STAMP, OR SIGN BELOW THIS LINE
RESERVED FOR FINANCIAL INSTITUTION USE

b.

ENDORSE HERE
X   *Pay to the order of*
Kelsey Sarner
Matthew Worns
DO NOT WRITE, STAMP, OR SIGN BELOW THIS LINE
RESERVED FOR FINANCIAL INSTITUTION USE

c.

ENDORSE HERE
X   *For deposit only to*
the account of
Balsam Lake Accounting
Matthew Worns
DO NOT WRITE, STAMP, OR SIGN BELOW THIS LINE
RESERVED FOR FINANCIAL INSTITUTION USE

2., 3., 4a.

NO. 78 $ 162.00
Date: Oct. 30   2015
To: Corner Garage
For: Repairs

BAL. BRO'T. FOR'D.	1,805	75
AMT. DEPOSITED .... 10 30 2015 (Date)	489	00
SUBTOTAL	2,294	75
OTHER:		
SUBTOTAL	2,294	75
AMT. THIS CHECK	162	00
BAL. CAR'D. FOR'D.	2,132	75

Balsam Lake Accounting   NO. 78   93-109/918
154 Main Street
Balsam Lake, WI 54810-3982   Oct. 30   20 15

PAY TO THE ORDER OF   Corner Garage $ 162.00

One hundred sixty-two and 00/100 —————— DOLLARS

Peoples national bank   *For Classroom Use Only*
Balsam Lake, WI 54810

FOR Repairs   *Matthew Worns*

⑈091004329⑈ 291⑈36118⑈

4b.

NO. 79 $ 92.00
Date: Oct. 30   2015
To: St. Croix Supplies
For: Supplies

BAL. BRO'T. FOR'D.	2,132	75
AMT. DEPOSITED .... (Date)	0	00
SUBTOTAL	2,132	75
OTHER:		
SUBTOTAL	2,132	75
AMT. THIS CHECK	92	00
BAL. CAR'D. FOR'D.	2,040	75

Balsam Lake Accounting   NO. 79   93-109/918
154 Main Street
Balsam Lake, WI 54810-3982   Oct. 30   20 15

PAY TO THE ORDER OF   St. Croix Supply $ 92.00

Ninety-two and 00/100 —————— DOLLARS

Peoples national bank   *For Classroom Use Only*
Balsam Lake, WI 54810

FOR Supplies   *Matthew Worns*

⑈091004329⑈ 291⑈36118⑈

Endorsing and writing checks

1. **a.**

ENDORSE HERE
X
DO NOT WRITE, STAMP, OR SIGN BELOW THIS LINE
RESERVED FOR FINANCIAL INSTITUTION USE

b.

ENDORSE HERE
X
DO NOT WRITE, STAMP, OR SIGN BELOW THIS LINE
RESERVED FOR FINANCIAL INSTITUTION USE

2., 3., 4a.

NO. **345** $ _____

Date: _____ 20___

To: _____

For: _____

BAL. BRO'T. FOR'D. . . . .

AMT. DEPOSITED . . . . [Date]

SUBTOTAL . . . .

OTHER:

_____

_____

SUBTOTAL . . . .

AMT. THIS CHECK . . . .

BAL. CAR'D. FOR'D. . . . .

CENTURIA HAIR CARE   NO. **345**   79-1058 / 918
1250 State Street
Centuria, WI 54824-7264   _____ 20 ____

PAY TO THE
ORDER OF _____ $ _____

_____ DOLLARS

County Bank   *For Classroom Use Only*
Dresser, WI 54009

FOR _____   _____

⑆091004329⑆ 291⑈36118⑈

4b.

NO. **346** $ _____

Date: _____ 20___

To: _____

For: _____

BAL. BRO'T. FOR'D. . . . .

AMT. DEPOSITED . . . . [Date]

SUBTOTAL . . . .

OTHER:

_____

_____

SUBTOTAL . . . .

AMT. THIS CHECK . . . .

BAL. CAR'D. FOR'D. . . . .

CENTURIA HAIR CARE   NO. **346**   79-1058 / 918
1250 State Street
Centuria, WI 54824-7264   _____ 20 ____

PAY TO THE
ORDER OF _____ $ _____

_____ DOLLARS

County Bank   *For Classroom Use Only*
Dresser, WI 54009

FOR _____   _____

⑆091004329⑆ 291⑈36118⑈

5-2 WORK TOGETHER, p. 128

Reconciling a bank statement and recording a bank service charge

1.

RECONCILIATION OF BANK STATEMENT

July 29, 2015
(Date)

Balance On Check Stub No. 106 .... $ 1575 00

DEDUCT BANK CHARGES:

Description	Amount
Service charge	$ 2 00

Total bank charges ▶ 2 00

Balance On Bank Statement .... $ 1,528 00

ADD OUTSTANDING DEPOSITS:

Date	Amount
7/28/15	$ 150 00

Total outstanding deposits ▶ 150 00

SUBTOTAL .... $ 1,678 00

DEDUCT OUTSTANDING CHECKS:

Ck. No.	Amount	Ck. No.	Amount
103	70 00		
105	35 00		

Total outstanding checks ▶ 105 00

Adjusted Check Stub Balance .... $ 1573 00

Adjusted Bank Balance .... $ 1,573 00

2.

NO. **106** $ _____

Date: _____ 20 _ _

To: _____

For: _____

BAL. BRO'T. FOR'D.	1575	00
AMT. DEPOSITED .... [Date]		
SUBTOTAL	1575	00
OTHER: Service charge		
_____	2	00
SUBTOTAL	1573	00
AMT. THIS CHECK		
BAL. CAR'D. FOR'D.		

3.

JOURNAL   PAGE 14

	DATE	ACCOUNT TITLE	DOC. NO.	POST. REF.	GENERAL DEBIT	GENERAL CREDIT	SALES CREDIT	CASH DEBIT	CASH CREDIT	
14	Jul 29	Miscellaneous Expense	M44		2 00				2 00	14
15										15
16										16

Reconciling a bank statement and recording a bank service charge

1.

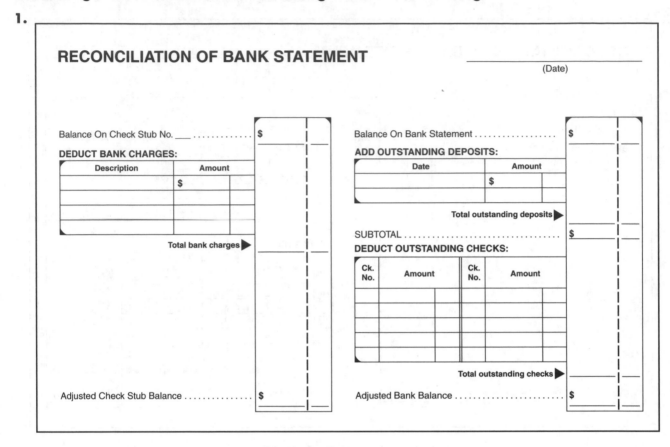

RECONCILIATION OF BANK STATEMENT _____
(Date)

Balance On Check Stub No. ___ .... $ _____

DEDUCT BANK CHARGES:

Description	Amount
	$

Total bank charges ▶

Adjusted Check Stub Balance .... $ _____

Balance On Bank Statement .... $ _____

ADD OUTSTANDING DEPOSITS:

Date	Amount
	$

Total outstanding deposits ▶

SUBTOTAL .... $ _____

DEDUCT OUTSTANDING CHECKS:

Ck. No.	Amount	Ck. No.	Amount

Total outstanding checks ▶

Adjusted Bank Balance .... $ _____

2.

NO. **119** $ _____
Date: _____ 20 _ _
To: _____
For: _____
_____

BAL. BRO'T. FOR'D. ....
AMT. DEPOSITED .... Date
SUBTOTAL ....
OTHER:

_____
_____

SUBTOTAL ....
AMT. THIS CHECK ....
BAL. CAR'D. FOR'D. ....

3.

JOURNAL   PAGE

	DATE	ACCOUNT TITLE	DOC. NO.	POST. REF.	GENERAL DEBIT	GENERAL CREDIT	SALES CREDIT	CASH DEBIT	CASH CREDIT	
					1	2	3	4	5	
17										17
18										18
19										19

5-3 WORK TOGETHER, p. 133

Recording dishonored checks, electronic funds transfers, and debit card purchases

JOURNAL PAGE ___

	DATE	ACCOUNT TITLE	DOC. NO.	POST. REF.	GENERAL DEBIT	GENERAL CREDIT	SALES CREDIT	CASH DEBIT	CASH CREDIT	
3	Mar 15	Accts. Rec.-Christopher Ikola	M121		73 00				73 00	3
4	16	Accts Pay.-Spinoza Enterprises	M122		135 00				135 00	4
5	17	Supplies	M123		31 00				31 00	5
6										6
7										7
8										8
9										9
10										10
11										11
12										12
13										13
14										14
15										15
16										16
17										17
18										18

Recording dishonored checks, electronic funds transfers, and debit card purchases

JOURNAL PAGE

	DATE	ACCOUNT TITLE	DOC. NO.	POST. REF.	GENERAL DEBIT	GENERAL CREDIT	SALES CREDIT	CASH DEBIT	CASH CREDIT	
15										15
16										16
17										17
18										18
19										19
20										20
21										21
22										22
23										23
24										24
25										25
26										26
27										27
28										28
29										29
30										30

5-4 WORK TOGETHER, p. 138

Establishing and replenishing a petty cash fund

JOURNAL PAGE

	DATE	ACCOUNT TITLE	DOC. NO.	POST. REF.	GENERAL DEBIT	GENERAL CREDIT	SALES CREDIT	CASH DEBIT	CASH CREDIT	
1	Jul 3	Petty Cash	C57		250 00				250 00	1
2	31	Supplies	C97		25 00				78 00	2
3		Miscellaneous Expense			8 00					3
4		Repairs			45 00					4
5										5
6										6
7										7
8										8
9										9
10										10
11										11
12										12
13										13
14										14
15										15
16										16
17										17

Establishing and replenishing a petty cash fund

JOURNAL

PAGE

	DATE	ACCOUNT TITLE	DOC. NO.	POST. REF.	GENERAL		SALES CREDIT	CASH	
					1 DEBIT	2 CREDIT	3	4 DEBIT	5 CREDIT
1									
2									
3									
4									
5									
6									
7									
8									
9									
10									
11									
12									
13									
14									
15									
16									
17									

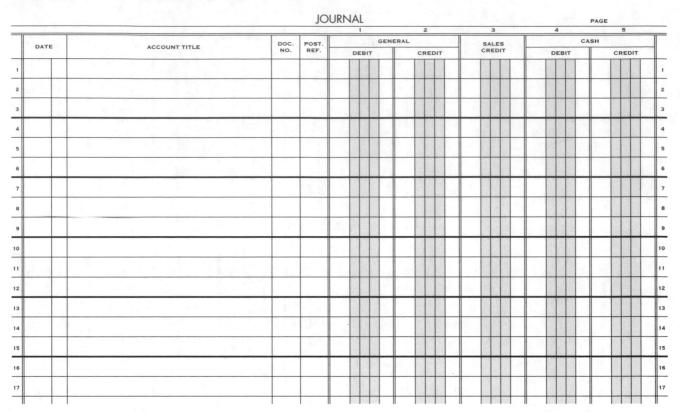

5-6 CHALLENGE PROBLEM, p. 142

Reconciling a bank statement and recording a bank service charge

1., 2.

SECURITY NATIONAL BANK
Pittsburgh, PA 15209-7634

STATEMENT OF ACCOUNT FOR
GolfPro
119 Matlock Street
Pittsburgh, PA 15237-4403

ACCOUNT NUMBER
398-24534

STATEMENT DATE
August 28, 20 – –

BALANCE FROM PREVIOUS STATEMENT	NO. OF CHECKS	AMOUNT OF CHECKS	NO. OF DEPOSITS	AMOUNT OF DEPOSITS	SERVICE CHARGES	STATEMENT BALANCE
0.00	11	4,675.00	4	12,955.00	5.00	8,275.00

DATE	CHECK	AMOUNT	CHECK	AMOUNT	DEPOSITS	BALANCE
08/01/– –						0.00
08/01/– –					12,000.00	12,000.00
08/04/– –	151	1,577.00				10,423.00
08/08/– –	152	200.00			125.00	10,348.00
08/13/– –	154	250.00	156	135.00		9,963.00
08/15/– –	153	1,560.00	158	75.00	260.00	8,588.00
08/17/– –	155	205.00	159	98.00		8,285.00
08/18/– –	160	140.00				8,145.00
08/20/– –	157	250.00				7,895.00
08/22/– –					570.00	8,465.00
08/25/– –	162	185.00				8,280.00
08/27/– –	SC	5.00				8,275.00

PLEASE EXAMINE AT ONCE • IF NO ERRORS ARE REPORTED WITHIN 10 DAYS THE ACCOUNT WILL BE CONSIDERED CORRECT. REFER ANY DISCREPANCY TO OUR ACCOUNTING DEPARTMENT IMMEDIATELY.

GolfPro
119 Matlock Street
Pittsburgh, PA 15237–4403
NO. 151 8-17/430
August 1, 20 – –
PAY TO THE ORDER OF Montag Company $ 1,577.00

GolfPro
119 Matlock Street
Pittsburgh, PA 15237–4403
NO. 152 8-17/430
August 5, 20 – –
PAY TO THE ORDER OF Plain Company $ 200.00

GolfPro
119 Matlock Street
Pittsburgh, PA 15237–4403
NO. 153 8-17/430
August 8, 20 – –
PAY TO THE ORDER OF Thomson Company $ 1,560.00

GolfPro
119 Matlock Street
Pittsburgh, PA 15237–4403
NO. 154 8-17/430
August 8, 20 – –
PAY TO THE ORDER OF Metro Insurance Co. $ 250.00

GolfPro
119 Matlock Street
Pittsburgh, PA 15237–4403
NO. 155 8-17/430
August 10, 20 – –
PAY TO THE ORDER OF City Electric Company $ 205.00

GolfPro
119 Matlock Street
Pittsburgh, PA 15237–4403
NO. 156 8-17/430
August 10, 20 – –
PAY TO THE ORDER OF Patterson Supplies $ 135.00
One hundred thirty - five dollars XX DOLLARS
SECURITY NATIONAL BANK
Pittsburgh, PA 15209-7634
FOR payment on account John Walker
⑈043000177⑈ 398⑈24534⑈

GolfPro
119 Matlock Street
Pittsburgh, PA 15237–4403
NO. 157 8-17/430
August 13, 20 – –
PAY TO THE ORDER OF John Walker $ 250.00

GolfPro
119 Matlock Street
Pittsburgh, PA 15237–4403
NO. 158 8-17/430
August 14, 20 – –
PAY TO THE ORDER OF Pennsylvania Telephone Co. $ 75.00

GolfPro
119 Matlock Street
Pittsburgh, PA 15237–4403
NO. 159 8-17/430
August 15, 20 – –
PAY TO THE ORDER OF Ace Cleaning Company $ 98.00

GolfPro
119 Matlock Street
Pittsburgh, PA 15237–4403
NO. 160 8-17/430
August 15, 20 – –
PAY TO THE ORDER OF Tri-State Agency $ 140.00

GolfPro
119 Matlock Street
Pittsburgh, PA 15237–4403
NO. 162 8-17/430
August 22, 20 – –
PAY TO THE ORDER OF Dowd Company $ 185.00
One hundred eighty - five dollars 00 XX DOLLARS
SECURITY NATIONAL BANK
Pittsburgh, PA 15209-7634
FOR payment on account John Walker
⑈043000177⑈ 398⑈24534⑈

1., 2., 4.

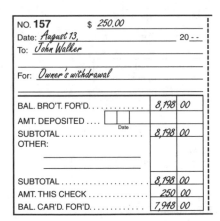

NO. **151**	$ *1,577.00*	
Date: *August 1,*		20 --
To: *Montag Company*		
For: *Supplies*		

BAL. BRO'T. FOR'D.		0	00
AMT. DEPOSITED ...	8 1 --	12,000	00
SUBTOTAL		12,000	00
OTHER:			
SUBTOTAL		12,000	00
AMT. THIS CHECK		1,577	00
BAL. CAR'D. FOR'D.		10,423	00

NO. **152**	$ *200.00*	
Date: *August 5,*		20 --
To: *Plain Company*		
For: *Rent*		

BAL. BRO'T. FOR'D.		10,423	00
AMT. DEPOSITED			
SUBTOTAL		10,423	00
OTHER:			
SUBTOTAL		10,423	00
AMT. THIS CHECK		200	00
BAL. CAR'D. FOR'D.		10,223	00

NO. **153**	$ *1,560.00*	
Date: *August 8,*		20 --
To: *Thomson Company*		
For: *Supplies*		

BAL. BRO'T. FOR'D.		10,223	00
AMT. DEPOSITED	8 8 --	125	00
SUBTOTAL		10,348	00
OTHER:			
SUBTOTAL		10,348	00
AMT. THIS CHECK		1,560	00
BAL. CAR'D. FOR'D.		8,788	00

NO. **154**	$ *250.00*	
Date: *August 8,*		20 --
To: *Metro Insurance Company*		
For: *Insurance*		

BAL. BRO'T. FOR'D.		8,788	00
AMT. DEPOSITED			
SUBTOTAL		8,788	00
OTHER:			
SUBTOTAL		8,788	00
AMT. THIS CHECK		250	00
BAL. CAR'D. FOR'D.		8,538	00

NO. **155**	$ *205.00*	
Date: *August 10,*		20 --
To: *City Electric Company*		
For: *Utilities*		

BAL. BRO'T. FOR'D.		8,538	00
AMT. DEPOSITED			
SUBTOTAL		8,538	00
OTHER:			
SUBTOTAL		8,538	00
AMT. THIS CHECK		205	00
BAL. CAR'D. FOR'D.		8,333	00

NO. **156**	$ *135.00*	
Date: *August 10,*		20 --
To: *Patterson Supplies*		
For: *Payment on account*		

BAL. BRO'T. FOR'D.		8,333	00
AMT. DEPOSITED			
SUBTOTAL		8,333	00
OTHER:			
SUBTOTAL		8,333	00
AMT. THIS CHECK		135	00
BAL. CAR'D. FOR'D.		8,198	00

NO. **157**	$ *250.00*	
Date: *August 13,*		20 --
To: *John Walker*		
For: *Owner's withdrawal*		

BAL. BRO'T. FOR'D.		8,198	00
AMT. DEPOSITED			
SUBTOTAL		8,198	00
OTHER:			
SUBTOTAL		8,198	00
AMT. THIS CHECK		250	00
BAL. CAR'D. FOR'D.		7,948	00

NO. **158**	$ *75.00*	
Date: *August 14,*		20 --
To: *Pennsylvania Telephone Company*		
For: *Utilities*		

BAL. BRO'T. FOR'D.		7,948	00
AMT. DEPOSITED			
SUBTOTAL		7,948	00
OTHER:			
SUBTOTAL		7,948	00
AMT. THIS CHECK		75	00
BAL. CAR'D. FOR'D.		7,873	00

NO. **159**	$ *98.00*	
Date: *August 15,*		20 --
To: *Ace Cleaning Company*		
For: *Cleaning*		

BAL. BRO'T. FOR'D.		7,873	00
AMT. DEPOSITED			
SUBTOTAL		7,873	00
OTHER:			
SUBTOTAL		7,873	00
AMT. THIS CHECK		98	00
BAL. CAR'D. FOR'D.		7,775	00

5-6 CHALLENGE PROBLEM (continued)

1., 2., 4.

NO. **160**	$ *140.00*	
Date: *August 15,*		20 - -
To: *Tri-State Agency*		
For: *Miscellaneous*		
BAL. BRO'T. FOR'D.	7,775	00
AMT. DEPOSITED . . . . 8 15 - - (Date)	260	00
SUBTOTAL	8,035	00
OTHER:		
SUBTOTAL	8,035	00
AMT. THIS CHECK	140	00
BAL. CAR'D. FOR'D.	7,895	00

NO. **161**	$ *375.00*	
Date: *August 19,*		20 - -
To: *Pittsburgh Enquirer*		
For: *Advertising*		
BAL. BRO'T. FOR'D.	7,895	00
AMT. DEPOSITED . . . . (Date)		
SUBTOTAL	7,895	00
OTHER:		
SUBTOTAL	7,895	00
AMT. THIS CHECK	375	00
BAL. CAR'D. FOR'D.	7,520	00

NO. **162**	$ *185.00*	
Date: *August 22,*		20 - -
To: *Dowd Company*		
For: *Payment on account*		
BAL. BRO'T. FOR'D.	7,520	00
AMT. DEPOSITED . . . . 8 22 - - (Date)	570	00
SUBTOTAL	8,090	00
OTHER:		
SUBTOTAL	8,090	00
AMT. THIS CHECK	185	00
BAL. CAR'D. FOR'D.	7,905	00

NO. **163**	$ *17.00*	
Date: *August 23,*		20 - -
To: *Jason North*		
For: *Miscellaneous*		
BAL. BRO'T. FOR'D.	7,905	00
AMT. DEPOSITED . . . . (Date)		
SUBTOTAL	7,905	00
OTHER:		
SUBTOTAL	7,905	00
AMT. THIS CHECK	17	00
BAL. CAR'D. FOR'D.	7,888	00

NO. **164**	$ *250.00*	
Date: *August 28,*		20 - -
To: *John Walker*		
For: *Owner's withdrawal*		
BAL. BRO'T. FOR'D.	7,888	00
AMT. DEPOSITED . . . . 8 28 - - (Date)	430	00
SUBTOTAL	8,318	00
OTHER:		
SUBTOTAL	8,318	00
AMT. THIS CHECK	250	00
BAL. CAR'D. FOR'D.	8,068	00

NO. **165**	$	
Date:		20 - -
To:		
For:		
BAL. BRO'T. FOR'D.	8,068	00
AMT. DEPOSITED . . . . (Date)		
SUBTOTAL	8,068	00
OTHER:		
SUBTOTAL		
AMT. THIS CHECK		
BAL. CAR'D. FOR'D.		

2.

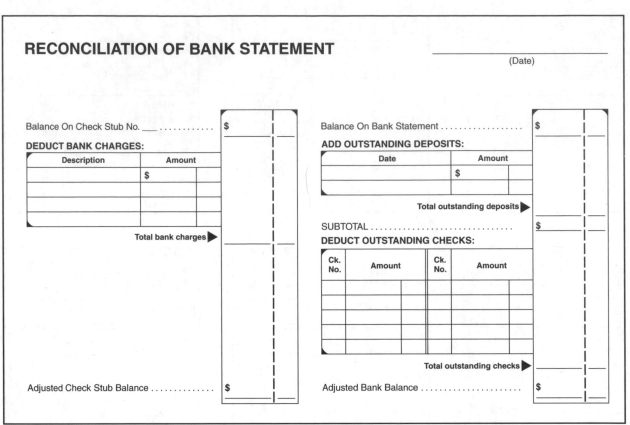

RECONCILIATION OF BANK STATEMENT

_____
(Date)

Balance On Check Stub No. ___ . . . . $

DEDUCT BANK CHARGES:

Description	Amount	
	$	

Total bank charges ▶

Adjusted Check Stub Balance . . . . $

Balance On Bank Statement . . . . $

ADD OUTSTANDING DEPOSITS:

Date	Amount	
	$	

Total outstanding deposits ▶

SUBTOTAL . . . . $

DEDUCT OUTSTANDING CHECKS:

Ck. No.	Amount	Ck. No.	Amount

Total outstanding checks ▶

Adjusted Bank Balance . . . . $

3.

JOURNAL   PAGE

	DATE	ACCOUNT TITLE	DOC. NO.	POST. REF.	GENERAL DEBIT	GENERAL CREDIT	SALES CREDIT	CASH DEBIT	CASH CREDIT	
1										1
2										2
3										3
4										4
5										5
6										6
7										7
8										8
9										9
10										10
11										11
12										12
13										13
14										14
15										15
16										16

Study Guide 6

Name	Perfect Score	Your Score
Identifying Accounting Terms	8 Pts.	
Analyzing Accounting Practices Related to a Work Sheet	17 Pts.	
Analyzing Adjustments and Extending Account Balances on a Work Sheet	16 Pts.	
Total	41 Pts.	

Part One—Identifying Accounting Terms

Directions: Select the one term in Column I that best fits each definition in Column II. Print the letter identifying your choice in the Answers column.

Column I	Column II	Answers
A. adjustments	1. The length of time for which a business summarizes and reports financial information. (p. 152)	1. _C_
B. balance sheet	2. A columnar accounting form used to summarize the general ledger information needed to prepare financial statements. (p. 153)	2. _H_
C. fiscal period	3. A proof of equality of debits and credits in a general ledger. (p. 154)	3. _G_
D. income statement	4. Changes recorded on a work sheet to update general ledger accounts at the end of a fiscal period. (p. 157)	4. _A_
E. net income	5. A financial statement that reports assets, liabilities, and owner's equity on a specific date. (p. 162)	5. _B_
F. net loss	6. A financial statement showing the revenue and expenses for a fiscal period. (p. 163)	6. _D_
G. trial balance	7. The difference between total revenue and total expenses when total revenue is greater. (p. 164)	7. _E_
H. work sheet	8. The difference between total revenue and total expenses when total expenses are greater. (p. 165)	8. _F_

Part Two—Analyzing Accounting Practices Related to a Work Sheet

Directions: Place a *T* for True or an *F* for False in the Answers column to show whether each of the following statements is true or false.

Answers

1. The accounting concept Consistent Reporting is being applied when a delivery business reports the number of deliveries made one year and the amount of revenue received for deliveries made the next year. (p. 152)

   1. _____

2. An accounting period is also known as a fiscal period. (p. 152)

   2. _____

3. Journals, ledgers, and work sheets are considered permanent records. (p. 153)

   3. _____

4. All general ledger account titles are listed on a trial balance in the same order as listed on the chart of accounts. (p. 154)

   4. _____

5. The four questions asked when analyzing an adjustment are: Why? Where? When? and How? (p. 158)

   5. _____

6. The two accounts affected by the adjustment for supplies are Supplies and Supplies Expense. (p. 158)

   6. _____

7. The two accounts affected by the adjustment for insurance are Prepaid Insurance Expense and Insurance. (p. 159)

   7. _____

8. Totaling and ruling the Adjustments columns of a work sheet are necessary to prove the equality of debits and credits. (p. 160)

   8. _____

9. Two financial statements are prepared from the information on the work sheet. (p. 162)

   9. _____

10. Net income on a work sheet is calculated by subtracting the Income Statement Credit column total from the Income Statement Debit column total. (p. 164)

    10. _____

11. If errors are found on a work sheet, they must be erased and corrected before any further work is completed. (p. 167)

    11. _____

12. When two column totals are not in balance on the work sheet, the difference between the two totals is calculated and checked. (p. 167)

    12. _____

13. If the difference between the totals of Debit and Credit columns on a work sheet can be evenly divided by 9, then the error is most likely in addition. (p. 167)

    13. _____

14. If there are errors in the work sheet's Trial Balance columns, it might be because not all general ledger account balances were copied in the Trial Balance column correctly. (p. 168)

    14. _____

15. Errors in general ledger accounts should never be erased. (p. 169)

    15. _____

16. Most errors occur in doing arithmetic. (p. 169)

    16. _____

17. The best way to prevent errors is to use a calculator. (p. 169)

    17. _____

Part Three—Analyzing Adjustments and Extending Account Balances on a Work Sheet

Directions: For each account listed below, determine in which work sheet column(s) an amount typically will be written. Place a check mark in the proper Answers column to show your answer.

	Adjustments Debit Credit (pp. 157–160)		Income Statement Debit Credit (p. 163)		Balance Sheet Debit Credit (p. 162)	
1. Cash	___	___	___	___	___	___
2. Petty Cash	___	___	___	___	___	___
3. Accounts Receivable— Imagination Station	___	___	___	___	___	___
4. Supplies	___	___	___	___	___	___
5. Prepaid Insurance	___	___	___	___	___	___
6. Accounts Payable— Suburban Office Supplies	___	___	___	___	___	___
7. J. Nichols, Capital	___	___	___	___	___	___
8. J. Nichols, Drawing	___	___	___	___	___	___
9. Income Summary	___	___	___	___	___	___
10. Sales	___	___	___	___	___	___
11. Advertising Expense	___	___	___	___	___	___
12. Insurance Expense	___	___	___	___	___	___
13. Miscellaneous Expense	___	___	___	___	___	___
14. Rent Expense	___	___	___	___	___	___
15. Supplies Expense	___	___	___	___	___	___
16. Utilities Expense	___	___	___	___	___	___

6-1 Recording the trial balance on a work sheet
6-2 Planning adjustments on a work sheet
6-3 Completing a work sheet

Golden Tan

Work Sheet

For Month Ended February 28, 2015

	ACCOUNT TITLE	TRIAL BALANCE DEBIT	TRIAL BALANCE CREDIT	ADJUSTMENTS DEBIT	ADJUSTMENTS CREDIT	INCOME STATEMENT DEBIT	INCOME STATEMENT CREDIT	BALANCE SHEET DEBIT	BALANCE SHEET CREDIT
1	Cash	9800.00						9800.00	
2	Petty Cash	150.00						150.00	
3	Accts. Rec.–Ruby Prince	2795.00						2795.00	
4	Supplies	456.00			(a)131.00			325.00	
5	Prepaid Insurance	750.00			(b)250.00			500.00	
6	Accts. Pay.–Richard Navarro		555.00						555.00
7	Gary Baldwin, Capital		14885.00						14885.00
8	Gary Baldwin, Drawing	3400.00						3400.00	
9	Income Summary								
10	Sales		4320.00				4320.00		
11						931.00			
12				(b)250.00		250.00			
13						378.00			
14				(a)131.00		131.00			
15						1100.00			
16		19760.00	19760.00	381.00	381.00	2790.00	4320.00	16970.00	15440.00
17						1530.00			1530.00
18						4320.00	4320.00	16970.00	16970.00
19									

6-1 Recording the trial balance on a work sheet
6-2 Planning adjustments on a work sheet
6-3 Completing a work sheet

ACCOUNT TITLE	TRIAL BALANCE		ADJUSTMENTS		INCOME STATEMENT		BALANCE SHEET	
	DEBIT	CREDIT	DEBIT	CREDIT	DEBIT	CREDIT	DEBIT	CREDIT
Cash								
Petty Cash								
Supplies								
Prepaid								

6-4 WORK TOGETHER, p. 170

Finding and correcting errors in accounting records

1., 2.   **GENERAL LEDGER**

ACCOUNT Cash   ACCOUNT NO. 110

DATE		ITEM	POST. REF.	DEBIT	CREDIT	BALANCE DEBIT	BALANCE CREDIT
20-- Sept.	1		1	4 0 0 0 00		4 0 0 0 00	
	30		2	7 0 0 0 00		15 0 0 0 00	
	30		2		6 7 5 0 00	8 0 0 0 00	

ACCOUNT Accounts Receivable—Sharon Mann   ACCOUNT NO. 120

DATE		ITEM	POST. REF.	DEBIT	CREDIT	BALANCE DEBIT	BALANCE CREDIT
20-- Sept.	12		1	1 0 0 0 00		1 0 0 0 00	

ACCOUNT Supplies   ACCOUNT NO. 130

DATE		ITEM	POST. REF.	DEBIT	CREDIT	BALANCE DEBIT	BALANCE CREDIT
20-- Sept.	2		1	6 0 0 00		6 0 0 00	
	25		2	4 25 00		7 25 00	

ACCOUNT Prepaid Insurance   ACCOUNT NO. 140

DATE		ITEM	POST. REF.	DEBIT	CREDIT	BALANCE DEBIT	BALANCE CREDIT
20-- Sept.	3		1	1 5 0 00		1 5 0 00	
	20		2	1 5 0 00		4 0 0 00	

ACCOUNT Accounts Payable—Powers Supply   ACCOUNT NO. 210

DATE		ITEM	POST. REF.	DEBIT	CREDIT	BALANCE DEBIT	BALANCE CREDIT
20-- Sept.	4		1		3 0 0 00		3 0 0 00
	15		2	1 5 0 00			1 5 0 00

ACCOUNT Paul Coty, Capital   ACCOUNT NO. 310

DATE		ITEM	POST. REF.	DEBIT	CREDIT	BALANCE DEBIT	BALANCE CREDIT
20-- Sept.	1		1		5 0 0 0 00		5 0 0 0 00

1., 2.   GENERAL LEDGER

ACCOUNT Paul Coty, Drawing   ACCOUNT NO. 320

DATE	ITEM	POST. REF.	DEBIT	CREDIT	BALANCE DEBIT	BALANCE CREDIT
Sept. 30		2	300 00		300 00	

ACCOUNT Income Summary   ACCOUNT NO. 330

DATE	ITEM	POST. REF.	DEBIT	CREDIT	BALANCE DEBIT	BALANCE CREDIT

ACCOUNT Sales   ACCOUNT NO. 410

DATE	ITEM	POST. REF.	DEBIT	CREDIT	BALANCE DEBIT	BALANCE CREDIT
Sept. 30		2		1900 00		1875 00

ACCOUNT Insurance Expense   ACCOUNT NO. 510

DATE	ITEM	POST. REF.	DEBIT	CREDIT	BALANCE DEBIT	BALANCE CREDIT

ACCOUNT Miscellaneous Expense   ACCOUNT NO. 520

DATE	ITEM	POST. REF.	DEBIT	CREDIT	BALANCE DEBIT	BALANCE CREDIT
Sept. 9		1	150 00		150 00	
27		2	25 00		125 00	

ACCOUNT Supplies Expense   ACCOUNT NO. 530

DATE	ITEM	POST. REF.	DEBIT	CREDIT	BALANCE DEBIT	BALANCE CREDIT

6-4 **WORK TOGETHER (continued)**

1.   **ERRORS**

1.

LeafyLift

Work Sheet

For Month Ended September 30, 20 - -

	ACCOUNT TITLE	TRIAL BALANCE DEBIT	TRIAL BALANCE CREDIT	ADJUSTMENTS DEBIT	ADJUSTMENTS CREDIT	INCOME STATEMENT DEBIT	INCOME STATEMENT CREDIT	BALANCE SHEET DEBIT	BALANCE SHEET CREDIT
1	Cash	8000.00						8000.00	
2	Accts. Rec.—Sharon Mann	1000.00						1000.00	
3	Supplies	725.00		(a) 390.00				1115.00	
4	Prepaid Insurance	400.00		(b) 95.00				495.00	
5	Accts. Pay.—Powers Supply		150.00						150.00
6	Paul Coty, Capital		5000.00						5000.00
7	Paul Coty, Drawing	300.00							300.00
8	Income Summary								
9	Sales		1875.00				1875.00		
10	Insurance Expense				(b) 95.00		95.00		
11	Miscellaneous Expense	125.00				152.00			
12	Supplies Expense				(a) 390.00		390.00		
13		10550.00	7025.00	485.00	485.00	152.00	2360.00	10610.00	5450.00
14	Net Income					2208.00			5160.00
15						2360.00	2360.00	10610.00	10610.00
16									
17									
18									
19									
20									
21									

6-4 WORK TOGETHER (concluded)

3.

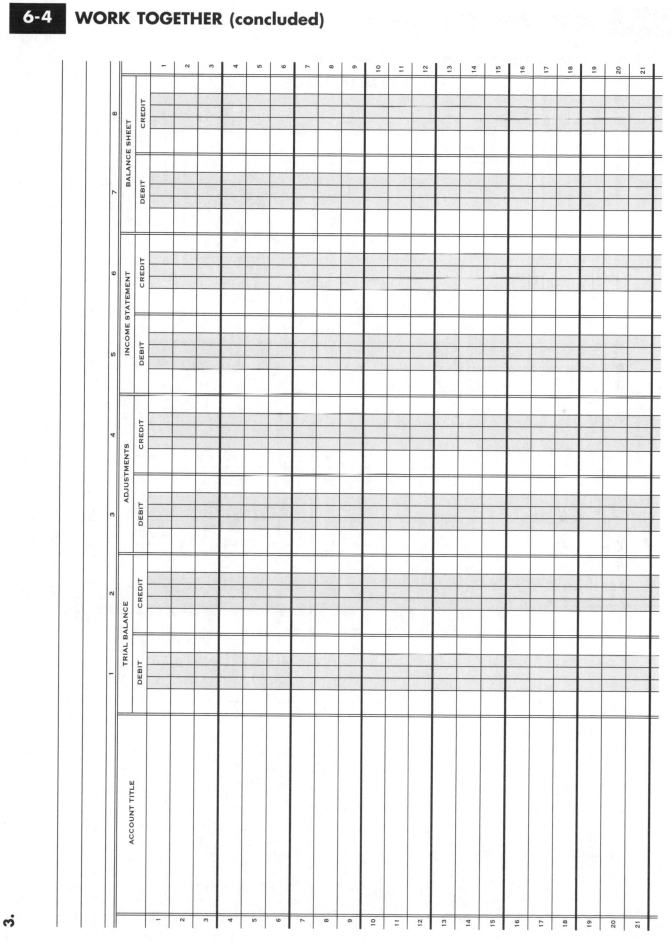

Finding and correcting errors in accounting records

1., 2. **GENERAL LEDGER**

ACCOUNT Cash ACCOUNT NO. 110

DATE		ITEM	POST. REF.	DEBIT	CREDIT	BALANCE DEBIT	BALANCE CREDIT
20-- Nov.	1		1	12 000 00		12 000 00	
	30		2	6 495 00		18 945 00	
	30		2		5 550 00	13 395 00	

ACCOUNT Supplies ACCOUNT NO. 120

DATE		ITEM	POST. REF.	DEBIT	CREDIT	BALANCE DEBIT	BALANCE CREDIT
20-- Nov.	2		1	300 00		300 00	
	25		2	100 00		1 300 00	

ACCOUNT Prepaid Insurance ACCOUNT NO. 130

DATE		ITEM	POST. REF.	DEBIT	CREDIT	BALANCE DEBIT	BALANCE CREDIT
20-- Nov.	3		1	350 00		530 00	

ACCOUNT Accounts Payable—NW Electric ACCOUNT NO. 210

DATE		ITEM	POST. REF.	DEBIT	CREDIT	BALANCE DEBIT	BALANCE CREDIT
20-- Nov.	4		1		400 00		400 00
	15		2	150 00			550 00

ACCOUNT Nadine Fritz, Capital ACCOUNT NO. 310

DATE		ITEM	POST. REF.	DEBIT	CREDIT	BALANCE DEBIT	BALANCE CREDIT
20-- Nov.	1		1		12 000 00		12 000 00

6-4 **ON YOUR OWN (continued)**

1., 2. **GENERAL LEDGER**

ACCOUNT Nadine Fritz, Drawing ACCOUNT NO. 320

DATE	ITEM	POST. REF.	DEBIT	CREDIT	BALANCE DEBIT	BALANCE CREDIT
20-- Nov. 30		2	3 0 0 00		3 0 0 00	

ACCOUNT Income Summary ACCOUNT NO. 330

DATE	ITEM	POST. REF.	DEBIT	CREDIT	BALANCE DEBIT	BALANCE CREDIT

ACCOUNT Sales ACCOUNT NO. 410

DATE	ITEM	POST. REF.	DEBIT	CREDIT	BALANCE DEBIT	BALANCE CREDIT
20-- Nov. 30		2		1 9 5 0 00		1 9 5 0 00

ACCOUNT Insurance Expense ACCOUNT NO. 510

DATE	ITEM	POST. REF.	DEBIT	CREDIT	BALANCE DEBIT	BALANCE CREDIT

ACCOUNT Miscellaneous Expense ACCOUNT NO. 520

DATE	ITEM	POST. REF.	DEBIT	CREDIT	BALANCE DEBIT	BALANCE CREDIT
20-- Nov. 9		1	1 5 0 00		1 5 0 00	
27		2	5 5 00		9 5 00	

ACCOUNT Supplies Expense ACCOUNT NO. 530

DATE	ITEM	POST. REF.	DEBIT	CREDIT	BALANCE DEBIT	BALANCE CREDIT

1. **ERRORS**

6-4 ON YOUR OWN (continued)

2.

Your Personal Trainer

Work Sheet

For Month Ended November 30, 20 – –

	ACCOUNT TITLE	TRIAL BALANCE DEBIT	TRIAL BALANCE CREDIT	ADJUSTMENTS DEBIT	ADJUSTMENTS CREDIT	INCOME STATEMENT DEBIT	INCOME STATEMENT CREDIT	BALANCE SHEET DEBIT	BALANCE SHEET CREDIT
1	Cash	13 395 00						13 395 00	
2	Supplies	1 30 00		(a) 90 00				2 20 00	
3	Prepaid Insurance	5 30 00		(b) 1 04 00				6 43 00	
4	Accts. Pay.—NW Electric		5 50 00						5 50 00
5	Nadine Fritz, Capital		12 000 00						12 000 00
6	Nadine Fritz, Drawing	3 00 00							3 00 00
7	Income Summary								
8	Sales		1 950 00				1 950 00		
9	Insurance Expense				(b) 1 04 00		1 04 00		
10	Miscellaneous Expense	95 00				59 00			
11	Supplies Expense				(a) 90 00		90 00		
12		14 450 00	14 500 00	1 94 00	1 94 00	59 00	2 144 00	14 258 00	12 850 00
13	Net Income					2 085 00			1 408 00
14						2 144 00	2 144 00	14 258 00	14 258 00
15									
16									
17									
18									
19									
20									
21									
22									

3.

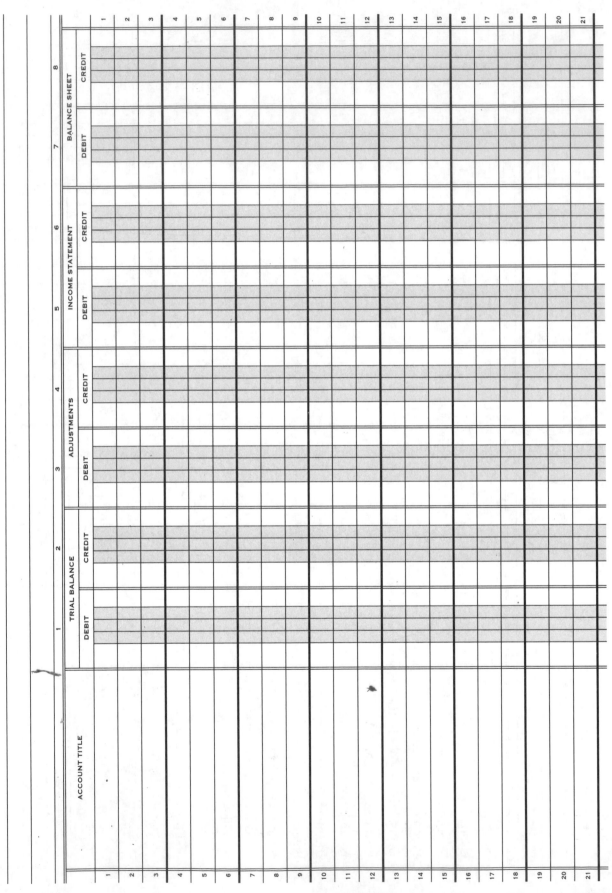

6-4 APPLICATION PROBLEM (continued)

1., 2.   GENERAL LEDGER

ACCOUNT Ervin Watkins, Drawing   ACCOUNT NO. 320

DATE		ITEM	POST. REF.	DEBIT	CREDIT	BALANCE DEBIT	BALANCE CREDIT
20-- Apr.	30		2	6 0 0 00		6 0 0 00	

ACCOUNT Income Summary   ACCOUNT NO. 330

DATE		ITEM	POST. REF.	DEBIT	CREDIT	BALANCE DEBIT	BALANCE CREDIT

ACCOUNT Sales   ACCOUNT NO. 410

DATE		ITEM	POST. REF.	DEBIT	CREDIT	BALANCE DEBIT	BALANCE CREDIT
20-- Apr.	30		2		9 0 0 00		9 9 0 00

ACCOUNT Insurance Expense   ACCOUNT NO. 510

DATE		ITEM	POST. REF.	DEBIT	CREDIT	BALANCE DEBIT	BALANCE CREDIT

ACCOUNT Miscellaneous Expense   ACCOUNT NO. 520

DATE		ITEM	POST. REF.	DEBIT	CREDIT	BALANCE DEBIT	BALANCE CREDIT
20-- Apr.	9		1	3 5 0 00			3 5 0 00
	27		2	1 2 5 00			2 2 5 00

ACCOUNT Supplies Expense   ACCOUNT NO. 530

DATE		ITEM	POST. REF.	DEBIT	CREDIT	BALANCE DEBIT	BALANCE CREDIT

1.   **ERRORS**

6-4 APPLICATION PROBLEM (continued)

1.

EverClean

Work Sheet

For Month Ended April 30, 20 – –

	ACCOUNT TITLE	TRIAL BALANCE DEBIT (1)	TRIAL BALANCE CREDIT (2)	ADJUSTMENTS DEBIT (3)	ADJUSTMENTS CREDIT (4)	INCOME STATEMENT DEBIT (5)	INCOME STATEMENT CREDIT (6)	BALANCE SHEET DEBIT (7)	BALANCE SHEET CREDIT (8)
1	Cash	7 9 6 5 00						7 9 5 6 00	
2	Supplies	5 0 00							2 5 0 00
3	Prepaid Insurance	6 3 0 00		(b) 2 1 0 00	(b) 3 0 0 00			2 4 0 00	
4	Accts. Pay.—Archer Supplies		5 0 0 00						5 0 0 00
5	Ervin Watkins, Capital		5 8 0 0 00						5 8 0 0 00
6	Ervin Watkins, Drawing	6 0 0 00						6 0 0 00	
7	Income Summary								
8	Sales		9 9 0 00				9 9 0 00		
9	Insurance Expense				(b) 2 1 0 00		2 1 0 00		
10	Miscellaneous Expense	2 2 5 00				2 2 5 00			
11	Supplies Expense			(b) 3 0 0 00		3 0 0 00			
12		9 4 7 0 00	7 2 9 0 00	5 1 0 00	5 1 0 00	5 2 5 00	1 2 0 0 00	8 7 9 6 00	6 5 5 0 00
13	Net Income					6 7 5 00			2 2 4 6 00
14						1 2 0 0 00	1 2 0 0 00	8 7 9 6 00	8 7 9 6 00
15									
16									
17									
18									
19									
20									
21									

3.

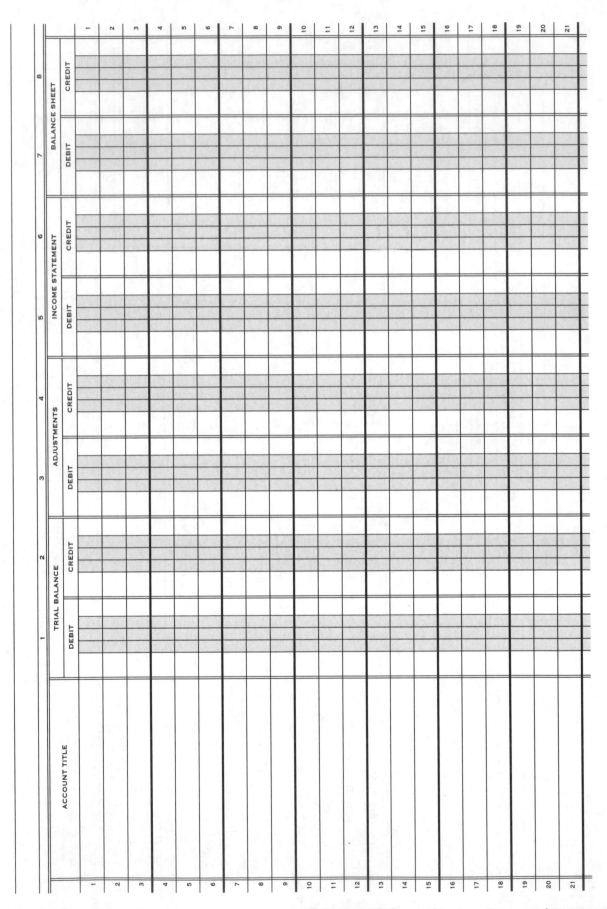

Study Guide 7

Name	Perfect Score	Your Score
Identifying Accounting Concepts and Practices	20 Pts.	
Analyzing an Income Statement	15 Pts.	
Analyzing Income Statement Procedures	5 Pts.	
Total	40 Pts.	

Part One—Identifying Accounting Concepts and Practices

Directions: Place a *T* for True or an *F* for False in the Answers column to show whether each of the following statements is true or false.

Answers

1. The Adequate Disclosure accounting concept is applied when financial statements contain all information necessary to understand a business's financial condition. (p. 180)   1. _____

2. Stakeholders are any persons or groups who will be affected by an action. (p. 181)   2. _____

3. An income statement reports information over a period of time, indicating the financial progress of a business in earning a net income or a net loss. (p. 182)   3. _____

4. The Matching Expenses with Revenue accounting concept is applied when the revenue earned and the expenses incurred to earn that revenue are reported in the same fiscal period. (p. 182)   4. _____

5. Information needed to prepare an income statement comes from the trial balance columns and the income statement columns of a work sheet. (p. 182)   5. _____

6. The income statement for a service business has five sections: heading, revenue, expenses, net income or loss, and capital. (p. 182)   6. _____

7. The income statement's account balances are obtained from the work sheet's Income Statement columns. (p. 182)   7. _____

8. The net income on an income statement is verified by checking the balance sheet. (p. 183)   8. _____

9. Single lines ruled across an amount column of an income statement indicate that amounts are to be added. (p. 183)   9. _____

10. A component percentage is the percentage relationship between one financial statement item and the total that includes that item. (p. 184)   10. _____

11. Component percentages on an income statement are calculated by dividing sales and total expenses by net income. (p. 184)   11. _____

12. All companies should have a total expenses component percentage that is not more than 80.0%. (p. 184)   12. _____

13. When a business has two different sources of revenue, a separate income statement should be prepared for each kind of revenue. (p. 185)   13. _____

14. An amount written in parentheses on a financial statement indicates an estimate. (p. 185)   14. _____

15. A balance sheet reports financial information on a specific date and includes the assets, liabilities, and owner's equity. (p. 187)   15. _____

16. A balance sheet reports information about the elements of the accounting equation. (p. 188)   16. _____

17. The owner's capital amount reported on a balance sheet is calculated as: capital account balance plus drawing account balance, less net income. (p. 189)   17. _____

18. The position of the total asset line on the balance sheet is determined after the equities section is prepared. (p. 189)   18. _____

19. Double lines are ruled across the balance sheet columns to show that the column totals have been verified as correct. (p. 189)   19. _____

20. The owner's equity section of a balance sheet may report different kinds of details about owner's equity, depending on the need of the business. (p. 190)   20. _____

Part Two—Analyzing an Income Statement

Directions: The parts of the income statement below are identified with capital letters. Decide the location of each of the following items. Print the letter identifying your choice in the Answers column.

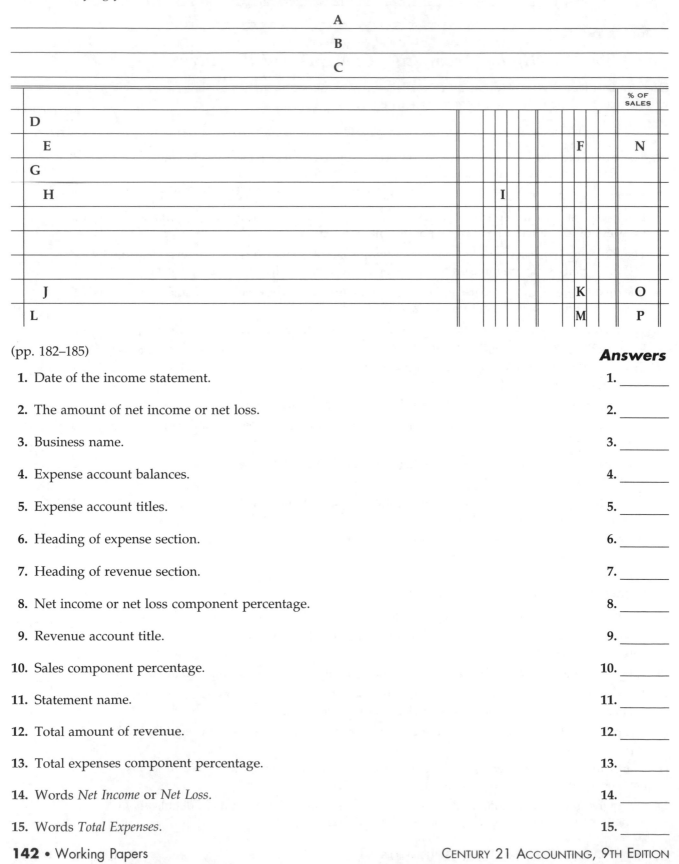

(pp. 182–185)

Answers

1. Date of the income statement.   1. _____

2. The amount of net income or net loss.   2. _____

3. Business name.   3. _____

4. Expense account balances.   4. _____

5. Expense account titles.   5. _____

6. Heading of expense section.   6. _____

7. Heading of revenue section.   7. _____

8. Net income or net loss component percentage.   8. _____

9. Revenue account title.   9. _____

10. Sales component percentage.   10. _____

11. Statement name.   11. _____

12. Total amount of revenue.   12. _____

13. Total expenses component percentage.   13. _____

14. Words *Net Income* or *Net Loss.*   14. _____

15. Words *Total Expenses.*   15. _____

Part Three—Analyzing Income Statement Procedures

Directions: For each of the following items, select the choice that best completes the statement. Print the letter identifying your choice in the Answers column.

Answers

1. The date on a monthly income statement prepared on July 31 is written as (A) For Month Ended July 31, 20–– (B) July 31, 20–– (C) 20––, July 31 (D) none of the above. (p. 182)

   1. _____

2. Information needed to prepare an income statement's revenue section is obtained from a work sheet's Account Title column and (A) Income Statement Debit column (B) Income Statement Credit column (C) Balance Sheet Debit column (D) Balance Sheet Credit column. (p. 183)

   2. _____

3. Information needed to prepare an income statement's expense section is obtained from a work sheet's Account Title column and (A) Income Statement Debit column (B) Income Statement Credit column (C) Balance Sheet Debit column (D) Balance Sheet Credit column. (p. 183)

   3. _____

4. The amount of net income calculated on an income statement is correct if (A) it is the same as net income shown on the work sheet (B) debits equal credits (C) it is the same as the balance sheet (D) none of the above. (p. 183)

   4. _____

5. The formula for calculating the net income component percentage is (A) net income divided by total sales equals net income component percentage (B) total sales divided by total expenses equals net income component percentage (C) total sales minus total expenses divided by net income equals total net income percentage (D) none of the above. (p. 184)

   5. _____

Study Skills

Effective Listening

Every day we hear thousands of words, and we quickly forget most of them. There is little reason to remember most of what we hear. However, we forget many things that we should remember. In order to remember the important things, we must learn to listen effectively.

Become Involved

To retain the important points that we hear, we must become actively involved in the subject. We should try to hold a "mental conversation" with the speaker. We must keep our attention on the subject and try to anticipate what we think the speaker will say next. We should ask ourselves questions that the speaker should answer in the next few sentences.

Play Detective

As we listen, we can "play detective." We can examine every piece of evidence that the speaker presents. We can look for problems in logic or conclusions that are not supported by the evidence presented.

Avoid Distractions

As we are listening, we should not allow ourselves to be distracted. Something like the color of the speaker's clothing can distract us if we are not alert. The speaker's accent may keep us from concentrating on the ideas if we allow it to do so. If we realize that we are not paying attention or daydreaming, we must call our attention back to the subject immediately.

Disagreements

We will often disagree with what a speaker is saying. However, we should not stop listening. We can tell ourselves, "That's not what I think" and immediately return our attention to the subject. We must not allow difference of opinion to keep us from getting the point of a talk.

Conclusion

A passive listener will not gain everything from a talk. A good listener participates actively. Effective listening requires self-control and concentration. It is a skill that each of us should work hard to attain. With practice, we can all be good listeners.

Name _____ Date _____ Class _____

Preparing an income statement

ACCOUNT TITLE	INCOME STATEMENT DEBIT	INCOME STATEMENT CREDIT	BALANCE SHEET DEBIT	BALANCE SHEET CREDIT	
	5	6	7	8	
11 Sales		5 5 1 1 00			11
12 Advertising Expense	8 2 1 00				12
13 Insurance Expense	3 0 0 00				13
14 Miscellaneous Expense	3 4 7 00				14
15 Supplies Expense	7 1 3 00				15
16	2 1 8 1 00	5 5 1 1 00	11 0 6 0 00	7 7 3 0 00	16
17 Net Income	3 3 3 0 00			3 3 3 0 00	17
18	5 5 1 1 00	5 5 1 1 00	11 0 6 0 00	11 0 6 0 00	18
19					19
20					20
21					21
22					22

% OF SALES

Preparing an income statement

	ACCOUNT TITLE	INCOME STATEMENT DEBIT	INCOME STATEMENT CREDIT	BALANCE SHEET DEBIT	BALANCE SHEET CREDIT	
12	Sales		3 8 4 7 00			12
13	Insurance Expense	2 5 0 00				13
14	Miscellaneous Expense	9 8 00				14
15	Supplies Expense	3 7 7 00				15
16	Utilities Expense	1 2 2 0 00				16
17		1 9 4 5 00	3 8 4 7 00	8 4 0 6 00	6 5 0 4 00	17
18	Net Income	1 9 0 2 00			1 9 0 2 00	18
19		3 8 4 7 00	3 8 4 7 00	8 4 0 6 00	8 4 0 6 00	19
20						20
21						21
22						22
23						23

			% OF SALES

7-2 WORK TOGETHER, p. 192

Preparing a balance sheet

	ACCOUNT TITLE	BALANCE SHEET DEBIT	BALANCE SHEET CREDIT	
1	Cash	9 5 0 0 00		1
2	Petty Cash	1 0 0 00		2
3	Accts. Rec.—Betsy Russell	1 6 5 0 00		3
4	Accts. Rec.—Charles Healy	1 4 0 3 00		4
5	Supplies	2 2 0 00		5
6	Prepaid Insurance	6 4 0 00		6
7	Accts. Pay.—Lindgren Supply		5 4 8 00	7
8	Accts. Pay.—Taxes By Thomas		1 1 1 00	8
9	Ken Cherniak, Capital		11 8 1 0 00	9
10	Ken Cherniak, Drawing	8 5 5 00		10
11	Income Summary			11
18		14 3 6 8 00	12 4 6 9 00	18
19	Net Income		1 8 9 9 00	19
20		14 3 6 8 00	14 3 6 8 00	20
21				21
22				22

Preparing a balance sheet

	ACCOUNT TITLE	7 BALANCE SHEET DEBIT	8 BALANCE SHEET CREDIT	
1	Cash	5 3 0 0 00		1
2	Petty Cash	2 5 0 00		2
3	Accts. Rec.—K. Hartwood	5 5 2 00		3
4	Accts. Rec.—Ruth Kabila	1 8 7 00		4
5	Supplies	3 4 3 00		5
6	Prepaid Insurance	9 0 0 00		6
7	Accts. Pay.—Sam's Supply		1 6 5 00	7
8	Accts. Pay.—Ella's on Eaton		1 6 0 00	8
9	Anne Olson, Capital		6 2 1 0 00	9
10	Anne Olson, Drawing	1 2 0 0 00		10
16		8 7 3 2 00	6 5 3 5 00	16
17	Net Income		2 1 9 7 00	17
18		8 7 3 2 00	8 7 3 2 00	18
19				19
20				20
21				21

Name	Perfect Score	Your Score
Identifying Accounting Terms	6 Pts.	
Analyzing Accounts Affected by Adjusting and Closing Entries	14 Pts.	
Analyzing Adjusting and Closing Entries	9 Pts.	
Identifying the Accounting Cycle for a Service Business	8 Pts.	
Total	37 Pts.	

Part One—Identifying Accounting Terms

Directions: Select the one term in Column I that best fits each definition in Column II. Print the letter identifying your choice in the Answers column.

Column I	Column II	Answers
A. accounting cycle	1. Journal entries recorded to update general ledger accounts at the end of a fiscal period. (p. 202)	1. _____
B. adjusting entries	2. Accounts used to accumulate information from one fiscal period to the next. (p. 206)	2. _____
C. closing entries	3. Accounts used to accumulate information until it is transferred to the owner's capital account. (p. 206)	3. _____
D. permanent accounts	4. Journal entries used to prepare temporary accounts for a new fiscal period. (p. 206)	4. _____
E. post-closing trial balance	5. A trial balance prepared after the closing entries are posted. (p. 216)	5. _____
F. temporary accounts	6. The series of accounting activities included in recording financial information for a fiscal period. (p. 217)	6. _____

Part Two—Analyzing Accounts Affected by Adjusting and Closing Entries

Directions: Use the partial chart of accounts given below. For each adjusting or closing entry described, decide which accounts are debited and credited. Write the account numbers identifying your choice in the proper Answers column.

Account Title	Acct. No.
Supplies	150
Prepaid Insurance	160
J. Nichols, Capital	310
J. Nichols, Drawing	320
Income Summary	330
Sales	410
Advertising Expense	510
Insurance Expense	520
Supplies Expense	550

	Accounts to Be	
	Debited	**Credited**
1–2. Adjusting entry for Supplies. (p. 203)	1. _____	2. _____
3–4. Adjusting entry for Prepaid Insurance. (p. 204)	3. _____	4. _____
5–6. Closing entry for Sales. (p. 208)	5. _____	6. _____
7–8. Closing entry for all expense accounts. (p. 209)	7. _____	8. _____
9–10. Closing entry for Income Summary with a net income. (p. 210)	9. _____	10. _____
11–12. Closing entry for Income Summary with a net loss. (p. 210)	11. _____	12. _____
13–14. Closing entry for owner's drawing account. (p. 211)	13. _____	14. _____

Part Three—Analyzing Adjusting and Closing Entries

Directions: For each of the following items, select the choice that best completes the statement. Print the letter identifying your choice in the Answers column.

Answers

1. Which accounting concept applies when a work sheet is prepared at the end of each fiscal cycle to summarize the general ledger information needed to prepare financial statements? (A) Business Entity (B) Accounting Period Cycle (C) Adequate Disclosure (D) Consistent Reporting (p. 202)

   1. _____

2. Which accounting concept applies when expenses are reported in the same fiscal period that they are used to produce revenue? (A) Business Entity (B) Going Concern (C) Matching Expenses with Revenue (D) Adequate Disclosure (p. 202)

   2. _____

3. Information needed for journalizing the adjusting entries is obtained from the (A) general ledger account Balance columns (B) income statement (C) work sheet's Adjustments columns (D) balance sheet. (p. 204)

   3. _____

4. After adjusting entries are posted, the supplies account balance will be equal to (A) the cost of supplies used during the fiscal period (B) the cost of the supplies on hand at the end of the fiscal period (C) zero (D) none of these. (p. 204)

   4. _____

5. When revenue is greater than total expenses, resulting in a net income, the income summary account has a (A) debit balance (B) credit balance (C) normal debit balance (D) normal credit balance. (p. 207)

   5. _____

6. Information needed for recording the closing entries is obtained from the (A) general ledger accounts' Debit Balance columns (B) work sheet's Income Statement and Balance Sheet columns (C) balance sheet (D) income statement. (p. 207)

   6. _____

7. Income Summary is (A) an asset account (B) a liability account (C) a temporary account (D) a permanent account. (p. 207)

   7. _____

8. After the closing entries are posted, the owner's capital account balance should be the same as (A) shown on the balance sheet for the fiscal period (B) shown in the work sheet's Balance Sheet Debit column (C) shown in the work sheet's Balance Sheet Credit column (D) shown in the work sheet's Income Statement Debit column. (p. 211)

   8. _____

9. The accounts listed on a post-closing trial balance are (A) general ledger accounts with balances after the closing entries are posted (B) all general ledger accounts (C) those that have no balances after adjusting and closing entries (D) those that appear in the work sheet's Trial Balance columns. (p. 216)

   9. _____

Part Four—Identifying the Accounting Cycle for a Service Business

Directions: Arrange the series of accounting activities listed below for the accounting cycle for a service business. Indicate the sequence of the steps by writing a number from 1 to 8 to the left of each activity. (p. 217)

Answers

1. _____ A work sheet, including a trial balance, is prepared from the general ledger.

2. _____ Transactions, from information on source documents, are recorded in a journal.

3. _____ Source documents are checked for accuracy, and transactions are analyzed into debit and credit parts.

4. _____ Adjusting and closing entries are posted to the general ledger.

5. _____ Financial statements are prepared from the work sheet.

6. _____ Adjusting and closing entries are journalized from the work sheet.

7. _____ A post-closing trial balance of the general ledger is prepared.

8. _____ Journal entries are posted to the general ledger.

8-1 and 8-2   WORK TOGETHER, pp. 205, 212

8-1 Journalizing and posting adjusting entries
8-2 Journalizing and posting closing entries

	ACCOUNT TITLE	ADJUSTMENTS DEBIT	ADJUSTMENTS CREDIT	INCOME STATEMENT DEBIT	INCOME STATEMENT CREDIT	BALANCE SHEET DEBIT	BALANCE SHEET CREDIT	
1	Cash					7350 00		1
2	Accts. Rec.—Romelle Woods					372 00		2
3	Accts. Rec.—Wyatt Ames					88 00		3
4	Supplies		(a) 713 00			250 00		4
5	Prepaid Insurance		(b) 300 00			900 00		5
6	Accts. Pay.—Colin Gas						975 00	6
7	Accts. Pay.—Grand Uniforms						212 00	7
8	Darlene Wong, Capital						6543 00	8
9	Darlene Wong, Drawing					2100 00		9
10	Income Summary							10
11	Sales				5511 00			11
12	Advertising Expense			821 00				12
13	Insurance Expense	(b) 300 00		300 00				13
14	Miscellaneous Expense			347 00				14
15	Supplies Expense	(a) 713 00		713 00				15
16		1013 00	1013 00	2181 00	5511 00	11060 00	7730 00	16
17	Net Income			3330 00			3330 00	17
18				5511 00	5511 00	11060 00	11060 00	18
19								19
20								20
21								21
22								22
23								23

JOURNAL

PAGE 4

	DATE	ACCOUNT TITLE	DOC. NO.	POST. REF.	GENERAL DEBIT	GENERAL CREDIT	SALES CREDIT	CASH DEBIT	CASH CREDIT
1	20--	Adjusting Entries							
2	Jul 31	Supplies Expense			713 00				
3		Supplies				713 00			
4	31	Insurance Expense			300 00				
5		Prepaid Insurance				300 00			
6		Closing Entries							
7	31	Sales			5 511 00				
8		Income Summary				5 700 00			
9	31	Income Summary			2 181 00				
10		Advertising Expense				821 00			
11		Insurance Expense				300 00			
12		Miscellaneous Expense				347 00			
13		Supplies Expense				713 00			
14	31	Income Summary			3 330 00				
15		Darlene Wong Capital				3 330 00			
16	31	Darlene Wong Capital			2 100 00				
17		Darlene Wong Drawing				2 100 00			
18									
19									
20									
21									
22									
23									
24									

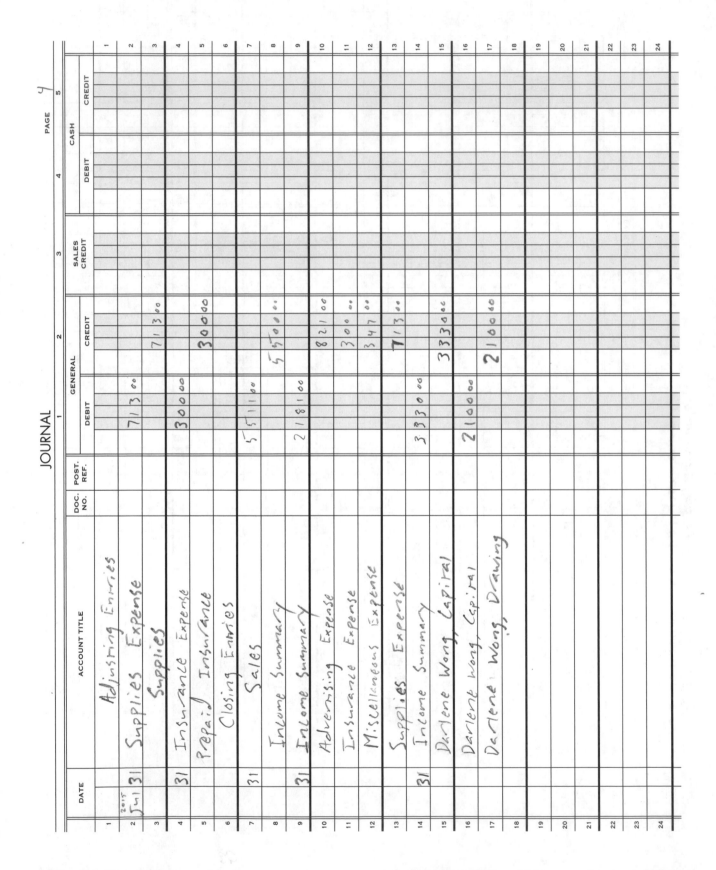

8-1 and 8-2   WORK TOGETHER (continued)

GENERAL LEDGER

ACCOUNT Cash   ACCOUNT NO. 110

DATE		ITEM	POST. REF.	DEBIT	CREDIT	BALANCE	
						DEBIT	CREDIT
July 31	Balance		✔			7 3 5 0 00	

ACCOUNT Accounts Receivable—Romelle Woods   ACCOUNT NO. 120

DATE		ITEM	POST. REF.	DEBIT	CREDIT	BALANCE	
						DEBIT	CREDIT
July 31	Balance		✔			3 7 2 00	

ACCOUNT Accounts Receivable—Wyatt Ames   ACCOUNT NO. 130

DATE		ITEM	POST. REF.	DEBIT	CREDIT	BALANCE	
						DEBIT	CREDIT
July 31	Balance		✔			8 8 00	

ACCOUNT Supplies   ACCOUNT NO. 140

DATE		ITEM	POST. REF.	DEBIT	CREDIT	BALANCE	
						DEBIT	CREDIT
July 31	Balance		✔			9 6 3 00	

ACCOUNT Prepaid Insurance   ACCOUNT NO. 150

DATE		ITEM	POST. REF.	DEBIT	CREDIT	BALANCE	
						DEBIT	CREDIT
July 31	Balance		✔			1 2 0 0 00	

ACCOUNT Accounts Payable—Colin Gas   ACCOUNT NO. 210

DATE		ITEM	POST. REF.	DEBIT	CREDIT	BALANCE	
						DEBIT	CREDIT
July 31	Balance		✔				9 7 5 00

GENERAL LEDGER

ACCOUNT Accounts Payable—Grand Uniforms   ACCOUNT NO. 220

DATE		ITEM	POST. REF.	DEBIT	CREDIT	BALANCE	
						DEBIT	CREDIT
July 20--	31	Balance	✔				2 1 2 00

ACCOUNT Darlene Wong, Capital   ACCOUNT NO. 310

DATE		ITEM	POST. REF.	DEBIT	CREDIT	BALANCE	
						DEBIT	CREDIT
July 20--	31	Balance	✔				6 5 4 3 00

ACCOUNT Darlene Wong, Drawing   ACCOUNT NO. 320

DATE		ITEM	POST. REF.	DEBIT	CREDIT	BALANCE	
						DEBIT	CREDIT
July 20--	31	Balance	✔			2 1 0 0 00	

ACCOUNT Income Summary   ACCOUNT NO. 330

DATE		ITEM	POST. REF.	DEBIT	CREDIT	BALANCE	
						DEBIT	CREDIT

ACCOUNT Sales   ACCOUNT NO. 410

DATE		ITEM	POST. REF.	DEBIT	CREDIT	BALANCE	
						DEBIT	CREDIT
July 20--	31	Balance	✔				5 5 1 1 00

ACCOUNT Advertising Expense   ACCOUNT NO. 510

DATE		ITEM	POST. REF.	DEBIT	CREDIT	BALANCE	
						DEBIT	CREDIT
July 20--	31	Balance	✔			8 2 1 00	

8-1 and 8-2 WORK TOGETHER (concluded)

GENERAL LEDGER

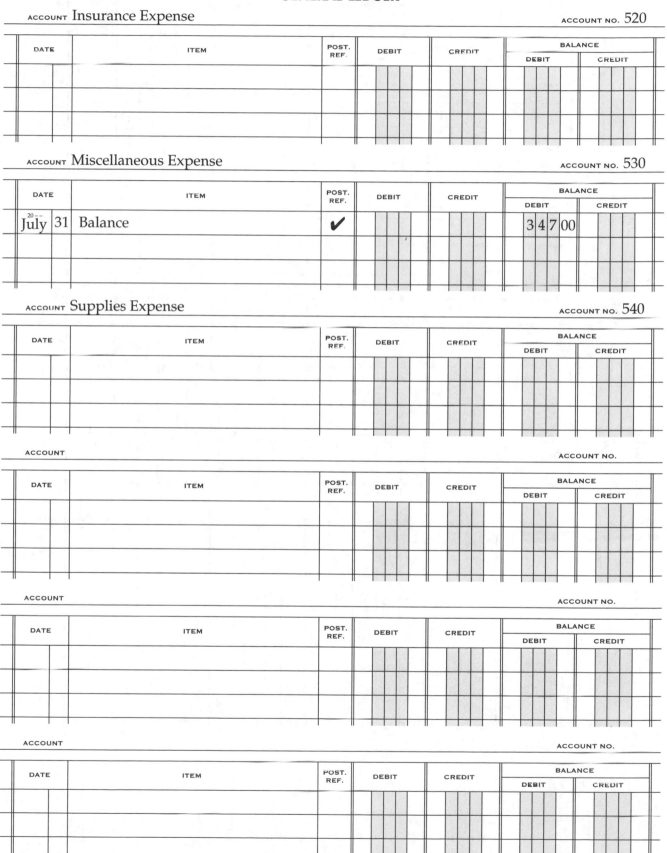

ACCOUNT Insurance Expense   ACCOUNT NO. 520

DATE	ITEM	POST. REF.	DEBIT	CREDIT	BALANCE DEBIT	BALANCE CREDIT

ACCOUNT Miscellaneous Expense   ACCOUNT NO. 530

DATE	ITEM	POST. REF.	DEBIT	CREDIT	BALANCE DEBIT	BALANCE CREDIT
July 31	Balance	✔			3 4 7 00	

ACCOUNT Supplies Expense   ACCOUNT NO. 540

DATE	ITEM	POST. REF.	DEBIT	CREDIT	BALANCE DEBIT	BALANCE CREDIT

ACCOUNT   ACCOUNT NO.

DATE	ITEM	POST. REF.	DEBIT	CREDIT	BALANCE DEBIT	BALANCE CREDIT

ACCOUNT   ACCOUNT NO.

DATE	ITEM	POST. REF.	DEBIT	CREDIT	BALANCE DEBIT	BALANCE CREDIT

ACCOUNT   ACCOUNT NO.

DATE	ITEM	POST. REF.	DEBIT	CREDIT	BALANCE DEBIT	BALANCE CREDIT

8-1 Journalizing and posting adjusting entries
8-2 Journalizing and posting closing entries

	ACCOUNT TITLE	ADJUSTMENTS DEBIT	ADJUSTMENTS CREDIT	INCOME STATEMENT DEBIT	INCOME STATEMENT CREDIT	BALANCE SHEET DEBIT	BALANCE SHEET CREDIT	
1	Cash					6116 00		1
2	Petty Cash					200 00		2
3	Accts. Rec.—Jodi Ford					317 00		3
4	Accts. Rec.—Midville Center					148 00		4
5	Supplies		(a) 377 00			225 00		5
6	Prepaid Insurance		(b) 250 00			400 00		6
7	Accts. Pay.—Beauty Supply Co.						422 00	7
8	Accts. Pay.—Midwest Towel						182 00	8
9	Kelley Cooper, Capital						5900 00	9
10	Kelley Cooper, Drawing					1000 00		10
11	Income Summary							11
12	Sales				3847 00			12
13	Insurance Expense	(b) 250 00		250 00				13
14	Miscellaneous Expense			98 00				14
15	Supplies Expense	(a) 377 00		377 00				15
16	Utilities Expense			1220 00				16
17		627 00	627 00	1945 00	3847 00	8406 00	6504 00	17
18	Net Income			1902 00			1902 00	18
19				3847 00	3847 00	8406 00	8406 00	19
20								20
21								21
22								22

8-1 and 8-2   ON YOUR OWN (continued)

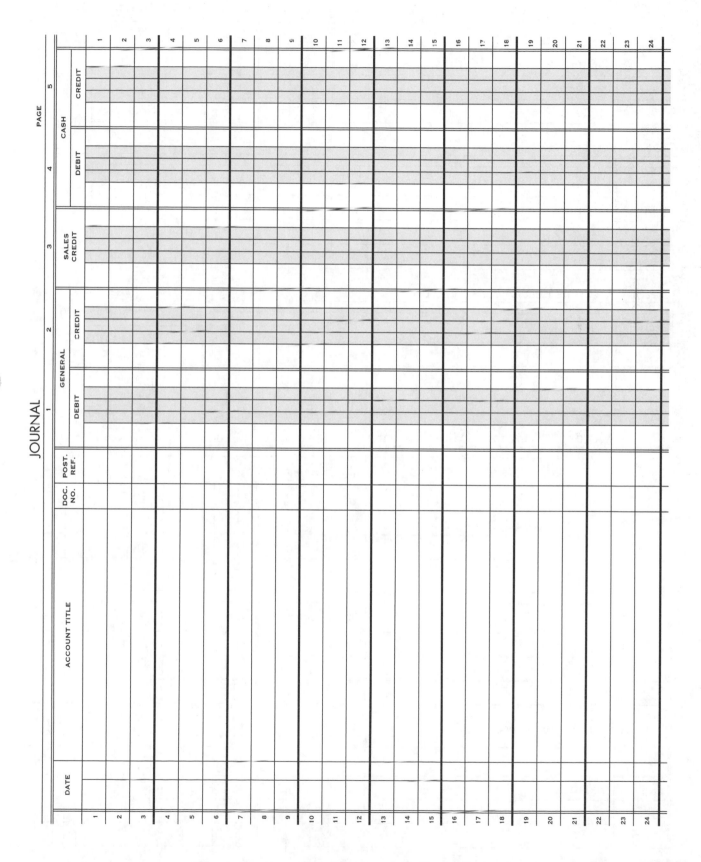

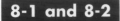

GENERAL LEDGER

ACCOUNT Cash   ACCOUNT NO. 110

DATE		ITEM	POST. REF.	DEBIT	CREDIT	BALANCE DEBIT	BALANCE CREDIT
20-- Feb.	28	Balance	✔			6 1 1 6 00	

ACCOUNT Petty Cash   ACCOUNT NO. 120

DATE		ITEM	POST. REF.	DEBIT	CREDIT	BALANCE DEBIT	BALANCE CREDIT
20-- Feb.	28	Balance	✔			2 0 0 00	

ACCOUNT Accounts Receivable—Jodi Ford   ACCOUNT NO. 130

DATE		ITEM	POST. REF.	DEBIT	CREDIT	BALANCE DEBIT	BALANCE CREDIT
20-- Feb.	28	Balance	✔			3 1 7 00	

ACCOUNT Accounts Receivable—Midville Center   ACCOUNT NO. 140

DATE		ITEM	POST. REF.	DEBIT	CREDIT	BALANCE DEBIT	BALANCE CREDIT
20-- Feb.	28	Balance	✔			1 4 8 00	

ACCOUNT Supplies   ACCOUNT NO. 150

DATE		ITEM	POST. REF.	DEBIT	CREDIT	BALANCE DEBIT	BALANCE CREDIT
20-- Feb.	28	Balance	✔			6 0 2 00	

ACCOUNT Prepaid Insurance   ACCOUNT NO. 160

DATE		ITEM	POST. REF.	DEBIT	CREDIT	BALANCE DEBIT	BALANCE CREDIT
20-- Feb.	28	Balance	✔			6 5 0 00	

8-1 and 8-2 ON YOUR OWN (continued)

GENERAL LEDGER

ACCOUNT Accounts Payable—Beauty Supply Co. ACCOUNT NO. 210

DATE	ITEM	POST. REF.	DEBIT	CREDIT	BALANCE DEBIT	BALANCE CREDIT
Feb. 28	Balance	✔				4 2 2 00

ACCOUNT Accounts Payable—Midwest Towel ACCOUNT NO. 220

DATE	ITEM	POST. REF.	DEBIT	CREDIT	BALANCE DEBIT	BALANCE CREDIT
Feb. 28	Balance	✔				1 8 2 00

ACCOUNT Kelley Cooper, Capital ACCOUNT NO. 310

DATE	ITEM	POST. REF.	DEBIT	CREDIT	BALANCE DEBIT	BALANCE CREDIT
Feb. 28	Balance	✔				5 9 0 0 00

ACCOUNT Kelley Cooper, Drawing ACCOUNT NO. 320

DATE	ITEM	POST. REF.	DEBIT	CREDIT	BALANCE DEBIT	BALANCE CREDIT
Feb. 28	Balance	✔			1 0 0 0 00	

ACCOUNT Income Summary ACCOUNT NO. 330

DATE	ITEM	POST. REF.	DEBIT	CREDIT	BALANCE DEBIT	BALANCE CREDIT

ACCOUNT Sales ACCOUNT NO. 410

DATE	ITEM	POST. REF.	DEBIT	CREDIT	BALANCE DEBIT	BALANCE CREDIT
Feb. 28	Balance	✔				3 8 4 7 00

GENERAL LEDGER

ACCOUNT Insurance Expense   ACCOUNT NO. 510

DATE	ITEM	POST. REF.	DEBIT	CREDIT	BALANCE DEBIT	BALANCE CREDIT

ACCOUNT Miscellaneous Expense   ACCOUNT NO. 520

DATE	ITEM	POST. REF.	DEBIT	CREDIT	BALANCE DEBIT	BALANCE CREDIT
20-- Feb. 28	Balance	✔			9 8 00	

ACCOUNT Supplies Expense   ACCOUNT NO. 530

DATE	ITEM	POST. REF.	DEBIT	CREDIT	BALANCE DEBIT	BALANCE CREDIT

ACCOUNT Utilities Expense   ACCOUNT NO. 540

DATE	ITEM	POST. REF.	DEBIT	CREDIT	BALANCE DEBIT	BALANCE CREDIT
20-- Feb. 28	Balance	✔			1 2 2 0 00	

ACCOUNT   ACCOUNT NO.

DATE	ITEM	POST. REF.	DEBIT	CREDIT	BALANCE DEBIT	BALANCE CREDIT

ACCOUNT   ACCOUNT NO.

DATE	ITEM	POST. REF.	DEBIT	CREDIT	BALANCE DEBIT	BALANCE CREDIT

8-3 WORK TOGETHER, p. 219

Preparing a post-closing trial balance

Darlene's Delivery Service
Post-Closing Trial Balance
July 31, 2015

ACCOUNT TITLE	DEBIT	CREDIT
Cash	7 350 00	
Accts. Rec. — Romelle Woods	3 72 00	
Accts. Rec. — Wyatt Ames	88 00	
Supplies	2 50 00	
Prepaid Insurance	9 00 00	
Accts. Pay. — Colin Gas		9 75 00
Accts. Pay. — Grand Uniforms		2 12 00
Darlene Wong, Capital		7 773 00
Totals	8 960 00	8 960 00

Preparing a post-closing trial balance

ACCOUNT TITLE	DEBIT	CREDIT

8-5 CHALLENGE PROBLEM, p. 223

Journalizing and posting adjusting and closing entries with two revenue accounts and a net loss; preparing a post-closing trial balance

1., 2.

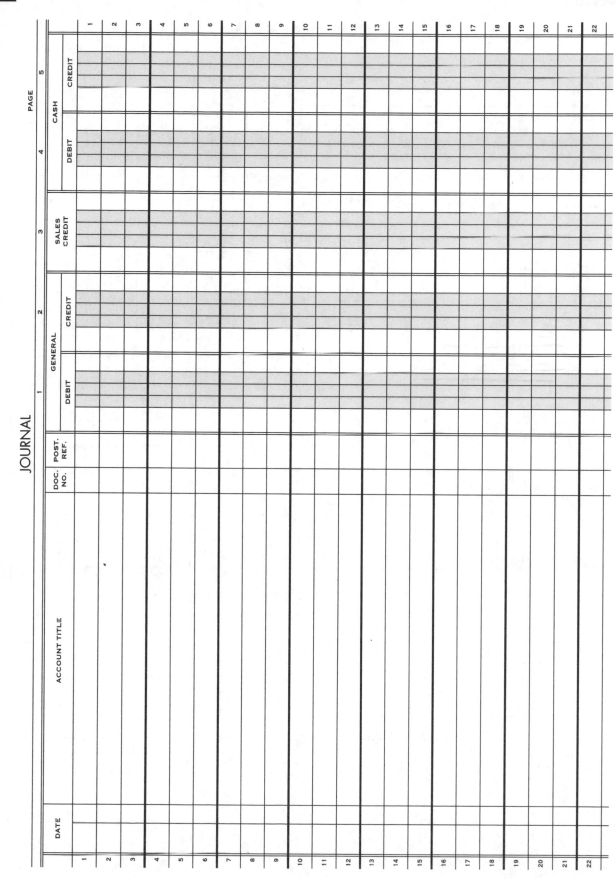

1., 2.

GENERAL LEDGER

ACCOUNT Cash   ACCOUNT NO. 110

DATE		ITEM	POST. REF.	DEBIT	CREDIT	BALANCE	
						DEBIT	CREDIT
Sept.	30	Balance	✔			1 8 9 8 00	

ACCOUNT Accounts Receivable—Sandra Rohe   ACCOUNT NO. 120

DATE		ITEM	POST. REF.	DEBIT	CREDIT	BALANCE	
						DEBIT	CREDIT
Sept.	30	Balance	✔			9 5 00	

ACCOUNT Supplies   ACCOUNT NO. 130

DATE		ITEM	POST. REF.	DEBIT	CREDIT	BALANCE	
						DEBIT	CREDIT
Sept.	30	Balance	✔			3 8 5 0 00	

ACCOUNT Prepaid Insurance   ACCOUNT NO. 140

DATE		ITEM	POST. REF.	DEBIT	CREDIT	BALANCE	
						DEBIT	CREDIT
Sept.	30	Balance	✔			1 6 0 0 00	

ACCOUNT Accounts Payable—Corner Garage   ACCOUNT NO. 210

DATE		ITEM	POST. REF.	DEBIT	CREDIT	BALANCE	
						DEBIT	CREDIT
Sept.	30	Balance	✔				5 8 00

8-5 **CHALLENGE PROBLEM (continued)**

1., 2.   **GENERAL LEDGER**

ACCOUNT Accounts Payable—Broadway Gas   ACCOUNT NO. 220

DATE	ITEM	POST. REF.	DEBIT	CREDIT	BALANCE DEBIT	BALANCE CREDIT
Sept. 30	Balance	✔				1 1 0 00

ACCOUNT Accounts Payable—Esko Repair   ACCOUNT NO. 230

DATE	ITEM	POST. REF.	DEBIT	CREDIT	BALANCE DEBIT	BALANCE CREDIT
Sept. 30	Balance	✔				2 1 5 00

ACCOUNT Ryo Morrison, Capital   ACCOUNT NO. 310

DATE	ITEM	POST. REF.	DEBIT	CREDIT	BALANCE DEBIT	BALANCE CREDIT
Sept. 30	Balance	✔				4 0 0 0 00

ACCOUNT Ryo Morrison, Drawing   ACCOUNT NO. 320

DATE	ITEM	POST. REF.	DEBIT	CREDIT	BALANCE DEBIT	BALANCE CREDIT
Sept. 30	Balance	✔			1 0 0 00	

ACCOUNT Income Summary   ACCOUNT NO. 330

DATE	ITEM	POST. REF.	DEBIT	CREDIT	BALANCE DEBIT	BALANCE CREDIT

ACCOUNT Sales—Lawn Care   ACCOUNT NO. 410

DATE	ITEM	POST. REF.	DEBIT	CREDIT	BALANCE DEBIT	BALANCE CREDIT
Sept. 30	Balance	✔				4 9 0 0 00

1., 2.   **GENERAL LEDGER**

ACCOUNT Sales—Shrub Care   ACCOUNT NO. 420

DATE	ITEM	POST. REF.	DEBIT	CREDIT	BALANCE DEBIT	BALANCE CREDIT
Sept. 30	Balance	✔				2 5 0 0 00

ACCOUNT Advertising Expense   ACCOUNT NO. 510

DATE	ITEM	POST. REF.	DEBIT	CREDIT	BALANCE DEBIT	BALANCE CREDIT
Sept. 30	Balance	✔			3 9 0 00	

ACCOUNT Insurance Expense   ACCOUNT NO. 520

DATE	ITEM	POST. REF.	DEBIT	CREDIT	BALANCE DEBIT	BALANCE CREDIT

ACCOUNT Miscellaneous Expense   ACCOUNT NO. 530

DATE	ITEM	POST. REF.	DEBIT	CREDIT	BALANCE DEBIT	BALANCE CREDIT
Sept. 30	Balance	✔			5 5 0 00	

ACCOUNT Rent Expense   ACCOUNT NO. 540

DATE	ITEM	POST. REF.	DEBIT	CREDIT	BALANCE DEBIT	BALANCE CREDIT
Sept. 30	Balance	✔			3 3 0 0 00	

ACCOUNT Supplies Expense   ACCOUNT NO. 550

DATE	ITEM	POST. REF.	DEBIT	CREDIT	BALANCE DEBIT	BALANCE CREDIT

8-5   **CHALLENGE PROBLEM (continued)**

3.

ACCOUNT TITLE	DEBIT	CREDIT

4.

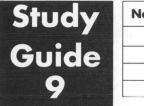
Study Guide 9

Part One—Identifying Accounting Terms

Directions: Select the one term in Column I that best fits each definition in Column II. Print the letter identifying your choice in the Answers column.

Column I	Column II	Answers
A. capital stock	1. An organization with the legal rights of a person and which many persons may own. (p. 234)	1. _____
B. cash discount	2. Each unit of ownership in a corporation. (p. 234)	2. _____
C. cash payments journal	3. Total shares of ownership in a corporation. (p. 234)	3. _____
	4. An owner of one or more shares of a corporation. (p. 234)	4. _____
D. contra account	5. The price a business pays for goods it purchases to sell. (p. 236)	5. _____
E. corporation	6. The amount added to the cost of merchandise to establish the selling price. (p. 236)	6. _____
F. cost of merchandise	7. A business from which merchandise is purchased or supplies or other assets are bought. (p. 236)	7. _____
G. debit memorandum	8. A transaction in which the merchandise purchased is to be paid for later. (p. 236)	8. _____
H. list price	9. An invoice used as a source document for recording a purchase on account transaction. (p. 238)	9. _____
I. markup	10. An agreement between a buyer and a seller about payment for merchandise. (p. 238)	10. _____
J. purchase invoice	11. A special journal used to record only cash payment transactions. (p. 242)	11. _____
K. purchase on account	12. A deduction that a vendor allows on the invoice amount to encourage prompt payment. (p. 242)	12. _____
L. purchases allowance	13. A cash discount on purchases taken by a customer. (p. 242)	13. _____
M. purchases discount	14. The retail price listed in a catalog or on an Internet site. (p. 244)	14. _____
N. purchases return	15. A reduction in the list price granted to customers. (p. 244)	15. _____
O. share of stock	16. An account that reduces a related account on a financial statement. (p. 245)	16. _____
P. stockholder	17. Credit allowed for the purchase price of returned merchandise, resulting in a decrease in the customer's accounts payable. (p. 256)	17. _____
Q. terms of sale	18. Credit allowed for part of the purchase price of merchandise that is not returned, resulting in a decrease in the customer's accounts payable. (p. 256)	18. _____
R. trade discount		
S. vendor	19. A form prepared by the customer showing the price deduction taken by the customer for returns and allowances. (p. 256)	19. _____

Part Two—Analyzing Accounting Concepts and Practices

Directions: Place a *T* for True or an *F* for False in the Answers column to show whether each of the following statements is true or false.

Answers

1. Unlike a proprietorship, a corporation exists independent of its owners. (p. 234) **1.** _____
2. A corporation can incur liabilities but cannot own property. (p. 234) **2.** _____
3. As in proprietorships, information in a corporation's accounting system is kept separate from the personal records of the owners, and this accounting concept application is called a Business Entity. (p. 234) **3.** _____
4. The selling price of merchandise must be greater than the cost of merchandise for a business to make a profit. (p. 236) **4.** _____
5. The cost account Purchases is used only to record the value of merchandise purchased. (p. 236) **5.** _____
6. When purchases are recorded at their cost, including any related shipping costs and taxes, the Historical Cost accounting concept is being applied. (p. 236) **6.** _____
7. Recording entries in a journal with special amount columns saves time. (p. 237) **7.** _____
8. All purchase transactions, including purchases made on account and purchases made for cash, are recorded in the purchases journal. (p. 237) **8.** _____
9. The source document for recording a purchase on account transaction is a memorandum describing the merchandise purchased. (p. 238) **9.** _____
10. By listing the quantity, the description, the price of each item, and the total amount purchased, the Objective Evidence concept is applied. (p. 238) **10.** _____
11. A purchase invoice usually lists only the total cost of the merchandise. (p. 238) **11.** _____
12. A purchase on account transaction increases the amount owed to a vendor. (p. 239) **12.** _____
13. A cash payments journal includes a special amount column for the cash account and the accounts payable account. (p. 242) **13.** _____
14. The source document for most cash payments is the check issued. (p. 242) **14.** _____
15. When supplies are purchased for use in the business, the amount is recorded in the purchases account. (p. 243) **15.** _____
16. A special journal entry is made to show the amount of a trade discount. (p. 244) **16.** _____
17. The terms of sale 2/15, n/30 mean that 2% of the invoice amount may be deducted if paid within 15 days of the invoice date or the total invoice amount must be paid within 30 days. (p. 245) **17.** _____
18. Purchase discounts are recorded in the general journal. (p. 245) **18.** _____
19. The contra account Purchases Discount has a normal credit balance. (p. 245) **19.** _____
20. The custodian prepares a petty cash report when the petty cash fund is to be replenished. (p. 248) **20.** _____
21. The petty cash account Cash Short and Over is a permanent account. (p. 249) **21.** _____
22. A journal is proved and ruled only at the end of a fiscal period. (p. 250) **22.** _____
23. To begin a new journal page, the totals from the previous journal page are carried forward to the next journal page. (p. 251) **23.** _____
24. Buying supplies on account is recorded in the general journal. (p. 254) **24.** _____
25. When store supplies are purchased on account, the Store Supplies account balance increases and the Accounts Payable account balance increases. (p. 255) **25.** _____
26. The source document for a purchases return is a check. (p. 256) **26.** _____
27. The normal account balance of Purchases Returns and Allowances is a credit. (p. 257) **27.** _____

Part Three—Analyzing Transactions Recorded in Special Journals

Directions: In Answers Column l, print the abbreviation for the journal in which each transaction is to be recorded. In Answers Columns 2 and 3, print the letters identifying the accounts to be debited and credited for each transaction.

PJ—Purchases journal; **GJ**—General journal; **CPJ**—Cash payments journal

Answers

Account Titles	Transactions	Journal	Debit	Credit
A. Accounts Payable	1–2–3. Purchased merchandise on account from Wixom Sports. (p. 239)	1. _____	2. _____	3. _____
B. Cash	4–5–6. Paid cash for rent. (p. 243)	4. _____	5. _____	6. _____
C. Cash Short and Over	7–8–9. Purchased merchandise for cash. (p. 244)	7. _____	8. _____	9. _____
D. Miscellaneous Expense	10–11–12. Paid cash on account to Wixom Sports, less purchases discount. (p. 245)	10. _____	11. _____	12. _____
E. Petty Cash				
F. Purchases	13–14–15. Paid cash on account to Tri-County Suppliers. (p. 246)	13. _____	14. _____	15. _____
G. Purchases Discount	16–17–18. Paid cash to replenish the petty cash fund: supplies, miscellaneous, cash over. (p. 249)	16. _____	17. _____	18. _____
H. Purchases Returns and Allowances	19–20–21. Bought supplies on account from Yukon Outfitters. (p. 255)	19. _____	20. _____	21. _____
I. Rent Expense	22–23–24. Returned merchandise to Tri-County Suppliers. (p. 257)	22. _____	23. _____	24. _____
J. Supplies				
K. Tri-County Suppliers				
L. Wixom Sports				
M. Yukon Outfitters				

Study Skills

Skimming and Careful Reading

We must learn to use different techniques as we read. Sometimes we need to skim material very quickly, touching only the high points. At other times we need to read slowly and carefully, concentrating on every word.

Skimming

Skimming helps you gain a general understanding of what is contained in material without slow and careful reading. You may wish to skim a magazine article to determine if it contains information you want to read carefully later.

You can use skimming to preview an assignment before you read for details. You should first read the title and the introduction quickly. You should then read the main headings and glance through the paragraphs. By skimming first, you will know what is included before you become involved in the details.

If you own the book, you may wish to use a highlighter sparingly as you skim. This will help call your attention to certain parts of a selection later. If you highlight too much, it will be of little help to you.

You can also use skimming to review material that you have studied previously. Before an exam, for example, you may want to read quickly through the material to be sure that you have not forgotten any important points.

Careful Reading

Many times you will be responsible for every detail in a reading assignment. You may have to remember names, dates, and facts that are of great importance. Before you read for details, you should skim the material first to gain an overview. Then you should read it slowly and carefully.

As you read carefully, you should ask yourself what is included in each paragraph. If you can summarize each paragraph as you read, you will have a good understanding. Then you should determine if you can remember names, dates, and other details. If you cannot, you should read the material again, concentrating on the details while keeping the overall picture in mind.

Conclusion

Skimming and careful reading are techniques that will be extremely useful to you in the future. You should know which technique to use and be sure to use it properly. Skimming will give you an overall view of the material. Careful reading will ensure that you know the details.

9-1 WORK TOGETHER, p. 241

Journalizing purchases using a purchases journal

PURCHASES JOURNAL   PAGE _____

	DATE	ACCOUNT CREDITED	PURCH. NO.	POST. REF.	PURCHASES DR. ACCTS. PAY. CR.	
1						1
2						2
3						3
4						4
5						5
6						6
7						7
8						8
9						9
10						10
11						11
12						12
13						13
14						14
15						15
16						16
17						17
18						18
19						19
20						20
21						21
22						22
23						23
24						24
25						25
26						26
27						27
28						28
29						29
30						30
31						31
32						32
33						33

Journalizing purchases using a purchases journal

PURCHASES JOURNAL   PAGE

	DATE		ACCOUNT CREDITED	PURCH. NO.	POST. REF.	PURCHASES DR. ACCTS. PAY. CR.		
1								1
2								2
3								3
4								4
5								5
6								6
7								7
8								8
9								9
10								10
11								11
12								12
13								13
14								14
15								15
16								16
17								17
18								18
19								19
20								20
21								21
22								22
23								23
24								24
25								25
26								26
27								27
28								28
29								29
30								30
31								31
32								32
33								33

9-2 **WORK TOGETHER, p. 247**

Journalizing cash payments using a cash payments journal

CASH PAYMENTS JOURNAL

PAGE _____

DATE	ACCOUNT TITLE	CK. NO.	POST. REF.	GENERAL DEBIT	GENERAL CREDIT	ACCOUNTS PAYABLE DEBIT	PURCHASES DISCOUNT CREDIT	CASH CREDIT
1								
2								
3								
4								
5								
6								
7								
8								
9								
10								
11								
12								
13								
14								
15								
16								
17								
18								
19								
20								
21								
22								
23								
24								

Journalizing cash payments using a cash payments journal

CASH PAYMENTS JOURNAL

PAGE

| | | | | | GENERAL | | ACCOUNTS PAYABLE DEBIT | PURCHASES DISCOUNT CREDIT | CASH CREDIT | |
DATE	ACCOUNT TITLE	CK. NO.	POST. REF.	DEBIT	CREDIT				
									1
									2
									3
									4
									5
									6
									7
									8
									9
									10
									11
									12
									13
									14
									15
									16
									17
									18
									19
									20
									21
									22
									23
									24

9-3 WORK TOGETHER, p. 253

Performing other cash payments journal operations

CASH PAYMENTS JOURNAL PAGE 5

	DATE	ACCOUNT TITLE	CK. NO.	POST. REF.	GENERAL DEBIT	GENERAL CREDIT	ACCOUNTS PAYABLE DEBIT	PURCHASES DISCOUNT CREDIT	CASH CREDIT	
23	27	Supplies	534		234 30				234 30	23
24	27	Ace Manufacturing	535				189 60	3 79	185 81	24
25					18 486 85	458 56	16 483 50	251 34	34 260 45	25

CASH PAYMENTS JOURNAL PAGE

	DATE	ACCOUNT TITLE	CK. NO.	POST. REF.	GENERAL DEBIT	GENERAL CREDIT	ACCOUNTS PAYABLE DEBIT	PURCHASES DISCOUNT CREDIT	CASH CREDIT	
1										1
2										2
3										3
4										4
5										5
6										6

PETTY CASH REPORT

Date: _____   Custodian: _____

	Explanation	Reconciliation	Replenish Amount
Fund Total Payments:	_____		
	_____		
	_____		
Less:	Total payments		
Equals:	Recorded amount on hand		
Less:	Actual amount on hand		
Equals:	Cash short (over)		
Amount to Replenish			

Column Title	Debit Column Totals	Credit Column Totals
General Debit	_____	
General Credit		_____
Accounts Payable Debit	_____	
Purchases Discount Credit		_____
Cash Credit		_____
Totals	_____	_____

Performing other cash payments journal operations

CASH PAYMENTS JOURNAL   PAGE 11

	DATE	ACCOUNT TITLE	CK. NO.	POST. REF.	GENERAL DEBIT	GENERAL CREDIT	ACCOUNTS PAYABLE DEBIT	PURCHASES DISCOUNT CREDIT	CASH CREDIT	
23	28	Advertising Expense	625		1 5 0 0 00				1 5 0 0 00	23
24	28	GRF Manufacturing, Inc.	626				2 5 1 8 00	5 0 36	2 4 6 7 64	24
25					25 6 2 4 85	9 5 8 48	35 1 4 2 50	4 9 2 15	59 3 1 6 72	25

CASH PAYMENTS JOURNAL   PAGE

	DATE	ACCOUNT TITLE	CK. NO.	POST. REF.	GENERAL DEBIT	GENERAL CREDIT	ACCOUNTS PAYABLE DEBIT	PURCHASES DISCOUNT CREDIT	CASH CREDIT	
1										1
2										2
3										3
4										4
5										5
6										6
7										7

PETTY CASH REPORT

Date: _____   Custodian: _____

Explanation	Reconciliation	Replenish Amount
Fund Total Payments: _____		
_____		
_____		
_____		
Less: Total payments		→
Equals: Recorded amount on hand		
Less: Actual amount on hand		
Equals: Cash short (over)		→
Amount to Replenish		

Column Title	Debit Column Totals	Credit Column Totals
General Debit	_____	
General Credit		_____
Accounts Payable Debit	_____	
Purchases Discount Credit		_____
Cash Credit		_____
Totals	_____	_____

9-4 **WORK TOGETHER and ON YOUR OWN, p. 258**

Journalizing other transactions using a general journal

GENERAL JOURNAL

PAGE _____

	DATE		ACCOUNT TITLE	DOC. NO.	POST. REF.	DEBIT	CREDIT	
1								1
2								2
3								3
4								4
5								5
6								6
7								7
8								8
9								9
10								10
11								11
12								12
13								13
14								14
15								15
16								16
17								17
18								18
19								19
20								20
21								21
22								22
23								23
24								24

Journalizing purchases using a purchases journal

PURCHASES JOURNAL   PAGE

	DATE	ACCOUNT CREDITED	PURCH. NO.	POST. REF.	PURCHASES DR. ACCTS. PAY. CR.	
1						1
2						2
3						3
4						4
5						5
6						6
7						7
8						8
9						9
10						10
11						11
12						12
13						13
14						14
15						15
16						16
17						17
18						18
19						19
20						20
21						21
22						22
23						23
24						24
25						25
26						26
27						27
28						28
29						29
30						30
31						31
32						32
33						33

9-2 APPLICATION PROBLEM, p. 260

Journalizing cash payments using a cash payments journal

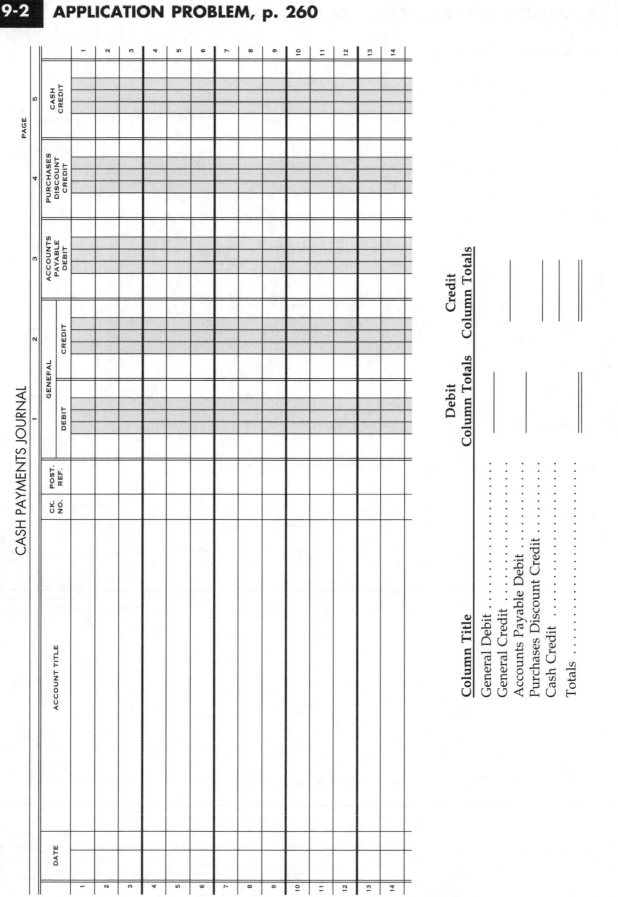

CASH PAYMENTS JOURNAL

	Debit Column Totals	Credit Column Totals
Column Title		
General Debit		
General Credit		
Accounts Payable Debit		
Purchases Discount Credit		
Cash Credit		
Totals		

Note: Line 12 of the journal and the journal proof above are completed in Application Problem 9-4.

9-3 APPLICATION PROBLEM, p. 261

Preparing a petty cash report

PETTY CASH REPORT			
Date: _____		Custodian: _____	
Explanation		Reconciliation	Replenish Amount
Fund Total Payments: _____			
_____			
_____			
_____			
Less: Total payments		_____ →	
Equals: Recorded amount on hand		_____	
Less: Actual amount on hand		_____	
Equals: Cash short (over)		_____ →	
Amount to Replenish			

9-4 APPLICATION PROBLEM, p. 261

Performing additional cash payments journal operations

4.

PETTY CASH REPORT			
Date: _____		Custodian: _____	
Explanation		Reconciliation	Replenish Amount
Fund Total Payments: _____			
_____			
_____			
_____			
Less: Total payments		_____ →	
Equals: Recorded amount on hand		_____	
Less: Actual amount on hand		_____	
Equals: Cash short (over)		_____ →	
Amount to Replenish			

9-4 APPLICATION PROBLEM (concluded)

3., 5., 6., 7.

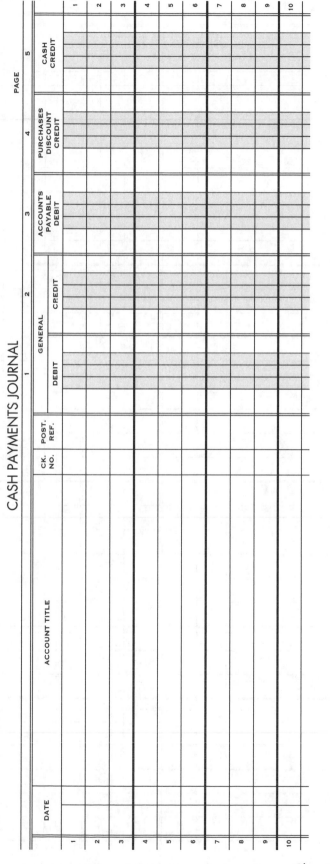

CASH PAYMENTS JOURNAL

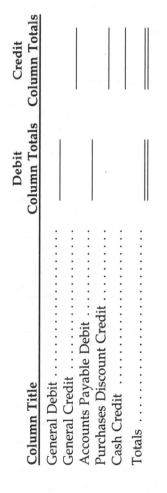

Column Title	Debit Column Totals	Credit Column Totals
General Debit		
General Credit		
Accounts Payable Debit		
Purchases Discount Credit		
Cash Credit		
Totals		

Journalizing other transactions using a general journal

GENERAL JOURNAL   PAGE ____

	DATE		ACCOUNT TITLE	DOC. NO.	POST. REF.	DEBIT	CREDIT	
1								1
2								2
3								3
4								4
5								5
6								6
7								7
8								8
9								9
10								10
11								11
12								12
13								13
14								14
15								15
16								16
17								17
18								18
19								19
20								20
21								21
22								22
23								23
24								24
25								25
26								26
27								27
28								28
29								29
30								30
31								31
32								32
33								33

9-6   **MASTERY PROBLEM, pp. 262, 263**

Journalizing purchases, cash payments, and other transactions

1., 2.

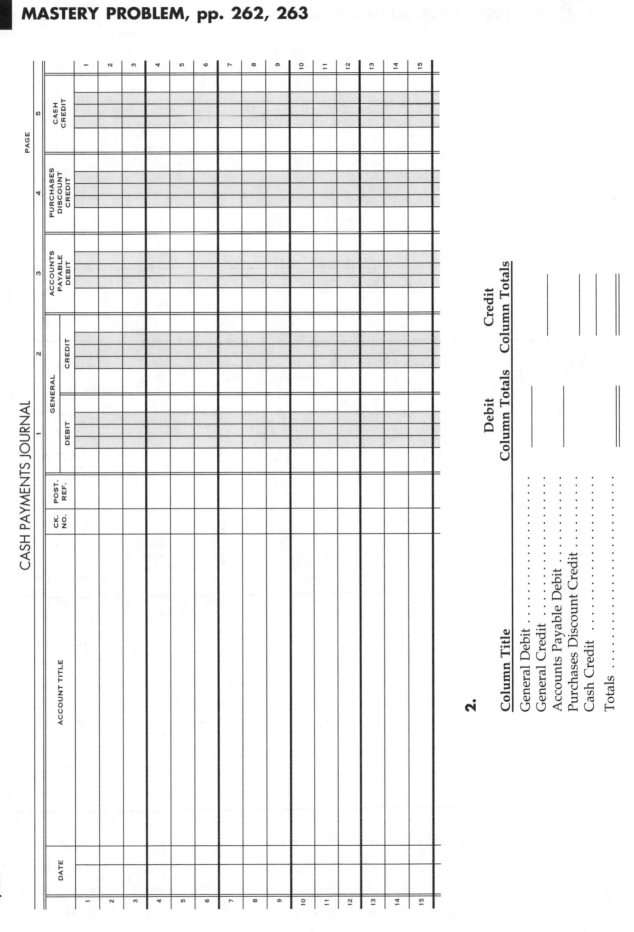

CASH PAYMENTS JOURNAL

	DATE	ACCOUNT TITLE	CK. NO.	POST. REF.	GENERAL DEBIT	GENERAL CREDIT	ACCOUNTS PAYABLE DEBIT	PURCHASES DISCOUNT CREDIT	CASH CREDIT	
1										1
2										2
3										3
4										4
5										5
6										6
7										7
8										8
9										9
10										10
11										11
12										12
13										13
14										14
15										15

PAGE 5

2.

Column Title	Debit Column Totals	Credit Column Totals
General Debit		
General Credit		
Accounts Payable Debit		
Purchases Discount Credit		
Cash Credit		
Totals		

1., 5.

PURCHASES JOURNAL

PAGE

	DATE	ACCOUNT CREDITED	PURCH. NO.	POST. REF.	PURCHASES DR. ACCTS. PAY. CR.	
1						1
2						2
3						3
4						4
5						5
6						6
7						7
8						8
9						9
10						10
11						11
12						12
13						13
14						14

1.

GENERAL JOURNAL

PAGE

	DATE	ACCOUNT TITLE	DOC. NO.	POST. REF.	DEBIT	CREDIT	
1							1
2							2
3							3
4							4
5							5
6							6
7							7
8							8
9							9
10							10
11							11
12							12
13							13
14							14

9-6 MASTERY PROBLEM (concluded)

3., 4., 6., 7.

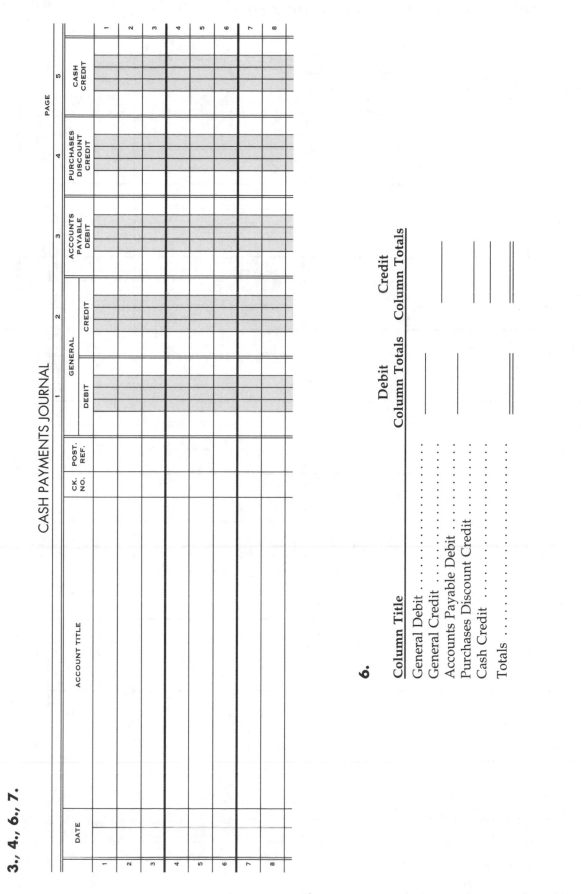

CASH PAYMENTS JOURNAL

6.

Column Title	Debit Column Totals	Credit Column Totals
General Debit		
General Credit		
Accounts Payable Debit		
Purchases Discount Credit		
Cash Credit		
Totals		

CHALLENGE PROBLEM, p. 263

Journalizing purchases, cash payments, and other transactions

1.

PURCHASES JOURNAL

PAGE

	DATE		ACCOUNT CREDITED	PURCH. NO.	POST. REF.	PURCHASES DR. ACCTS. PAY. CR.	
1							1
2							2
3							3
4							4
5							5
6							6
7							7
8							8
9							9
10							10
11							11
12							12
13							13
14							14
15							15
16							16
17							17
18							18
19							19
20							20
21							21
22							22
23							23
24							24
25							25

9-7 CHALLENGE PROBLEM (continued)

1.

CASH PAYMENTS JOURNAL

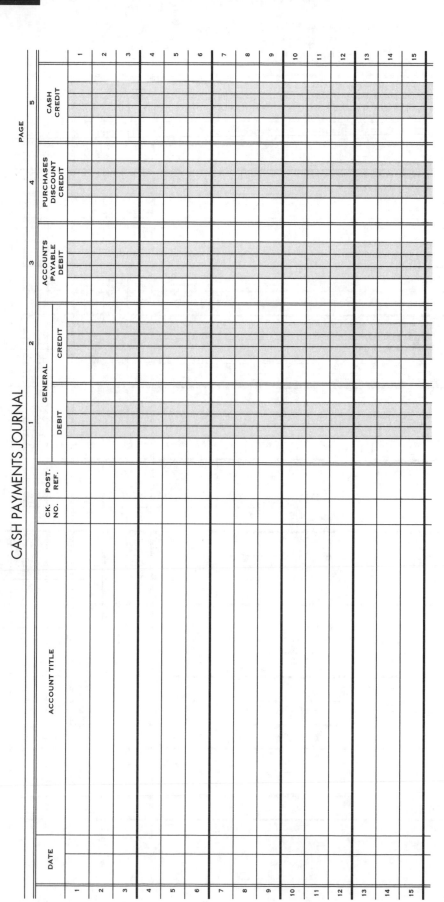

1.

GENERAL JOURNAL

PAGE

	DATE	ACCOUNT TITLE	DOC. NO.	POST. REF.	DEBIT	CREDIT	
1							1
2							2
3							3
4							4
5							5
6							6
7							7
8							8
9							9
10							10
11							11
12							12
13							13
14							14
15							15
16							16
17							17
18							18
19							19
20							20
21							21
22							22
23							23
24							24
25							25
26							26
27							27
28							28
29							29
30							30
31							31

9-7 **CHALLENGE PROBLEM (concluded)**

2.

_____

_____

_____

_____

_____

_____

_____

_____

_____

_____

_____

_____

_____

_____

_____

_____

_____

_____

_____

_____

_____

_____

_____

_____

_____

_____

_____

_____

_____

_____

_____

_____

_____

_____

_____

_____

USING SOURCE DOCUMENTS, p. 265

Journalizing purchases, cash payments, and other transactions from source documents

Suddard Industries 1423 Commercial Road Bell City, LA 70630-6213	INVOICE	REC'D 10/03/-- P324 Form *1*

TO: Messler Sailing
    142 River Street
    Naperville, IL 60540-3172

DATE: *9/30/--*
INV. NO. *6234*
TERMS: *30 days*
ACCT. NO. *2450*

QUANTITY	CAT. NO.	DESCRIPTION	UNIT PRICE	TOTAL
25	4323	jib sheet	$ 45.00	$ 1,125.00
20	4233	jib halyard	$ 55.00	$ 1,100.00
		TOTAL		$ 2,225.00

NO. **458**	$ *1,520.00*	Form *2*	
Date: *October 4*		20 --	
To: *Seaside Manufacturing*			
For: *On account*			

BAL. BRO'T. FOR'D. . . .	12,485	25
AMT. DEPOSITED		
SUBTOTAL	12,485	25
OTHER:		
SUBTOTAL	12,485	25
AMT. THIS CHECK	1,520	00
BAL. CAR'D. FOR'D.	10,965	25

USING SOURCE DOCUMENTS (continued)

Messler Sailing

MEMORANDUM   Form _3_

NO.   39

DATE   October 4, 20--

Attached invoice from Sullivan
Supply Co. is for store supplies,
bought on account, $105.00

DEBIT MEMORANDUM NO. 25   Form _4_

| DATE |
| October 8, 20-- |

| TO |
| Seaside Manufacturing |
| 1430 Industrial Road |
| Ocean City, WA 98569-2198 |

Messler Sailing
142 River Street
Naperville, IL 60540-3172

| ACCOUNT NO. |
| 2040 |

QUANTITY	CAT. NO.	DESCRIPTION	UNIT PRICE	TOTAL
11	JS-342	Life preservers damaged in transit	$ 25.00	$ 275.00

NO. **459** $ *625.00* Form _5_		
Date: *October 10* 20--		
To: *Willcutt & Bishop*		
For: *Office Supplies*		
BAL. BRO'T. FOR'D...	10,965	25
AMT. DEPOSITED .... 10 09 20- Date	1,264	00
SUBTOTAL	12,229	25
OTHER:		
SUBTOTAL	12,229	25
AMT. THIS CHECK	625	00
BAL. CAR'D. FOR'D...........	11,604	25

REC'D 10/11/-- P325

INVOICE

Form __6__

Aquatic Manufacturing
42 Industrial Road
Stratford, CA 93266-4762

DATE:	10/8/--
INV. NO.	15484
TERMS:	2/10, n/30
ACCT. NO.	1420

TO: Messler Sailing
142 River Street
Naperville, IL 60540-3172

QUANTITY	CAT. NO.	DESCRIPTION	UNIT PRICE	TOTAL
5	532	Fiberglass repair kit	$ 60.00	$ 300.00
10	6346	U-bolts, 1"	$ 16.00	$ 160.00
20	6347	U-bolts, 2"	$ 23.00	$ 460.00
		TOTAL		$ 920.00

Messler Sailing

MEMORANDUM Form __7__

NO. 40

DATE October 12, 20--

Attached invoice from Office
Zone is for office supplies,
bought on account, $95.00

NO. **460**	$ 425.00	Form __8__
Date: October 15		20 --
To: Northern Electric		
For: Utilities		

BAL. BRO'T. FOR'D. . . .	11,604	25
AMT. DEPOSITED . . . . Date		
SUBTOTAL	11,604	25
OTHER:		
SUBTOTAL	11,604	25
AMT. THIS CHECK	425	00
BAL. CAR'D. FOR'D.	11,179	25

USING SOURCE DOCUMENTS (continued)

NO. **461** $ *901.60*   Form *9*
Date: *October 19*   20 - -
To: *Aquatic Manufacturing*

For: *On account; $920.00 less*
    2% cash discount

BAL. BRO'T. FOR'D. . .	11,179	25
AMT. DEPOSITED . . . . *10 18 20 -*	546	50
SUBTOTAL	11,725	75
OTHER:		
SUBTOTAL	11,725	75
AMT. THIS CHECK	901	60
BAL. CAR'D. FOR'D.	10,824	15

NORTHERN SAIL COMPANY
253 Beach Blvd.
Boston, MA 02169-5029

INVOICE

REC'D 10/20/-- P326

Form *10*

TO: Messler Sailing
142 River Street
Naperville, IL 60540-3172

DATE: *10/18/--*
INV. NO.   *895*
TERMS: *30 days*
ACCT. NO.   *1820*

QUANTITY	CAT. NO.	DESCRIPTION	UNIT PRICE	TOTAL
2	B-23	Viking-16 mainsail	$ 1,599.00	$ 3,198.00
3	B-44	Sunset-13 mainsail	$ 459.00	$ 1,377.00
		TOTAL		$ 4,575.00

NO. **462**	$ *2,560.00*	Form *11*

Date: *October 20* 20 *--*

To: *WRRX Radio*

For: *Advertising*

BAL. BRO'T. FOR'D. . .		10,824 15
AMT. DEPOSITED	Date	
SUBTOTAL		10,824 15
OTHER:		
SUBTOTAL		10,824 15
AMT. THIS CHECK		2,560 00
BAL. CAR'D. FOR'D.		8,264 15

DEBIT MEMORANDUM NO. 26   Form *12*

DATE
October 22, 20--

Messler Sailing
142 River Street
Naperville, IL 60540-3172

TO
Aquatic Manufacturing
42 Industrial Road
Stratford, CA 93266-4762

ACCOUNT NO.
1420

QUANTITY	CAT. NO.	DESCRIPTION	UNIT PRICE	TOTAL
2	532	*Fiberglass repair kit missing components*	$ 60.00	$ 120.00

USING SOURCE DOCUMENTS (continued)

NO. **463**	$ _224.00_	Form _13_
Date: _October 22_		20 - -
To: _Michigan Sail Co._		
For: _Purchases_		

BAL. BRO'T. FOR'D...	8,264	15
AMT. DEPOSITED .... 10 22 20—	1,421	08
SUBTOTAL	9,685	23
OTHER:		
SUBTOTAL	9,685	23
AMT. THIS CHECK	224	00
BAL. CAR'D. FOR'D...........	9,461	23

NO. **464**	$ _2,225.00_	Form _14_
Date: _October 29_		20 - -
To: _Suddard Industries_		
For: _On account_		

BAL. BRO'T. FOR'D...	9,461	23
AMT. DEPOSITED	9,461	23
SUBTOTAL	9,461	23
OTHER:		
SUBTOTAL	9,461	23
AMT. THIS CHECK	2,225	00
BAL. CAR'D. FOR'D...........	7,236	23

NO. **465**	$ _112.94_	Form _15_
Date: _October 31_		20 - -
To: _Mary Donovan, Petty Cash_		
For: _Petty cash; office supplies, $23.45;_		
store supplies, $65.25; misc. expense, $25.11;		
cash over, $0.87		

BAL. BRO'T. FOR'D...	7,236	23
AMT. DEPOSITED 10 30 20-	648	22
SUBTOTAL	7,884	45
OTHER:		
SUBTOTAL	7,884	45
AMT. THIS CHECK	112	94
BAL. CAR'D. FOR'D...........	7,771	51

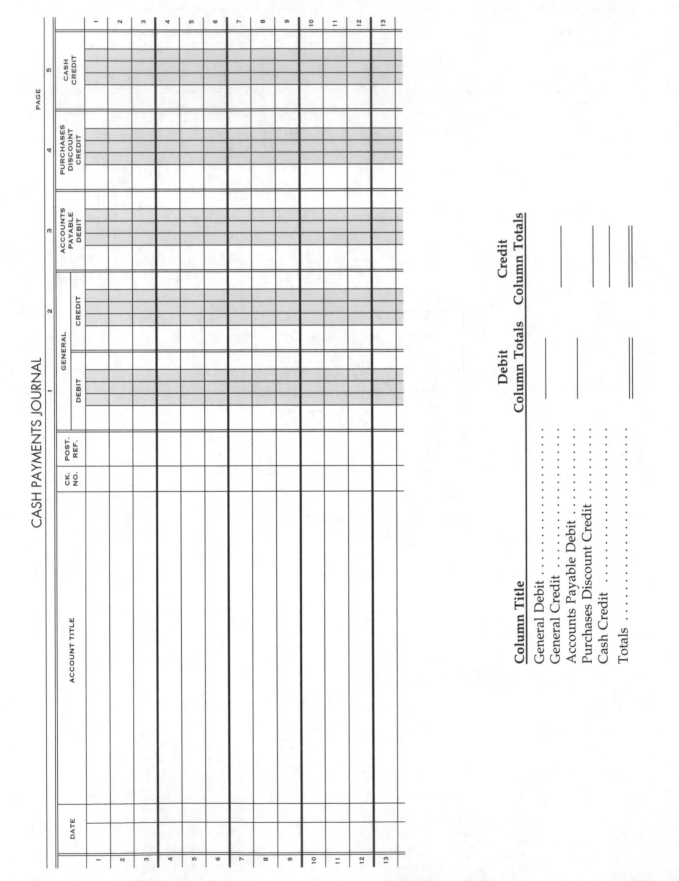

CASH PAYMENTS JOURNAL

Column Title	Debit Column Totals	Credit Column Totals
General Debit		
General Credit		
Accounts Payable Debit		
Purchases Discount Credit		
Cash Credit		
Totals		

Name _____ Date _____ Class _____

USING SOURCE DOCUMENTS (concluded)

PURCHASES JOURNAL   PAGE

	DATE	ACCOUNT CREDITED	PURCH. NO.	POST. REF.	PURCHASES DR. ACCTS. PAY. CR.	
1						1
2						2
3						3
4						4
5						5
6						6
7						7
8						8
9						9

GENERAL JOURNAL   PAGE

	DATE	ACCOUNT TITLE	DOC. NO.	POST. REF.	DEBIT	CREDIT	
1							1
2							2
3							3
4							4
5							5
6							6
7							7
8							8
9							9
10							10
11							11
12							12

Name	Perfect Score	Your Score
Identifying Accounting Terms	14 Pts.	
Analyzing Sales and Cash Receipts	24 Pts.	
Analyzing Transactions Recorded in Special Journals	15 Pts.	
Total	53 Pts.	

Part One—Identifying Accounting Terms

Directions: Select the term in Column I that best fits each definition in Column II.
Print the letter identifying your choice in the Answers column.

Column I	Column II	Answers
A. batch report	**1.** A person or business to whom merchandise or services are sold. (p. 270)	1. _____
B. batching out	**2.** A tax on a sale of merchandise or services. (p. 270)	2. _____
C. cash receipts journal	**3.** A special journal used to record only sales of merchandise on account. (p. 272)	3. _____
D. cash sale	**4.** A sale in which cash is received for the total amount of the sale at the time of the transaction. (p. 276)	4. _____
E. credit card sale	**5.** A sale in which a credit card is used for the total amount of the sale at the time of the transaction. (p. 276)	5. _____
F. credit memorandum	**6.** A computer used to collect, store, and report all the information of a sales transaction. (p. 276)	6. _____
G. customer	**7.** The report that summarizes the cash and credit card sales of a point-of-sale terminal. (p. 276)	7. _____
H. point-of-sale (POS) terminal	**8.** A report of credit card sales produced by a point-of-sale terminal. (p. 278)	8. _____
	9. The process of preparing a batch report of credit card sales from a point-of-sale terminal. (p. 278)	9. _____
I. sales allowance	**10.** A special journal used to record only cash receipt transactions. (p. 278)	10. _____
J. sales discount	**11.** A cash discount on sales taken by a customer. (p. 278)	11. _____
K. sales journal	**12.** Credit allowed a customer for the sales price of returned merchandise, resulting in a decrease in the vendor's accounts receivable. (p. 285)	12. _____
L. sales return	**13.** Credit allowed a customer for part of the sales price of merchandise that is not returned, resulting in a decrease in the vendor's accounts receivable. (p. 285)	13. _____
M. sales tax	**14.** A form prepared by the vendor showing the amount deducted for returns and allowances. (p. 285)	14. _____
N. terminal summary		

Part Two—Analyzing Sales and Cash Receipts

Directions: Place a *T* for True or an *F* for False in the Answers column to show whether each of the following statements is true or false.

1. Most states do not require a business to collect sales tax from customers. (p. 270) 1. _____

2. Sales tax rates are usually stated as a percentage of sales. (p. 270) 2. _____

3. A sale of merchandise increases the revenue of a business. (p. 271) 3. _____

4. The Realization of Revenue accounting concept is applied when a sale is recorded at the time the sale is made. (p. 271) 4. _____

5. A sale on account is not the same as a charge sale. (p. 271) 5. _____

6. A credit card sale is a sale in which cash is received for the total amount of the sale at the time of the transaction. (p. 276) 6. _____

7. A cash sale is a sale in which a credit card is used for the total amount of the sale at the time of the transaction. (p. 276) 7. _____

8. At the end of the week, all credit card slips are gathered together, sorted by issuing bank, and mailed individually to each of the banks to collect payment. (p. 278) 8. _____

9. All cash receipts, including cash sales and credit card sales, are recorded in the cash receipts journal. (p. 278) 9. _____

10. The total of a terminal summary can be recorded as a single cash sales transaction. (p. 279) 10. _____

11. For cash and credit card sales, the asset account Cash is debited for the total of sales and sales tax, but the revenue account Sales is credited only for the total of sales. (p. 279) 11. _____

12. The revenue account Sales has a normal credit balance. (p. 279) 12. _____

13. The liability account Sales Tax Payable has a normal debit balance. (p. 279) 13. _____

14. The source document for cash received on account from a customer is a receipt. (p. 280) 14. _____

15. When cash is received on account, the cash account balance increases and the accounts receivable account balance increases. (p. 280) 15. _____

16. When a sales discount is taken, a customer pays less cash than the invoice amount previously recorded in the sales account. (p. 281) 16. _____

17. The account Sales Discount increases sales. (p. 282) 17. _____

18. Maintaining a separate account for sales discounts provides business managers with information to evaluate whether a sales discount is a cost-effective method. (p. 282) 18. _____

19. If a customer does not pay the amount owed within the sales discount period, the full invoice amount is due. (p. 282) 19. _____

20. After the cash receipts journal is proved at the end of the month, cash is proved. (p. 283) 20. _____

21. All transactions can be recorded in a special journal. (p. 285) 21. _____

22. Credit may be granted to a customer only when merchandise is returned. (p. 285) 22. _____

23. Sales returns and sales allowances increase the amount of sales. (p. 285) 23. _____

24. The account Sales Returns and Allowances is a contra account. (p. 285) 24. _____

Part Three—Analyzing Transactions Recorded in Special Journals

Directions: In Answers Column l, print the abbreviation for the journal in which each transaction is to be recorded. In Answers Columns 2 and 3, print the letters identifying the accounts to be debited and credited for each transaction.

SJ—Sales journal; **GJ**—General journal; **CRJ**—Cash receipts journal

Answers

Account Titles	Transactions	Journal	Debit	Credit
A. Accounts Receivable	**1–2–3.** Sold merchandise on account to Penny Kellar, plus sales tax. (p. 273)	1._____	2._____	3._____
B. Cash	**4–5–6.** Recorded cash and credit card sales, plus sales tax. (p. 279)	4._____	5._____	6._____
C. Penny Kellar				
D. Jim Tauras	**7–8–9.** Received cash on account from Jim Tauras. (p. 280)	7._____	8._____	9._____
E. Sales				
F. Sales Discount	**10–11–12.** Received cash on account from Penny Kellar, less sales discount. (p. 282)	10._____	11._____	12._____
G. Sales Returns and Allowances	**13–14–15.** Granted credit to Jim Tauras for merchandise returned, plus sales tax. (p. 286)	13._____	14._____	15._____
H. Sales Tax Payable				

Setting Priorities

Do you work hard every day but never seem to get your work completed? Do you spend hours on an assignment only to find that it is of little importance? Do you sometimes feel that you waste your time? If you answer yes to these questions, you should take a close look at your priorities.

You have only a limited amount of time available, and you will likely never be able to do everything you would like to do. Therefore, you must decide which things are the most important and concentrate on them.

Placing a Value on Jobs

There may be jobs that you do not enjoy doing, and under ordinary circumstances, you might put them off and complete other work instead. However, the things that you put off may be the most important things that you should do. They should be given a high priority.

There may be jobs that you enjoy doing, but these jobs might be of little real value to you in your personal, business, or school life. These activities should receive a low priority.

When you decide which jobs to spend your time on, you should look at each one and determine its overall value in relation to the other jobs that you should do.

Getting Your Jobs in Order

An easy method of setting priorities is to sit down every morning and list the things that you should do during the day. Let's suppose that your list contains six jobs. When you have decided what should be done, you should rank the jobs in order of importance. The most important should be first, and the least important should be last.

You should then begin working at the top of the list. As you do each task, mark it off. Perhaps you will be able to mark off all the items, but you may complete only three or four. This is satisfactory, however, because you used your time on the items of most importance. If you do not complete one or two jobs at the bottom of the list, do not worry. They were the least important.

Conclusion

You will probably never complete every job you want to do. If you do the most important things every day, however, you will accomplish a great deal. You will be successful because you have set your priorities correctly.

10-1 WORK TOGETHER, p. 275

Journalizing sales on account; proving and ruling a sales journal

1., 2.

SALES JOURNAL

PAGE _____

	DATE	ACCOUNT DEBITED	SALE NO.	POST. REF.	1 ACCOUNTS RECEIVABLE DEBIT	2 SALES CREDIT	3 SALES TAX PAYABLE CREDIT	
1								1
2								2
3								3
4								4
5								5
6								6
7								7
8								8
9								9
10								10
11								11
12								12
13								13
14								14
15								15

2.

Col. No.	Column Title	Debit Totals	Credit Totals
1	Accounts Receivable Debit	_____	
2	Sales Credit		_____
3	Sales Tax Payable Credit		_____
	Totals	_____	_____

Journalizing sales on account; proving and ruling a sales journal

1., 2.

SALES JOURNAL

PAGE

	DATE	ACCOUNT DEBITED	SALE NO.	POST. REF.	ACCOUNTS RECEIVABLE DEBIT (1)	SALES CREDIT (2)	SALES TAX PAYABLE CREDIT (3)	
1								1
2								2
3								3
4								4
5								5
6								6
7								7
8								8
9								9
10								10
11								11
12								12
13								13
14								14
15								15

2.

Col. No.	Column Title	Debit Totals	Credit Totals
1	Accounts Receivable Debit	_____	
2	Sales Credit		_____
3	Sales Tax Payable Credit		_____
	Totals	_____	_____

10-2 WORK TOGETHER, p. 284

Journalizing cash receipts; proving and ruling a cash receipts journal

1., 2., 4.

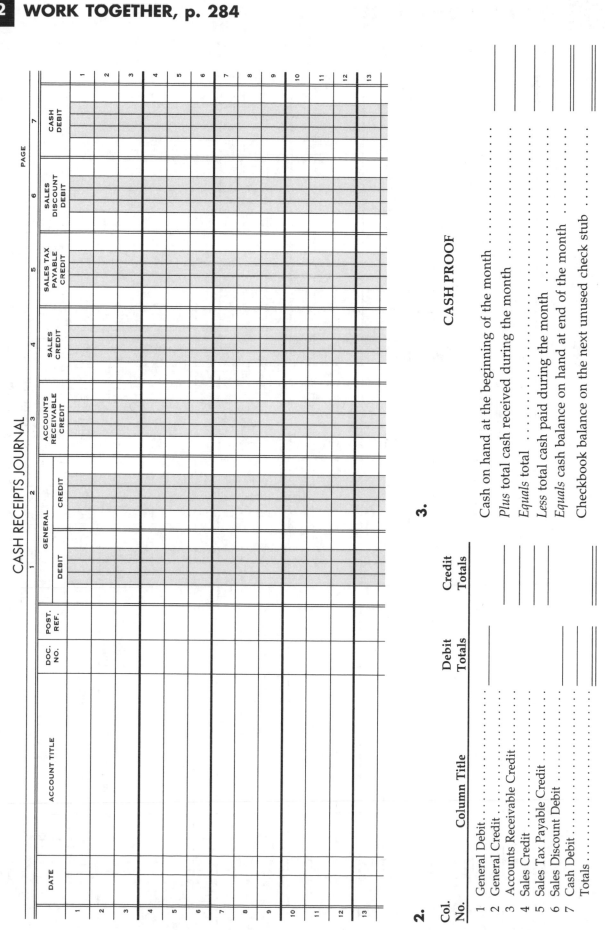

CASH RECEIPTS JOURNAL

PAGE 7

2.

Col. No.	Column Title	Debit Totals	Credit Totals
1	General Debit		
2	General Credit		
3	Accounts Receivable Credit		
4	Sales Credit		
5	Sales Tax Payable Credit		
6	Sales Discount Debit		
7	Cash Debit		
	Totals		

3.

CASH PROOF

Cash on hand at the beginning of the month ....
Plus total cash received during the month ....
Equals total ....
Less total cash paid during the month ....
Equals cash balance on hand at end of the month ....
Checkbook balance on the next unused check stub ....

Journalizing cash receipts; proving and ruling a cash receipts journal

1., 2., 4.

CASH RECEIPTS JOURNAL

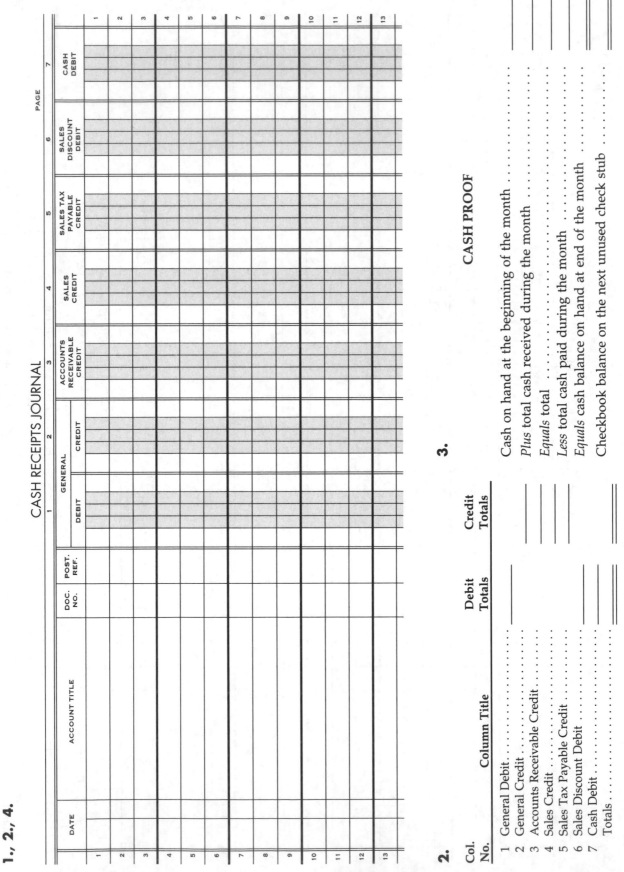

2.

Col. No.	Column Title	Debit Totals	Credit Totals
1	General Debit.........		
2	General Credit.........		
3	Accounts Receivable Credit.........		
4	Sales Credit.........		
5	Sales Tax Payable Credit.........		
6	Sales Discount Debit.........		
7	Cash Debit.........		
	Totals.........		

3.

CASH PROOF

Cash on hand at the beginning of the month........................

Plus total cash received during the month........................

Equals total ....

Less total cash paid during the month........................

Equals cash balance on hand at end of the month........................

Checkbook balance on the next unused check stub........................

10-3 WORK TOGETHER, p. 287

Journalizing sales returns and allowances using a general journal

1.

GENERAL JOURNAL | | | | | PAGE

	DATE	ACCOUNT TITLE	DOC. NO.	POST. REF.	DEBIT	CREDIT	
1							1
2							2
3							3
4							4
5							5
6							6
7							7
8							8
9							9
10							10
11							11
12							12
13							13
14							14
15							15
16							16
17							17
18							18
19							19
20							20
21							21
22							22
23							23
24							24
25							25

Journalizing sales returns and allowances using a general journal

1.

GENERAL JOURNAL

PAGE

	DATE		ACCOUNT TITLE	DOC. NO.	POST. REF.	DEBIT	CREDIT	
1								1
2								2
3								3
4								4
5								5
6								6
7								7
8								8
9								9
10								10
11								11
12								12
13								13
14								14
15								15
16								16
17								17
18								18
19								19
20								20
21								21
22								22
23								23
24								24
25								25

10-1 APPLICATION PROBLEM, p. 289

Journalizing sales on account; proving and ruling a sales journal

1., 2.

SALES JOURNAL   PAGE

	DATE		ACCOUNT DEBITED	SALE NO.	POST. REF.	ACCOUNTS RECEIVABLE DEBIT 1	SALES CREDIT 2	SALES TAX PAYABLE CREDIT 3	
1									1
2									2
3									3
4									4
5									5
6									6
7									7
8									8
9									9
10									10
11									11
12									12
13									13
14									14
15									15
16									16
17									17
18									18
19									19

2.

Col. No.	Column Title	Debit Totals	Credit Totals
1	Accounts Receivable Debit	_____	
2	Sales Credit		
3	Sales Tax Payable Credit		_____
	Totals	==========	==========

Journalizing cash receipts; proving and ruling a cash receipts journal

1., 2., 4.

CASH RECEIPTS JOURNAL

PAGE

				GENERAL		ACCOUNTS RECEIVABLE CREDIT	SALES CREDIT	SALES TAX PAYABLE CREDIT	SALES DISCOUNT DEBIT	CASH DEBIT	
DATE	ACCOUNT TITLE	DOC. NO.	POST. REF.	DEBIT	CREDIT						
					1	2	3	4	5	6	7	
											1
											2
											3
											4
											5
											6
											7
											8
											9
											10
											11
											12
											13
											14

2.

Col. No.	Column Title	Debit Totals	Credit Totals
1	General Debit		
2	General Credit		
3	Accounts Receivable Credit		
4	Sales Credit		
5	Sales Tax Payable Credit		
6	Sales Discount Debit		
7	Cash Debit		
	Totals		

3.

CASH PROOF

Cash on hand at the beginning of the month . . . .

Plus total cash received during the month . . . .

Equals total . . . .

Less total cash paid during the month . . . .

Equals cash balance on hand at end of the month . . . .

Checkbook balance on the next unused check stub . . . .

Name _____ Date _____ Class _____

Journalizing sales returns and allowances using a general journal

1.

GENERAL JOURNAL   PAGE _____

	DATE		ACCOUNT TITLE	DOC. NO.	POST. REF.	DEBIT	CREDIT	
1								1
2								2
3								3
4								4
5								5
6								6
7								7
8								8
9								9
10								10
11								11
12								12
13								13
14								14
15								15
16								16
17								17
18								18
19								19
20								20
21								21
22								22
23								23
24								24
25								25

Journalizing sales and cash receipts transactions; proving and ruling journals

1., 2., 3.

SALES JOURNAL

PAGE 19

	DATE		ACCOUNT DEBITED	SALE NO.	POST. REF.	1 ACCOUNTS RECEIVABLE DEBIT	2 SALES CREDIT	3 SALES TAX PAYABLE CREDIT	
1	20-- Oct.	24	Brought Forward		✔	1 4 9 6 6 70	1 4 5 2 1 55	4 4 5 15	1
2									2
3									3
4									4
5									5
6									6
7									7
8									8
9									9
10									10
11									11
12									12
13									13
14									14
15									15
16									16
17									17
18									18

2.

Col. No.	Column Title	Debit Totals	Credit Totals
1	Accounts Receivable Debit	_____	
2	Sales Credit		_____
3	Sales Tax Payable Credit		_____
	Totals	==========	==========

10-4 **MASTERY PROBLEM (continued)**

1., 4., 5., 6.

CASH RECEIPTS JOURNAL

PAGE 20

					1 GENERAL		3 ACCOUNTS RECEIVABLE CREDIT	4 SALES CREDIT	5 SALES TAX PAYABLE CREDIT	6 SALES DISCOUNT DEBIT	7 CASH DEBIT	
DATE	ACCOUNT TITLE	DOC. NO.	POST. REF.	DEBIT	CREDIT						
20-- Oct. 24	Brought Forward		✔			1215825	231541 2	9 2 6 16		36 2 3 8 53	1
											2
											3
											4
											5
											6
											7
											8
											9
											10
											11
											12
											13
											14

4.

Col. No.	Column Title	Debit Totals	Credit Totals
1	General Debit	_____	
2	General Credit		_____
3	Accounts Receivable Credit ...		_____
4	Sales Credit		_____
5	Sales Tax Payable Credit		_____
6	Sales Discount Debit	_____	
7	Cash Debit	_____	
	Totals	═══════	═══════

5.

CASH PROOF

Cash on hand at the beginning of the month .... _____

Plus total cash received during the month .... _____

Equals total .... _____

Less total cash paid during the month .... _____

Equals cash balance on hand at end of the month .... _____

Checkbook balance on the next unused check stub .... ════════════

1.

GENERAL JOURNAL

PAGE

	DATE	ACCOUNT TITLE	DOC. NO.	POST. REF.	DEBIT	CREDIT	
1							1
2							2
3							3
4							4
5							5
6							6
7							7
8							8
9							9
10							10
11							11
12							12
13							13
14							14
15							15
16							16
17							17
18							18
19							19
20							20
21							21
22							22
23							23
24							24
25							25

10-5 CHALLENGE PROBLEM, p. 291

Journalizing transactions; proving and ruling special journals

1., 2., 5.

SALES JOURNAL

PAGE _____

	DATE	ACCOUNT DEBITED	SALE NO.	POST. REF.	1 ACCOUNTS RECEIVABLE DEBIT	2 SALES CREDIT	3 SALES TAX PAYABLE CREDIT	
1								1
2								2
3								3
4								4
5								5
6								6
7								7
8								8
9								9
10								10
11								11
12								12
13								13
14								14
15								15
16								16
17								17
18								18

3.

Col. No.	Column Title	Debit Totals	Credit Totals
1	Accounts Receivable Debit	_____	
2	Sales Credit		_____
3	Sales Tax Payable Credit		_____
	Totals	=========	=========

1., 2., 5.

PURCHASES JOURNAL   PAGE

	DATE		ACCOUNT CREDITED	PURCH. NO.	POST. REF.	PURCHASES DR. ACCTS. PAY. CR.	
1							1
2							2
3							3
4							4
5							5
6							6
7							7
8							8
9							9
10							10
11							11
12							12
13							13
14							14
15							15
16							16
17							17
18							18
19							19
20							20
21							21
22							22
23							23
24							24
25							25

10-5 CHALLENGE PROBLEM (continued)

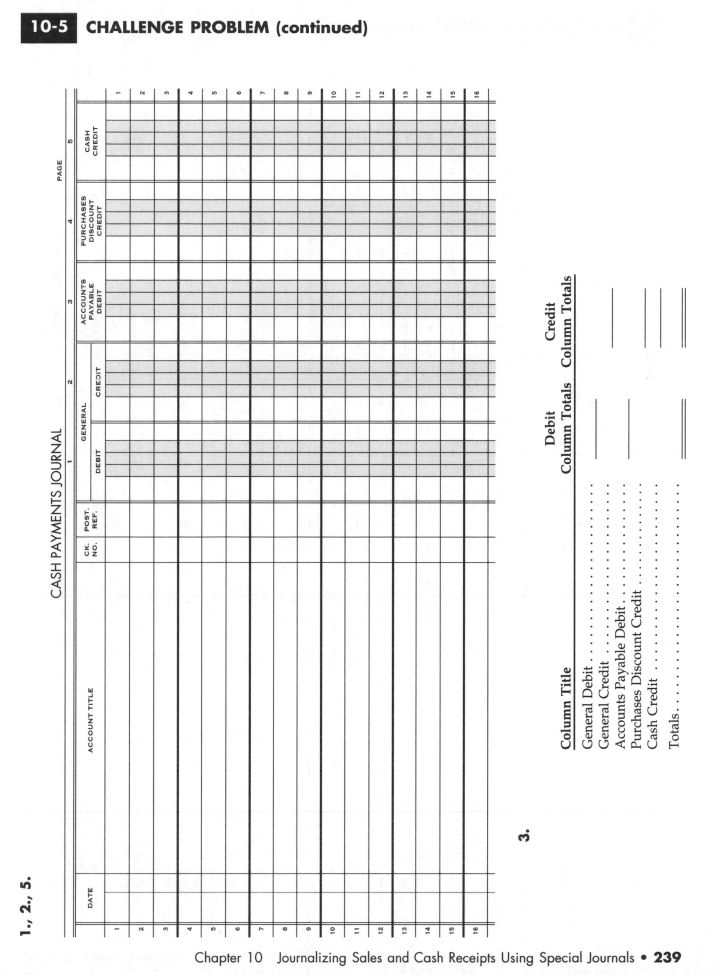

CASH PAYMENTS JOURNAL

1., 2., 5.

3.

Column Title	Debit Column Totals	Credit Column Totals
General Debit		
General Credit		
Accounts Payable Debit		
Purchases Discount Credit		
Cash Credit		
Totals		

1., 2., 5.

CASH RECEIPTS JOURNAL

PAGE 7

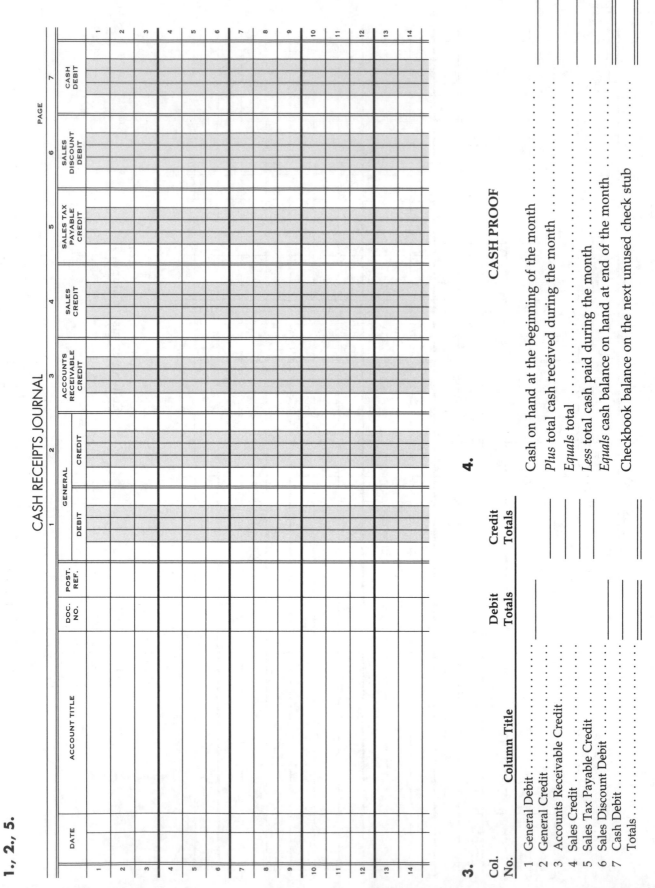

			1	2	3	4	5	6	7
			GENERAL		ACCOUNTS RECEIVABLE CREDIT	SALES CREDIT	SALES TAX PAYABLE CREDIT	SALES DISCOUNT DEBIT	CASH DEBIT
DATE	ACCOUNT TITLE	DOC. NO.	POST. REF.	DEBIT	CREDIT					

3.

Col. No.	Column Title	Debit Totals	Credit Totals
1	General Debit		
2	General Credit		
3	Accounts Receivable Credit		
4	Sales Credit		
5	Sales Tax Payable Credit		
6	Sales Discount Debit		
7	Cash Debit		
	Totals		

4.

CASH PROOF

Cash on hand at the beginning of the month . . . .
Plus total cash received during the month . . . .
Equals total . . . .
Less total cash paid during the month . . . .
Equals cash balance on hand at end of the month . . . .
Checkbook balance on the next unused check stub . . . .

10-5 CHALLENGE PROBLEM (concluded)

1.

GENERAL JOURNAL   PAGE _____

	DATE	ACCOUNT TITLE	DOC. NO.	POST. REF.	DEBIT	CREDIT	
1							1
2							2
3							3
4							4
5							5
6							6
7							7
8							8
9							9
10							10
11							11
12							12
13							13
14							14
15							15
16							16
17							17
18							18
19							19
20							20
21							21
22							22
23							23
24							24
25							25

Journalizing sales and cash receipts transactions; proving and ruling journals

NO.   **658**   Form *1*

DATE: *November 25*   20--
FROM: *Putt-A-Round*
FOR: *On Account*

On account $ *150.00*
Sales discount $ *3.00*

Cash received $ *147.00*

GOLFER'S PARADISE   Form *2*
142 Glade Road
Crossville, TN 38555-8102   NO. **443**

Sold to: Daniel Pearson   DATE: *11/27/--*
           2345 Lakeview Drive   TERMS: *30 days*
           Crossville, TN 38555-5819   CUST. NO.   *480*

CAT. NO.	DESCRIPTION	QUANTITY	UNIT PRICE	TOTAL
2432	*9 degree titanium driver*	*1*	$ *439.50*	$ *439.50*
745	*practice golf balls, dz.*	*5*	*10.00*	*50.00*
			SUBTOTAL	$ *489.50*
			TAX	*39.16*
			TOTAL	$ *528.66*

Serving Crossville and Fairfield Glade With All Your Recreational Equipment

USING SOURCE DOCUMENTS (continued)

Form __3__

CODE: 54
DATE: 11/27/--
TIME: 18:24

Credit Card 034
Sales 989.95
Sales Tax 79.20
Total 1,069.15

MasterCard 042
Sales 806.09
Sales Tax 64.49
Total 870.58

Cash 152
Sales 1,894.44
Sales Tax 151.56
Total 2,046.00

Totals
Sales 3,690.48
Sales Tax 295.25
Total 3,985.73

NO. **659** Form __4__

DATE: November 28 20--
FROM: Mary Ann Ingram
FOR: On Account

On account | $ 420.48
Sales discount |
Cash received | $ 420.48

CREDIT MEMORANDUM NO. 63 Form __5__

DATE
November 29, 20--

TO
Nelson Lang
354 Lang Drive
Crossville, TN 38555-2615

ACCOUNT NO.
340

GOLFER'S PARADISE
142 Glade Road
Crossville, TN 38555-8102

QUANTITY	CAT. NO.	DESCRIPTION	UNIT PRICE	TOTAL
2	643	golf bag	$130.00	$260.00

			SUBTOTAL	$260.00
			SALES TAX	20.80
			TOTAL	$280.80

USING SOURCE DOCUMENTS (continued)

GOLFER'S PARADISE
142 Glade Road
Crossville, TN 38555-8102

Form _6_

NO. **444**

Sold to: Janice Adams
594 Eagles Nest Road
Crossville, TN 38555-7364

DATE: 11/29/--
TERMS: 30 days
CUST. NO. 140

CAT. NO.	DESCRIPTION	QUANTITY	UNIT PRICE	TOTAL
BG-34	oversized irons, graphite shafts	1	$ 405.50	$ 405.50
			SUBTOTAL	$ 405.50
			TAX	32.44
			TOTAL	$ 437.94

Serving Crossville and Fairfield Glade With All Your Recreational Equipment

---

Form _7_

CODE: 55
DATE: 11/30/--
TIME: 18:45

Credit Card	005	
Sales		251.05
Sales Tax		20.08
Total		271.13

MasterCard	007	
Sales		315.15
Sales Tax		25.21
Total		340.36

Cash	062	
Sales		612.15
Sales Tax		48.97
Total		661.12

Totals		
Sales		1,178.35
Sales Tax		94.26
Total		1,272.61

USING SOURCE DOCUMENTS (continued)

1., 2., 3.

SALES JOURNAL   PAGE 18

	DATE	ACCOUNT DEBITED	SALE NO.	POST. REF.	ACCOUNTS RECEIVABLE DEBIT (1)	SALES CREDIT (2)	SALES TAX PAYABLE CREDIT (3)	
1	20-- Nov. 24	Brought Forward		✔	8 7 2 6 89	6 1 5 4 25	2 5 7 2 64	1
2								2
3								3
4								4
5								5
6								6

2.

Col. No.	Column Title	Debit Totals	Credit Totals
1	Accounts Receivable Debit	_____	
2	Sales Credit		_____
3	Sales Tax Payable Credit		_____
	Totals	==========	==========

1., 4., 6.

CASH RECEIPTS JOURNAL

PAGE 24

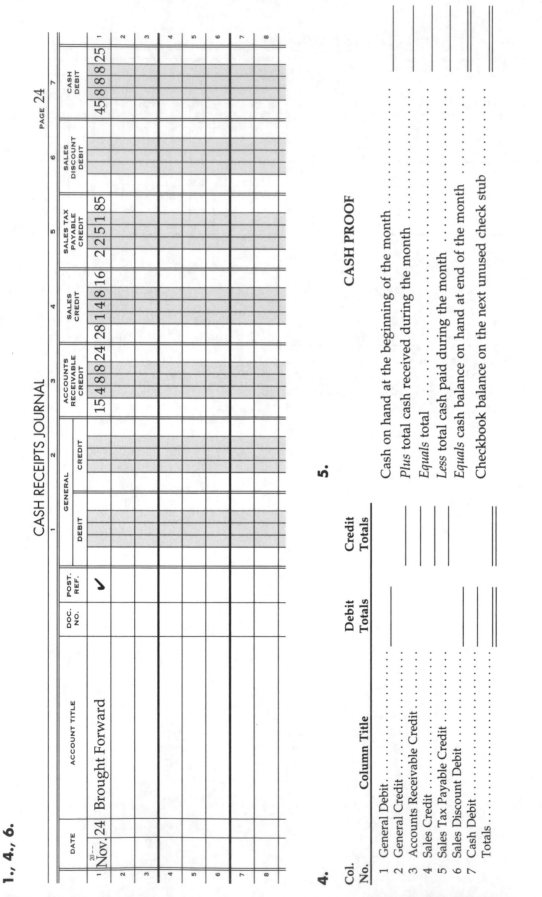

| | | | | 1 | 2 | 3 | 4 | 5 | 6 | 7 |
| | | | | GENERAL | | ACCOUNTS RECEIVABLE CREDIT | SALES CREDIT | SALES TAX PAYABLE CREDIT | SALES DISCOUNT DEBIT | CASH DEBIT |
DATE	ACCOUNT TITLE	DOC. NO.	POST. REF.	DEBIT	CREDIT					
20-- Nov. 24	Brought Forward		✔			15 4 8 8 24	28 1 4 8 16	2 2 5 1 85		45 8 8 8 25

4.

Col. No.	Column Title	Debit Totals	Credit Totals
1	General Debit		
2	General Credit		
3	Accounts Receivable Credit		
4	Sales Credit		
5	Sales Tax Payable Credit		
6	Sales Discount Debit		
7	Cash Debit		
	Totals		

5.

CASH PROOF

Cash on hand at the beginning of the month . . . .

Plus total cash received during the month . . . .

Equals total . . . .

Less total cash paid during the month . . . .

Equals cash balance on hand at end of the month . . . .

Checkbook balance on the next unused check stub . . . .

USING SOURCE DOCUMENTS (concluded)

1.

GENERAL JOURNAL   PAGE _____

	DATE		ACCOUNT TITLE	DOC. NO.	POST. REF.	DEBIT	CREDIT	
1								1
2								2
3								3
4								4
5								5
6								6

Name	Perfect Score	Your Score
Identifying Accounting Terms	6 Pts.	
Analyzing a Journal and Ledgers	21 Pts.	
Analyzing Posting and Subsidiary Ledgers	10 Pts.	
Total	37 Pts.	

Part One—Identifying Accounting Terms

Directions: Select the term in Column I that best fits each definition in Column II. Print the letter identifying your choice in the Answers column.

Column I	Column II	Answers
A. accounts payable ledger	**1.** A ledger that is summarized in a single general ledger account. (p. 298)	1. _____
B. accounts receivable ledger	**2.** A subsidiary ledger containing only accounts for vendors from whom items are purchased or bought on account. (p. 298)	2. _____
C. controlling account	**3.** A subsidiary ledger containing only accounts for charge customers. (p. 298)	3. _____
D. schedule of accounts payable	**4.** An account in a general ledger that summarizes all accounts in a subsidiary ledger. (p. 298)	4. _____
E. schedule of accounts receivable	**5.** A listing of vendor accounts, account balances, and total amounts due all vendors. (p. 305)	5. _____
F. subsidiary ledger	**6.** A listing of customer accounts, account balances, and total amount due from all customers. (p. 313)	6. _____

Part Two—Analyzing a Journal and Ledgers

Directions: Place a *T* for True or an *F* for False in the Answers column to show whether each of the following statements is true or false.

Answers

1. When using an accounts receivable ledger, the total amount due from all customers is summarized in a single general ledger account. (p. 298)

1. _____

2. Accounts are arranged in alphabetical order within the subsidiary ledgers. (p. 299)

2. _____

3. A change in the balance of a vendor account also changes the balance of the controlling account Accounts Payable. (p. 299)

3. _____

4. The total amount owed to all vendors is summarized in a single general ledger account, Accounts Payable. (p. 299)

4. _____

5. The number of entries that may be recorded on each ledger account form is limited to fifteen. (p. 300)

5. _____

6. The amount on each line of a purchases journal is posted as a credit to a vendor account in the accounts payable ledger. (p. 301)

6. _____

7. Posting frequently keeps each vendor account balance up to date. (p. 301)

7. _____

8. Entries in a general journal may affect account balances in an accounts payable ledger. (p. 303)

8. _____

9. A controlling account balance in a general ledger must equal the sum of all account balances in a subsidiary ledger. (p. 305)

9. _____

10. A schedule of accounts payable is prepared before all entries in a journal are posted. (p. 305)

10. _____

11. A change in the balance of a customer account does not affect the balance of the controlling account Accounts Receivable. (p. 307)

11. _____

12. The form used in the accounts receivable ledger has a Debit Balance column. (p. 308)

12. _____

13. Each amount in a sales journal's Accounts Receivable Debit column is posted as a credit to the customer account in the accounts receivable ledger. (p. 309)

13. _____

14. Each entry in the Accounts Receivable Credit column of the cash receipts journal is posted to the proper customer account in the accounts receivable ledger. (p. 310)

14. _____

15. The accounts receivable ledger is proved when the balance of Accounts Receivable in the general ledger is the same as the total of the schedule of accounts receivable. (p. 313)

15. _____

16. Each amount in the General columns of a cash payments journal is posted as a total at the end of the month. (p. 316)

16. _____

17. The monthly total of each special amount column in a cash payments journal is posted to a general ledger account. (p. 316)

17. _____

18. Transactions recorded in a general journal can affect both subsidiary ledger and general ledger accounts. (p. 318)

18. _____

19. A diagonal line in the Post. Ref. column allows the posting reference of two account numbers. (p. 318)

19. _____

20. Errors made in recording amounts in subsidiary ledgers always affect the general ledger controlling account. (p. 327)

20. _____

21. The steps for posting a journal entry to correct customer accounts are exactly the same as posting other transactions to subsidiary ledgers. (p. 328)

21. _____

Part Three—Analyzing Posting and Subsidiary Ledgers

Directions: For each item below, select the choice that best completes the statement. Print the letter identifying your choice in the Answers column.

Answers

1. When a debit is posted to the accounts payable ledger, the (A) debit amount is written in the Debit column of the account (B) cash account increases (C) controlling account is increased by the entry (D) all of the above. (p. 302)

1. _____

2. When a credit is posted to the accounts payable ledger, the (A) source document number and page number of the journal are written in the Post. Ref. column of the account (B) previous balance is added to the new amount posted in the Credit column (C) credit amount is written in the Debit column of the account (D) word *Balance* is written in the Item column. (p. 303)

2. _____

3. The total of all customer account balances in the accounts receivable ledger equals (A) the balance in the accounts receivable controlling account (B) the balance in the accounts payable controlling account (C) the cash account (D) none of these. (p. 307)

3. _____

4. A form in the accounts receivable ledger has (A) a Debit Balance column (B) a Credit Balance column (C) both Debit Balance and Credit Balance columns (D) none of these. (p. 308)

4. _____

5. The separate amounts in the Accounts Receivable Debit column of a sales journal are (A) posted individually to the general ledger (B) posted individually to the accounts receivable ledger (C) not posted to the general ledger (D) none of these. (p. 309)

5. _____

6. When all lines have been used in a ledger account form, a new page is prepared with the account name, account number, and (A) page number (B) account balance (C) company name (D) none of these. (p. 315)

6. _____

7. Posting the special amount column totals in the cash payments journal is done (A) weekly (B) daily (C) after each transaction (D) none of these. (p. 316)

7. _____

8. The total amount of the purchases journal is posted to the general ledger (A) daily (B) weekly (C) at the end of the month (D) none of these. (p. 321)

8. _____

9. A check mark is placed in parentheses below the General Debit and General Credit column totals in the journal to indicate that the two column totals are (A) posted individually (B) posted only as part of the column total (C) not posted (D) none of these. (p. 324)

9. _____

10. The journal that should be posted first is the (A) sales journal (B) purchases journal (C) general journal (D) cash payments journal. (p. 325)

10. _____

Study Skills

Handling Interruptions

Sometimes you will sit down to study and a family member will ask you an important question. Someone might ask you to run an errand. Occasionally a friend might call for assistance. It seems that interruptions occur quite regularly. There is no way to eliminate all interruptions, but you must learn to handle distractions if you are to complete all your work on schedule.

Establish a Formal Schedule
You can avoid many of the distractions you face daily if you establish regular study hours. You can post your study hours and keep your door closed while you are studying.

Telephone Calls
Some students simply do not answer the phone during study time. This may or may not be a good idea in a particular situation. There are certainly calls that you would welcome anytime, but most of them could be postponed without trouble. If your friends know that you have a regular study schedule, they should not be offended if you ask them to call before or after these hours.

Getting Back to Work
Perhaps the most important part of handling interruptions is getting back to work. When your study is interrupted, you must learn to control the length of time you lose. Most questions take only a moment to answer, but it is very easy to allow them to distract you for 10 or 15 minutes.

If you must stop to run an errand, note the time that you leave and hurry back to study with a minimum of delay. Students are often quite surprised when they realize that they lose an hour or two when they run an errand that should take only 15 or 20 minutes.

Looking for an Interruption
Sometimes we may find it difficult to get interested in an assignment, and we almost seem to look for something to postpone our study. We make a phone call when the call could easily wait. We pick up a magazine or a newspaper and begin reading when we should not do so.

If we find ourselves looking for a distraction, we must first realize that we are simply trying to postpone our work. Then we should force ourselves to get back to the subject immediately. The sooner we begin the work, the sooner we will finish.

A Key to Success
If you allow interruptions to interfere with your work on a regular basis, you will find that more and more interruptions occur. If you take steps to control interruptions, you will find that you will be less distracted. Handling interruptions is a key to accomplishing what you want to do in school.

11-1 WORK TOGETHER, p. 306

Posting to an accounts payable ledger

2.

PURCHASES JOURNAL PAGE 10

DATE	ACCOUNT CREDITED	PURCH. NO.	POST. REF.	PURCHASES DR. ACCTS. PAY. CR.
19	Regal Designs	89		1 4 0 3 20
31	Total			11 8 1 8 40

3.

CASH PAYMENTS JOURNAL PAGE 15

DATE	ACCOUNT TITLE	CK. NO.	POST. REF.	GENERAL DEBIT	GENERAL CREDIT	ACCOUNTS PAYABLE DEBIT	PURCHASES DISCOUNT CREDIT	CASH CREDIT
19	Supplies—Office	290		6960				6960
20	Electro-Graphics Supply	291				7 7 6 00		7 7 6 00
31	Totals			1 1 6 7 1 38	1 4 9 4 74	8 6 5 6 00	1 2 8 48	1 8 7 0 4 16

4.

GENERAL JOURNAL PAGE 11

DATE	ACCOUNT TITLE	DOC. NO.	POST. REF.	DEBIT	CREDIT
Oct. 12	Sales Returns and Allowances	CM29		5 2 00	
	Sales Tax Payable			3 12	
	Accounts Receivable/David Bishop				5 5 12
26	Supplies—Office	M32		2 5 4 4 00	
	Accounts Payable/Electro-Graphics Supply				2 5 4 4 00
28	Accounts Payable/Art and Things	DM37		1 2 5 00	
	Purchases Returns and Allowances				1 2 5 00

(Note: The journals in this problem are needed to complete Work Together 11-3 and 11-4. The general journal is also needed to complete Work Together 11-2.)

1., 2., 3., 4.   **ACCOUNTS PAYABLE LEDGER**

vendor Art and Things   vendor no. 210

DATE		ITEM	POST. REF.	DEBIT	CREDIT	CREDIT BALANCE
20-- Oct.	1	Balance	✔			8 7 3 00

vendor Can Do Graphics   vendor no. 220

DATE		ITEM	POST. REF.	DEBIT	CREDIT	CREDIT BALANCE
20-- Oct.	1	Balance	✔			1 8 1 4 00
	13		CP15	8 2 8 00		9 8 6 00

vendor Electro-Graphics Supply   vendor no. 230

DATE		ITEM	POST. REF.	DEBIT	CREDIT	CREDIT BALANCE
20-- Oct.	1	Balance	✔			7 7 6 00

vendor   vendor no.

DATE		ITEM	POST. REF.	DEBIT	CREDIT	CREDIT BALANCE

5.

11-1 ON YOUR OWN, p. 306

Posting to an accounts payable ledger

2.

PURCHASES JOURNAL PAGE 9

DATE	ACCOUNT CREDITED	PURCH. NO.	POST. REF.	PURCHASES DR. ACCTS. PAY. CR.	
14	Swann Industries	458		2485 00	11
30	Total			4857 25	22
					23

3.

CASH PAYMENTS JOURNAL PAGE 20

				1	2	3	4	5	
DATE	ACCOUNT TITLE	CK. NO.	POST. REF.	GENERAL DEBIT	GENERAL CREDIT	ACCOUNTS PAYABLE DEBIT	PURCHASES DISCOUNT CREDIT	CASH CREDIT	
21	Supplies—Store	647		124 20				124 20	18
22	Miller Supply	648				489 00		489 00	19
30	Totals			4215 82 5	1648 25	3323 72 6	425 22	7332 2 04	23
									24

4.

GENERAL JOURNAL PAGE 16

DATE	ACCOUNT TITLE	DOC. NO.	POST. REF.	DEBIT	CREDIT	
20-- Sept. 15	Sales Returns and Allowances	CM91		60 00		1
	Sales Tax Payable			4 20		2
	Accounts Receivable/Mary Burgin				64 20	3
27	Supplies—Store	M125		789 00		4
	Accounts Payable/Miller Supply				789 00	5
29	Accounts Payable/Franklin Mfg. Corp.			110 00		6
	Purchases Returns and Allowances				110 00	7

(Note: The journals in this problem are needed to complete On Your Own 11-3 and 11-4. The general journal is also needed to complete On Your Own 11-2.)

1., 2., 3., 4.   **ACCOUNTS PAYABLE LEDGER**

VENDOR Best Supply Co.   VENDOR NO. 210

DATE		ITEM	POST. REF.	DEBIT	CREDIT	CREDIT BALANCE
20-- Sept.	1	Balance	✔			
	3		P9		3 4 8 2 00	3 4 8 2 00

VENDOR Franklin Mfg. Corp.   VENDOR NO. 220

DATE		ITEM	POST. REF.	DEBIT	CREDIT	CREDIT BALANCE
20-- Sept.	1	Balance	✔			1 2 4 8 25

VENDOR Miller Supply   VENDOR NO. 230

DATE		ITEM	POST. REF.	DEBIT	CREDIT	CREDIT BALANCE
20-- Sept.	1	Balance	✔			4 8 9 00

VENDOR   VENDOR NO.

DATE		ITEM	POST. REF.	DEBIT	CREDIT	CREDIT BALANCE

5.

11-2 WORK TOGETHER, p. 314

Posting to an accounts receivable ledger

3.

CASH RECEIPTS JOURNAL

PAGE 12

				1 GENERAL		3 ACCOUNTS RECEIVABLE CREDIT	4 SALES CREDIT	5 SALES TAX PAYABLE CREDIT	6 SALES DISCOUNT DEBIT	7 CASH DEBIT	
DATE	ACCOUNT TITLE	DOC. NO.	POST. REF.	DEBIT	CREDIT						
21	Alfredo Lopez	R104				2 5 4 40				2 5 4 40	9
31	Totals					6 3 6 0 00	18 3 2 0 00	1 0 9 9 20	3 1 40	25 7 4 7 80	17
											18
											19

2.

SALES JOURNAL

PAGE 10

				1 ACCOUNTS RECEIVABLE DEBIT	2 SALES CREDIT	3 SALES TAX PAYABLE CREDIT	
DATE	ACCOUNT DEBITED	SALE NO.	POST. REF.				
20	Brandee Sparks	84		5 7 6 64	5 4 4 00	3 2 64	5
31	Totals			7 3 7 7 60	6 9 6 0 00	4 1 7 60	12
							13
							14

(Note: The journals in this problem are also needed to complete Work Together 11-4.)

1., 2., 3., 4.   **ACCOUNTS RECEIVABLE LEDGER**

CUSTOMER David Bishop   CUSTOMER NO. 110

DATE		ITEM	POST. REF.	DEBIT	CREDIT	DEBIT BALANCE
20-- Oct.	1	Balance	✔			5 8 7 25
	10		CR12		3 4 8 75	2 3 8 50

CUSTOMER Maria Farrell   CUSTOMER NO. 120

DATE		ITEM	POST. REF.	DEBIT	CREDIT	DEBIT BALANCE
20-- Oct.	1	Balance	✔			2 8 6 20

CUSTOMER Alfredo Lopez   CUSTOMER NO. 130

DATE		ITEM	POST. REF.	DEBIT	CREDIT	DEBIT BALANCE
20-- Oct.	1	Balance	✔			2 5 4 40
	12		S10	1 2 7 2 00		1 5 2 6 40

CUSTOMER   CUSTOMER NO.

DATE		ITEM	POST. REF.	DEBIT	CREDIT	DEBIT BALANCE

5.

11-2 ON YOUR OWN, p. 314

Posting to an accounts receivable ledger

2.

SALES JOURNAL   PAGE 9

DATE	ACCOUNT DEBITED	SALE NO.	POST. REF.	1 ACCOUNTS RECEIVABLE DEBIT	2 SALES CREDIT	3 SALES TAX PAYABLE CREDIT	
21	Davis Sullivan	354		1 4 7 0 50	1 3 7 4 30	9 6 20	8
30	Totals			30 1 1 8 36	28 1 4 8 00	1 9 7 0 36	17
							18
							19

3.

CASH RECEIPTS JOURNAL   PAGE 18

DATE	ACCOUNT TITLE	DOC. NO.	POST. REF.	1 GENERAL DEBIT	2 GENERAL CREDIT	3 ACCOUNTS RECEIVABLE CREDIT	4 SALES CREDIT	5 SALES TAX PAYABLE CREDIT	6 SALES DISCOUNT DEBIT	7 CASH DEBIT	
19	Harris Evans	R302				2 1 5 8 00				2 1 5 8 00	21
30	Totals					29 4 8 4 25	48 1 5 8 25	3 2 4 8 25	2 2 3 00	80 6 6 7 75	26
											27
											28
											29
											30

(Note: The journals used in this problem are also used to complete On Your Own 11-4.)

1., 2., 3., 4.   **ACCOUNTS RECEIVABLE LEDGER**

CUSTOMER Mary Burgin   CUSTOMER NO. 110

DATE		ITEM	POST. REF.	DEBIT	CREDIT	DEBIT BALANCE
Sept.	1	Balance	✔			1 5 4 8 00
	6		CR18		2 5 2 00	1 2 9 6 00

CUSTOMER Harris Evans   CUSTOMER NO. 120

DATE		ITEM	POST. REF.	DEBIT	CREDIT	DEBIT BALANCE
Sept.	1	Balance	✔			2 1 5 8 00
	13		S9	1 5 7 8 50		3 7 3 6 50

CUSTOMER Patrick Mussina   CUSTOMER NO. 130

DATE		ITEM	POST. REF.	DEBIT	CREDIT	DEBIT BALANCE
Sept.	1	Balance	✔			1 1 4 2 00

CUSTOMER   CUSTOMER NO.

DATE		ITEM	POST. REF.	DEBIT	CREDIT	DEBIT BALANCE

5.

11-3 and 11-4 WORK TOGETHER, pp. 319, 326

Posting to a general ledger

Posting special journals to a general ledger

1., 2., 3., 4., 5.   **GENERAL LEDGER**

ACCOUNT Cash   ACCOUNT NO. 1110

DATE		ITEM	POST. REF.	DEBIT	CREDIT	BALANCE	
						DEBIT	CREDIT
Oct. 20--	1	Balance	✔			13 2 3 5 58	

ACCOUNT Accounts Receivable   ACCOUNT NO. 1130

DATE		ITEM	POST. REF.	DEBIT	CREDIT	BALANCE	
						DEBIT	CREDIT
Oct. 20--	1	Balance	✔			1 3 3 9 85	

ACCOUNT   ACCOUNT NO.

DATE		ITEM	POST. REF.	DEBIT	CREDIT	BALANCE	
						DEBIT	CREDIT

ACCOUNT Accounts Payable   ACCOUNT NO. 2110

DATE		ITEM	POST. REF.	DEBIT	CREDIT	BALANCE	
						DEBIT	CREDIT
Oct. 20--	1	Balance	✔				2 5 1 7 80

(Note: The general ledger accounts used in this problem are needed to complete Work Together 11-4.)

ACCOUNT Sales Tax Payable   ACCOUNT NO. 2140

DATE		ITEM	POST. REF.	DEBIT	CREDIT	BALANCE DEBIT	BALANCE CREDIT
20-- Oct.	1	Balance	✔				1 4 1 0 00

ACCOUNT Sales   ACCOUNT NO. 4110

DATE		ITEM	POST. REF.	DEBIT	CREDIT	BALANCE DEBIT	BALANCE CREDIT
20-- Oct.	1	Balance	✔				233 3 3 5 00

ACCOUNT Sales Discount   ACCOUNT NO. 4120

DATE		ITEM	POST. REF.	DEBIT	CREDIT	BALANCE DEBIT	BALANCE CREDIT
20-- Oct.	1	Balance	✔			2 1 9 8 00	

ACCOUNT Sales Returns and Allowances   ACCOUNT NO. 4130

DATE		ITEM	POST. REF.	DEBIT	CREDIT	BALANCE DEBIT	BALANCE CREDIT
20-- Oct.	1	Balance	✔			9 0 3 00	

11-3 and 11-4 WORK TOGETHER (concluded)

ACCOUNT Purchases   ACCOUNT NO. 5110

DATE		ITEM	POST. REF.	DEBIT	CREDIT	BALANCE DEBIT	BALANCE CREDIT
20-- Oct.	1	Balance	✔			106 55 9 60	

ACCOUNT Purchases Discount   ACCOUNT NO. 5120

DATE		ITEM	POST. REF.	DEBIT	CREDIT	BALANCE DEBIT	BALANCE CREDIT
20-- Oct.	1	Balance	✔				1 2 5 8 85

ACCOUNT Purchases Returns and Allowances   ACCOUNT NO. 5130

DATE		ITEM	POST. REF.	DEBIT	CREDIT	BALANCE DEBIT	BALANCE CREDIT
20-- Oct.	1	Balance	✔				1 9 0 1 35

Posting to a general ledger
Posting special journals to a general ledger

1., 2., 3., 4., 5.   GENERAL LEDGER

ACCOUNT Cash   ACCOUNT NO. 1110

DATE	ITEM	POST. REF.	DEBIT	CREDIT	BALANCE DEBIT	BALANCE CREDIT
Sept. 1	Balance	✔			12 4 8 8 10	

ACCOUNT Accounts Receivable   ACCOUNT NO. 1130

DATE	ITEM	POST. REF.	DEBIT	CREDIT	BALANCE DEBIT	BALANCE CREDIT
Sept. 1	Balance	✔			11 1 1 1 00	

ACCOUNT   ACCOUNT NO.

DATE	ITEM	POST. REF.	DEBIT	CREDIT	BALANCE DEBIT	BALANCE CREDIT

ACCOUNT Accounts Payable   ACCOUNT NO. 2110

DATE	ITEM	POST. REF.	DEBIT	CREDIT	BALANCE DEBIT	BALANCE CREDIT
Sept. 1	Balance	✔				21 4 8 2 20

(Note: The general ledger accounts used in this problem are needed to complete On Your Own 11-4.)

11-3 and 11-4 ON YOUR OWN (continued)

ACCOUNT Sales Tax Payable   ACCOUNT NO. 2140

DATE		ITEM	POST. REF.	DEBIT	CREDIT	BALANCE	
						DEBIT	CREDIT
Sept.	1	Balance	✔				5 2 1 8 61

ACCOUNT Sales   ACCOUNT NO. 4110

DATE		ITEM	POST. REF.	DEBIT	CREDIT	BALANCE	
						DEBIT	CREDIT
Sept.	1	Balance	✔				408 7 4 2 25

ACCOUNT Sales Discount   ACCOUNT NO. 4120

DATE		ITEM	POST. REF.	DEBIT	CREDIT	BALANCE	
						DEBIT	CREDIT
Sept.	1	Balance	✔			2 1 9 8 00	

ACCOUNT Sales Returns and Allowances   ACCOUNT NO. 4130

DATE		ITEM	POST. REF.	DEBIT	CREDIT	BALANCE	
						DEBIT	CREDIT
Sept.	1	Balance	✔			5 1 2 3 00	

ACCOUNT Purchases   ACCOUNT NO. 5110

DATE		ITEM	POST. REF.	DEBIT	CREDIT	BALANCE	
						DEBIT	CREDIT
Sept. 20--	1	Balance	✔			212 1 8 4 66	

ACCOUNT Purchases Discount   ACCOUNT NO. 5120

DATE		ITEM	POST. REF.	DEBIT	CREDIT	BALANCE	
						DEBIT	CREDIT
Sept. 20--	1	Balance	✔				3 4 7 8 25

ACCOUNT Purchases Returns and Allowances   ACCOUNT NO. 5130

DATE		ITEM	POST. REF.	DEBIT	CREDIT	BALANCE	
						DEBIT	CREDIT
Sept. 20--	1	Balance	✔				3 2 7 6 00

11-5 WORK TOGETHER, p. 329

Journalizing and posting correcting entries affecting customer accounts

1.

GENERAL JOURNAL   PAGE 6

	DATE	ACCOUNT TITLE	DOC. NO.	POST. REF.	DEBIT	CREDIT	
6							6
7							7
8							8
9							9

2.   ACCOUNTS RECEIVABLE LEDGER

CUSTOMER Howell Clinic   CUSTOMER NO. 160

DATE	ITEM	POST. REF.	DEBIT	CREDIT	DEBIT BALANCE

CUSTOMER Howsley Dance Studio   CUSTOMER NO. 170

DATE		ITEM	POST. REF.	DEBIT	CREDIT	DEBIT BALANCE
20-- June	1	Balance	✔			4 1 4 99

Journalizing and posting correcting entries affecting customer accounts

1.

GENERAL JOURNAL   PAGE 7

	DATE	ACCOUNT TITLE	DOC. NO.	POST. REF.	DEBIT	CREDIT	
5							5
6							6
7							7
8							8
9							9
10							10

2.   **ACCOUNTS RECEIVABLE LEDGER**

CUSTOMER Keller Corp.   CUSTOMER NO. 140

DATE		ITEM	POST. REF.	DEBIT	CREDIT	DEBIT BALANCE
20-- July	1	Balance	✔			7 1 5 98

CUSTOMER Kellogg Co.   CUSTOMER NO. 150

DATE	ITEM	POST. REF.	DEBIT	CREDIT	DEBIT BALANCE

COPYRIGHT © SOUTH-WESTERN CENGAGE LEARNING

11-1 **APPLICATION PROBLEM, p. 331**

Posting to an accounts payable ledger

2.

PURCHASES JOURNAL   PAGE 10

	DATE		ACCOUNT CREDITED	PURCH. NO.	POST. REF.	PURCHASES DR. ACCTS. PAY. CR.	
1	Oct. 20--	4	Nutrition Center	78		2 0 1 6 00	1
2		20	Cornucopia, Inc.	79		4 5 8 4 00	2
3		25	Sports Nutrition	80		5 4 0 0 00	3
4		30	Healthy Foods	81		3 3 9 6 00	4

1., 2.   **ACCOUNTS PAYABLE LEDGER**

VENDOR   VENDOR NO.

DATE	ITEM	POST. REF.	DEBIT	CREDIT	CREDIT BALANCE

VENDOR   VENDOR NO.

DATE	ITEM	POST. REF.	DEBIT	CREDIT	CREDIT BALANCE

VENDOR						VENDOR NO.	
DATE	ITEM	POST. REF.	DEBIT	CREDIT	CREDIT BALANCE

VENDOR						VENDOR NO.	
DATE	ITEM	POST. REF.	DEBIT	CREDIT	CREDIT BALANCE

VENDOR						VENDOR NO.	
DATE	ITEM	POST. REF.	DEBIT	CREDIT	CREDIT BALANCE

11-1 **APPLICATION PROBLEM (continued)**

Posting to an accounts payable ledger

2.

CASH PAYMENTS JOURNAL   PAGE 10

DATE	ACCOUNT TITLE	CK. NO.	POST. REF.	GENERAL DEBIT	GENERAL CREDIT	ACCOUNTS PAYABLE DEBIT	PURCHASES DISCOUNT CREDIT	CASH CREDIT	
Oct. 3	Cornucopia, Inc.	184				3 0 9 0 00	6 1 80	3 0 2 8 20	1
6	Healthy Foods	185				5 0 6 4 00	1 0 1 28	4 9 6 2 72	2
15	Sports Nutrition	186				4 5 1 2 00		4 5 1 2 00	3
28	Nutrition Center	187				2 0 1 6 00		2 0 1 6 00	4
									5
									6
									7
									8

GENERAL JOURNAL   PAGE 10

DATE	ACCOUNT TITLE	DOC. NO.	POST. REF.	DEBIT	CREDIT	
Oct. 9	Supplies—Office	M26		9 6 00		1
	Accounts Payable/Office Center				9 6 00	2
25	Accounts Payable/Cornucopia, Inc.	DM36		1 2 4 00		3
	Purchases Returns and Allowances				1 2 4 00	4
						5
						6

3.

11-2 APPLICATION PROBLEM, p. 331

Posting to an accounts receivable ledger

2.

SALES JOURNAL PAGE 10

	DATE		ACCOUNT DEBITED	SALE NO.	POST. REF.	ACCOUNTS RECEIVABLE DEBIT	SALES CREDIT	SALES TAX PAYABLE CREDIT	
1	20-- Oct.	6	Southwest Community Club	69		3 0 0 1 92	2 8 3 2 00	1 6 9 92	1
2		9	Children's Center	70		1 7 5 5 36	1 6 5 6 00	9 9 36	2
3		12	Eastman Sports Arena	71		1 1 1 9 36	1 0 5 6 00	6 3 36	3
4		25	Maple Tree Club	72		2 5 4 4 00	2 4 0 0 00	1 4 4 00	4

1., 2. ACCOUNTS RECEIVABLE LEDGER

CUSTOMER CUSTOMER NO.

DATE	ITEM	POST. REF.	DEBIT	CREDIT	DEBIT BALANCE

CUSTOMER CUSTOMER NO.

DATE	ITEM	POST. REF.	DEBIT	CREDIT	DEBIT BALANCE

CUSTOMER CUSTOMER NO.

DATE	ITEM	POST. REF.	DEBIT	CREDIT	DEBIT BALANCE

CUSTOMER CUSTOMER NO.

DATE	ITEM	POST. REF.	DEBIT	CREDIT	DEBIT BALANCE

2.

GENERAL JOURNAL   PAGE 10

	DATE		ACCOUNT TITLE	DOC. NO.	POST. REF.	DEBIT	CREDIT	
1	Oct.	29	Sales Returns and Allowances	CM6		1 2 0 00		1
2			Sales Tax Payable			7 20		2
3			Accounts Receivable/Maple Tree Club		/		1 2 7 20	3
4								4
5								5
6								6
7								7
8								8
9								9
10								10
11								11
12								12
13								13
14								14
15								15
16								16
17								17
18								18
19								19
20								20
21								21
22								22
23								23
24								24
25								25
26								26
27								27
28								28
29								29
30								30
31								31
32								32
33								33

11-2 **APPLICATION PROBLEM (continued)**

2.

CASH RECEIPTS JOURNAL

PAGE 10

					GENERAL		ACCOUNTS RECEIVABLE CREDIT	SALES CREDIT	SALES TAX PAYABLE CREDIT	SALES DISCOUNT DEBIT	CASH DEBIT	
DATE		ACCOUNT TITLE	DOC. NO.	POST. REF.	DEBIT	CREDIT						
20-- Oct.	5	Children's Center	R170				4 4 1 6 00				4 4 1 6 00	1
	14	Eastman Sports Arena	R171				2 2 2 0 00				2 2 2 0 00	2
	24	Maple Tree Club	R172				3 5 2 8 00				3 5 2 8 00	3
												4
												5
												6
												7
												8
												9
												10
												11
												12
												13
												14
												15
												16
												17
												18
												19
												20
												21
												22
												23

3.

11-3 **APPLICATION PROBLEM, p. 332**

Posting to a general ledger

2.

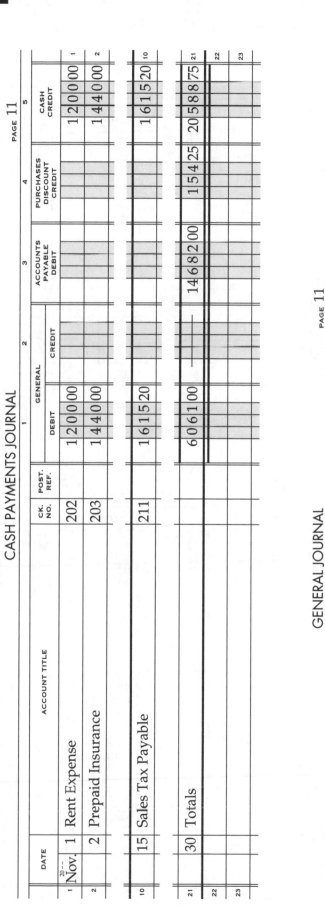

CASH PAYMENTS JOURNAL   PAGE 11

DATE		ACCOUNT TITLE	CK. NO.	POST. REF.	GENERAL DEBIT	GENERAL CREDIT	ACCOUNTS PAYABLE DEBIT	PURCHASES DISCOUNT CREDIT	CASH CREDIT	
20-- Nov.	1	Rent Expense	202		1 200 00				1 200 00	1
	2	Prepaid Insurance	203		1 440 00				1 440 00	2
	15	Sales Tax Payable	211		1 615 20				1 615 20	10
	30	Totals			6 061 00		14 682 00	154 25	20 588 75	21
										22
										23

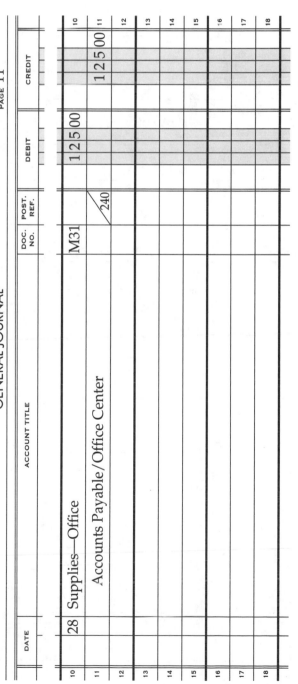

GENERAL JOURNAL   PAGE 11

DATE		ACCOUNT TITLE	DOC. NO.	POST. REF.	DEBIT	CREDIT	
	28	Supplies—Office	M31		125 00		10
		Accounts Payable/Office Center		240		125 00	11
							12
							13
							14
							15
							16
							17
							18

(Note: The ledger accounts used in this problem are also used in Application Problem 11-4.)

1., 2. **GENERAL LEDGER**

ACCOUNT _____ ACCOUNT NO. _____

DATE		ITEM	POST. REF.	DEBIT	CREDIT	BALANCE DEBIT	BALANCE CREDIT

ACCOUNT _____ ACCOUNT NO. _____

DATE		ITEM	POST. REF.	DEBIT	CREDIT	BALANCE DEBIT	BALANCE CREDIT

ACCOUNT _____ ACCOUNT NO. _____

DATE		ITEM	POST. REF.	DEBIT	CREDIT	BALANCE DEBIT	BALANCE CREDIT

ACCOUNT _____ ACCOUNT NO. _____

DATE		ITEM	POST. REF.	DEBIT	CREDIT	BALANCE DEBIT	BALANCE CREDIT

11-3 APPLICATION PROBLEM (continued)

ACCOUNT _____ ACCOUNT NO. _____

DATE	ITEM	POST. REF.	DEBIT	CREDIT	BALANCE	
					DEBIT	CREDIT

ACCOUNT _____ ACCOUNT NO. _____

DATE	ITEM	POST. REF.	DEBIT	CREDIT	BALANCE	
					DEBIT	CREDIT

ACCOUNT _____ ACCOUNT NO. _____

DATE	ITEM	POST. REF.	DEBIT	CREDIT	BALANCE	
					DEBIT	CREDIT

ACCOUNT _____ ACCOUNT NO. _____

DATE	ITEM	POST. REF.	DEBIT	CREDIT	BALANCE	
					DEBIT	CREDIT

ACCOUNT _____   ACCOUNT NO. _____

DATE	ITEM	POST. REF.	DEBIT	CREDIT	BALANCE	
					DEBIT	CREDIT

ACCOUNT _____   ACCOUNT NO. _____

DATE	ITEM	POST. REF.	DEBIT	CREDIT	BALANCE	
					DEBIT	CREDIT

ACCOUNT _____   ACCOUNT NO. _____

DATE	ITEM	POST. REF.	DEBIT	CREDIT	BALANCE	
					DEBIT	CREDIT

11-4 **APPLICATION PROBLEM, p. 332**

Posting special journal column totals to a general ledger

SALES JOURNAL

PAGE 11

DATE	ACCOUNT DEBITED	SALE NO.	POST. REF.	1 ACCOUNTS RECEIVABLE DEBIT	2 SALES CREDIT	3 SALES TAX PAYABLE CREDIT	
30	Totals			9 2 6 2 28	8 7 3 8 00	5 2 4 28	11
							12

PURCHASES JOURNAL

PAGE 11

DATE	ACCOUNT CREDITED	PURCH. NO.	POST. REF.	PURCHASES DR. ACCTS. PAY. CR.	
30	Total			16 1 6 5 80	13
					14

CASH RECEIPTS JOURNAL

PAGE 11

DATE	ACCOUNT TITLE	DOC. NO.	POST. REF.	1 GENERAL DEBIT	2 GENERAL CREDIT	3 ACCOUNTS RECEIVABLE CREDIT	4 SALES CREDIT	5 SALES TAX PAYABLE CREDIT	6 SALES DISCOUNT DEBIT	7 CASH DEBIT	
30	Totals					8 4 2 0 64	20 5 2 0 00	1 2 3 1 20	1 2 7 60	30 0 4 4 24	19
											20

APPLICATION PROBLEM, pp. 332, 333

Journalizing and posting correcting entries affecting customer accounts

1., 2.

GENERAL JOURNAL   PAGE

	DATE	ACCOUNT TITLE	DOC. NO.	POST. REF.	DEBIT	CREDIT	
1							1
2							2
3							3
4							4
5							5
6							6
7							7
8							8

11-5 APPLICATION PROBLEM (concluded)

2.   ACCOUNTS RECEIVABLE LEDGER

CUSTOMER Mark Ford   CUSTOMER NO. 145

DATE		ITEM	POST. REF.	DEBIT	CREDIT	DEBIT BALANCE
20-- July	1	Balance	✔			9 8 20

CUSTOMER Andrew Forde   CUSTOMER NO. 150

DATE		ITEM	POST. REF.	DEBIT	CREDIT	DEBIT BALANCE
20-- July	1	Balance	✔			1 2 8 00
	5		S12	2 5 3 32		3 8 1 32

CUSTOMER Daniel Patrick   CUSTOMER NO. 185

DATE		ITEM	POST. REF.	DEBIT	CREDIT	DEBIT BALANCE
20-- July	1	Balance	✔			6 0 00
	8		S12	3 8 4 50		4 4 4 50

CUSTOMER Sandy Patterson   CUSTOMER NO. 190

DATE		ITEM	POST. REF.	DEBIT	CREDIT	DEBIT BALANCE
20-- July	1	Balance	✔			1 2 5 00

Posting to general and subsidiary ledgers

1., 2.

SALES JOURNAL

	DATE		ACCOUNT DEBITED	SALE NO.	POST. REF.	ACCOUNTS RECEIVABLE DEBIT	SALES CREDIT	SALES TAX PAYABLE CREDIT	
						1	2	3	
1	Oct. 20--	4	Jerome Lewis	658		2 2 7 6 88	2 1 4 8 00	1 2 8 88	1
2		12	Douglas Rieves	659		3 7 3 12	3 5 2 00	2 1 12	2
3		15	Amy Carson	660		2 0 6 4 88	1 9 4 8 00	1 1 6 88	3
4		23	John Frazier	661		1 5 6 3 50	1 4 7 5 00	8 8 50	4
5		31	Totals			6 2 7 8 38	5 9 2 3 00	3 5 5 38	5
6									6
7									7
8									8
9									9
10									10
11									11
12									12
13									13
14									14
15									15
16									16
17									17
18									18

11-6 MASTERY PROBLEM (continued)

1., 2.

PURCHASES JOURNAL   PAGE 10

	DATE		ACCOUNT CREDITED	PURCH. NO.	POST. REF.	PURCHASES DR. ACCTS. PAY. CR.	
1	Oct.	5	Harman Supply	345		5 2 1 5 34	1
2		18	Mixon Industries	346		6 2 5 1 38	2
3		22	Alford Salvage	347		8 1 2 5 45	3
4		25	Reliable Auto	348		4 2 1 5 88	4
5		28	Harman Supply	349		3 6 4 8 80	5
6		30	Mixon Industries	350		2 5 1 5 84	6
7		31	Total			29 9 7 2 69	7
8							8
9							9
10							10
11							11
12							12
13							13
14							14
15							15
16							16
17							17
18							18
19							19
20							20
21							21
22							22
23							23
24							24
25							25

1.

GENERAL JOURNAL   PAGE 10

	DATE		ACCOUNT TITLE	DOC. NO.	POST. REF.	DEBIT	CREDIT	
1	Oct.	3	John Frazier	M77		8 2 5 00		1
2			Amy Carson				8 2 5 00	2
5		24	Accounts Payable/Alford Salvage	DM97		1 5 0 00		5
6			Purchases Returns and Allowances				1 5 0 00	6
7		25	Sales Returns and Allowances	CM151		3 0 0 00		7
8			Sales Tax Payable			1 8 00		8
9			Accounts Receivable/Jerome Lewis				3 1 8 00	9
10		28	Supplies—Store	M78		2 7 5 00		10
11			Accounts Payable/Mixon Industries				2 7 5 00	11
12								12
13								13

11-6 **MASTERY PROBLEM (continued)**

CASH RECEIPTS JOURNAL

PAGE 14

DATE	ACCOUNT TITLE	DOC. NO.	POST. REF.	GENERAL DEBIT	GENERAL CREDIT	ACCOUNTS RECEIVABLE CREDIT	SALES CREDIT	SALES TAX PAYABLE CREDIT	SALES DISCOUNT DEBIT	CASH DEBIT	
20-- Oct. 1	Jerome Lewis	R624				854 45				854 45	1
3	✔	TS30					5248 00	367 36		5615 36	2
10	✔	TS31					6004 00	420 28		6424 28	3
12	John Frazier	R625				2170 85			43 42	2127 43	4
17	✔	TS32					5495 00	384 65		5879 65	5
19	Douglas Rieves	R626				1694 34				1694 34	6
24	✔	TS33					5748 00	402 36		6150 36	7
26	Amy Carson	R627				420 25			8 41	411 84	8
31	✔	TS34					5258 00	368 06		5626 06	9
31	Totals					5139 89	27753 00	1942 71	51 83	34783 77	10
											11
											12
											13
											14

1., 2.

CASH PAYMENTS JOURNAL

PAGE 13

	DATE		ACCOUNT TITLE	CK. NO.	POST. REF.	GENERAL DEBIT	GENERAL CREDIT	ACCOUNTS PAYABLE DEBIT	PURCHASES DISCOUNT CREDIT	CASH CREDIT	
1	Oct.	2	Rent Expense	782		3 0 0 0 00				3 0 0 0 00	1
2		4	Utilities Expense	783		7 5 1 25				7 5 1 25	2
3		7	Alford Salvage	784				1 5 4 8 45	3 0 97	1 5 1 7 48	3
4		8	Mixon Industries	785				2 1 5 8 45	4 3 17	2 1 1 5 28	4
5		11	Harman Supply	790				1 4 1 7 25		1 4 1 7 25	5
6		12	Reliable Auto	787				3 5 1 5 34	7 0 31	3 4 4 5 03	6
7		13	Harman Supply	788				5 2 1 5 34		5 2 1 5 34	7
8		14	Advertising Expense	789		2 5 0 0 00				2 5 0 0 00	8
9		20	Miscellaneous Expense	786		2 3 4 25				2 3 4 25	9
10		24	Supplies—Store	791		3 5 2 25				3 5 2 25	10
11		27	Mixon Industries	792				6 2 5 1 38	1 2 5 03	6 1 2 6 35	11
12		30	Supplies—Office	793		4 2 5 17				4 2 5 17	12
13		31	Totals			7 2 6 2 92	—	20 1 0 6 21	2 6 9 48	27 0 9 9 65	13
14											14
15											15

11-6 MASTERY PROBLEM (continued)

1., 2.　　　　　　　　　　　　　　**GENERAL LEDGER**

ACCOUNT Cash　　　　　　　　　　　　　　　　　　　　ACCOUNT NO. 1110

DATE		ITEM	POST. REF.	DEBIT	CREDIT	BALANCE	
						DEBIT	CREDIT
20-- Oct.	1	Balance	✔			20 420 25	

ACCOUNT Accounts Receivable　　　　　　　　　　　　　　ACCOUNT NO. 1130

DATE		ITEM	POST. REF.	DEBIT	CREDIT	BALANCE	
						DEBIT	CREDIT
20-- Oct.	1	Balance	✔			5 139 89	

ACCOUNT Supplies—Office　　　　　　　　　　　　　　ACCOUNT NO. 1150

DATE		ITEM	POST. REF.	DEBIT	CREDIT	BALANCE	
						DEBIT	CREDIT
20-- Oct.	1	Balance	✔			2 514 20	

ACCOUNT Supplies—Store　　　　　　　　　　　　　　ACCOUNT NO. 1160

DATE		ITEM	POST. REF.	DEBIT	CREDIT	BALANCE	
						DEBIT	CREDIT
20-- Oct.	1	Balance	✔			2 514 00	

ACCOUNT Accounts Payable　　　　　　　　　　　　　　ACCOUNT NO. 2110

DATE		ITEM	POST. REF.	DEBIT	CREDIT	BALANCE	
						DEBIT	CREDIT
20-- Oct.	1	Balance	✔				8 639 49

ACCOUNT Sales Tax Payable ACCOUNT NO. 2120

DATE		ITEM	POST. REF.	DEBIT	CREDIT	BALANCE	
						DEBIT	CREDIT
20-- Oct.	1	Balance	✔				8 2 4 25

ACCOUNT Sales ACCOUNT NO. 4110

DATE		ITEM	POST. REF.	DEBIT	CREDIT	BALANCE	
						DEBIT	CREDIT
20-- Oct.	1	Balance	✔				214 7 1 5 25

ACCOUNT Sales Discount ACCOUNT NO. 4120

DATE		ITEM	POST. REF.	DEBIT	CREDIT	BALANCE	
						DEBIT	CREDIT
20-- Oct.	1	Balance	✔			5 0 1 35	

ACCOUNT Sales Returns and Allowances ACCOUNT NO. 4130

DATE		ITEM	POST. REF.	DEBIT	CREDIT	BALANCE	
						DEBIT	CREDIT
20-- Oct.	1	Balance	✔			1 5 9 3 50	

11-6 MASTERY PROBLEM (continued)

ACCOUNT Purchases   ACCOUNT NO. 5110

DATE		ITEM	POST. REF.	DEBIT	CREDIT	BALANCE	
						DEBIT	CREDIT
20-- Oct.	1	Balance	✔			140 6 8 4 34	

ACCOUNT Purchases Discount   ACCOUNT NO. 5120

DATE		ITEM	POST. REF.	DEBIT	CREDIT	BALANCE	
						DEBIT	CREDIT
20-- Oct.	1	Balance	✔				2 0 4 5 25

ACCOUNT Purchases Returns and Allowances   ACCOUNT NO. 5130

DATE		ITEM	POST. REF.	DEBIT	CREDIT	BALANCE	
						DEBIT	CREDIT
20-- Oct.	1	Balance	✔				2 4 7 7 00

ACCOUNT Advertising Expense   ACCOUNT NO. 6110

DATE		ITEM	POST. REF.	DEBIT	CREDIT	BALANCE	
						DEBIT	CREDIT
20-- Oct.	1	Balance	✔			25 8 4 8 45	

ACCOUNT Miscellaneous Expense   ACCOUNT NO. 6140

DATE		ITEM	POST. REF.	DEBIT	CREDIT	BALANCE	
						DEBIT	CREDIT
20-- Oct.	1	Balance	✔			1 5 8 4 00	

ACCOUNT Rent Expense   ACCOUNT NO. 6160

DATE		ITEM	POST. REF.	DEBIT	CREDIT	BALANCE	
						DEBIT	CREDIT
20-- Oct.	1	Balance	✔			30 0 0 0 00	

ACCOUNT Utilities Expense   ACCOUNT NO. 6190

DATE		ITEM	POST. REF.	DEBIT	CREDIT	BALANCE	
						DEBIT	CREDIT
20-- Oct.	1	Balance	✔			8 7 4 5 45	

11-6 MASTERY PROBLEM (continued)

1., 3.   ACCOUNTS RECEIVABLE LEDGER

CUSTOMER Amy Carson   CUSTOMER NO. 110

DATE		ITEM	POST. REF.	DEBIT	CREDIT	DEBIT BALANCE
20-- Oct.	1	Balance	✔			1 2 4 5 25

CUSTOMER John Frazier   CUSTOMER NO. 120

DATE		ITEM	POST. REF.	DEBIT	CREDIT	DEBIT BALANCE
20-- Oct.	1	Balance	✔			1 3 4 5 85

CUSTOMER Jerome Lewis   CUSTOMER NO. 130

DATE		ITEM	POST. REF.	DEBIT	CREDIT	DEBIT BALANCE
20-- Oct.	1	Balance	✔			8 5 4 45

CUSTOMER Douglas Rieves   CUSTOMER NO. 140

DATE		ITEM	POST. REF.	DEBIT	CREDIT	DEBIT BALANCE
20-- Oct.	1	Balance	✔			1 6 9 4 34

1., 3.   **ACCOUNTS PAYABLE LEDGER**

VENDOR Alford Salvage   VENDOR NO. 210

DATE		ITEM	POST. REF.	DEBIT	CREDIT	CREDIT BALANCE
20-- Oct.	1	Balance	✔			1 5 4 8 45

VENDOR Harman Supply   VENDOR NO. 220

DATE		ITEM	POST. REF.	DEBIT	CREDIT	CREDIT BALANCE
20-- Oct.	1	Balance	✔			1 4 1 7 25

VENDOR Mixon Industries   VENDOR NO. 230

DATE		ITEM	POST. REF.	DEBIT	CREDIT	CREDIT BALANCE
20-- Oct.	1	Balance	✔			2 1 5 8 45

VENDOR Reliable Auto   VENDOR NO. 240

DATE		ITEM	POST. REF.	DEBIT	CREDIT	CREDIT BALANCE
20-- Oct.	1	Balance	✔			3 5 1 5 34

11-7 **CHALLENGE PROBLEM, pp. 333, 334**

Journalizing and posting business transactions

1., 2.

SALES JOURNAL

PAGE

	DATE	ACCOUNT DEBITED	SALE NO.	POST. REF.	ACCOUNTS RECEIVABLE DEBIT 1	SALES CREDIT 2	SALES TAX PAYABLE CREDIT 3	
1								1
2								2
3								3
4								4
5								5

1., 3.

PURCHASES JOURNAL

PAGE

	DATE	ACCOUNT CREDITED	PURCH. NO.	POST. REF.	PURCHASES DR. ACCTS. PAY. CR.	
1						1
2						2
3						3
4						4
5						5

1.

GENERAL JOURNAL

PAGE

	DATE	ACCOUNT TITLE	DOC. NO.	POST. REF.	DEBIT	CREDIT	
1							1
2							2
3							3
4							4
5							5

2. Sales Journal Proof

Col. No.	Column Title	Debit Totals	Credit Totals
1	Accounts Receivable Debit	_____	
2	Sales Credit		_____
3	Sales Tax Payable Credit		_____
	Totals	_____	_____

1., 4., 6.

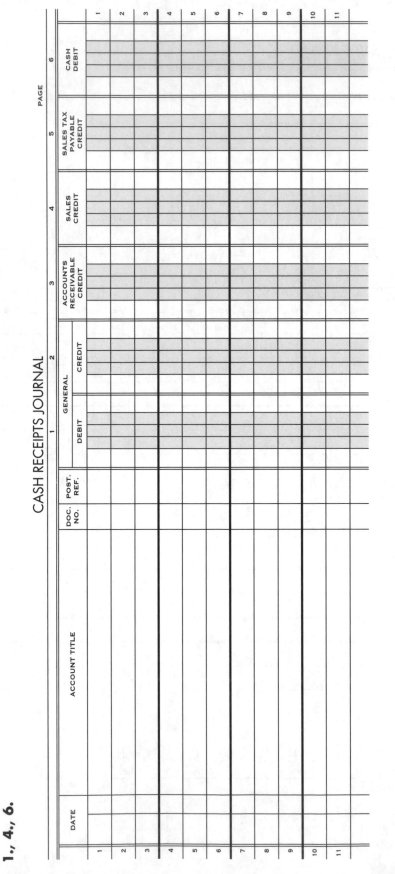

CASH RECEIPTS JOURNAL

4. Cash Receipts Journal Proof

Col. No.	Column Title	Debit Totals	Credit Totals
1	General Debit		
2	General Credit		
3	Accounts Receivable Credit		
4	Sales Credit		
5	Sales Tax Payable Credit		
6	Cash Debit		
	Totals		

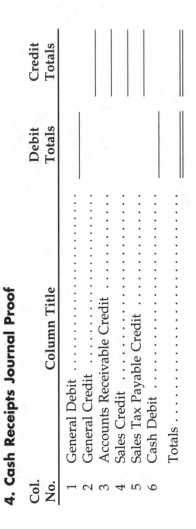

11-7 **CHALLENGE PROBLEM (continued)**

1., 4., 7.

CASH PAYMENTS JOURNAL

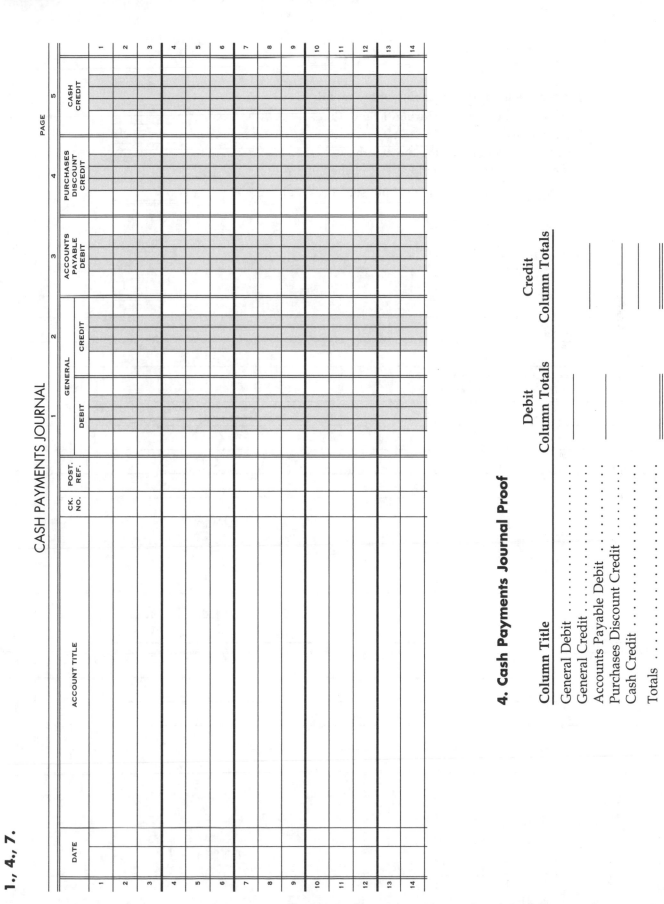

PAGE

| | | | GENERAL | | ACCOUNTS PAYABLE | PURCHASES DISCOUNT | CASH |
| DATE | ACCOUNT TITLE | CK. NO. | POST. REF. | DEBIT | CREDIT | DEBIT | CREDIT | CREDIT |

4. Cash Payments Journal Proof

Column Title	Debit Column Totals	Credit Column Totals
General Debit		
General Credit		
Accounts Payable Debit		
Purchases Discount Credit		
Cash Credit		
Totals		

5.

CASH PROOF

Cash on hand at the beginning of the month . . . . _____

Plus total cash received during the month . . . . _____

Equals total . . . . _____

Less total cash paid during the month . . . . _____

Equals cash balance on hand at end of the month . . . . _____

Checkbook balance on the next unused check stub . . . . _____

8.

11-7 CHALLENGE PROBLEM (continued)

1., 2., 3., 6., 7.   **GENERAL LEDGER**

ACCOUNT Cash   ACCOUNT NO. 1110

DATE		ITEM	POST. REF.	DEBIT	CREDIT	BALANCE	
						DEBIT	CREDIT
20-- Oct.	1	Balance	✔			20 2 2 0 00	

ACCOUNT Accounts Receivable   ACCOUNT NO. 1130

DATE		ITEM	POST. REF.	DEBIT	CREDIT	BALANCE	
						DEBIT	CREDIT
20-- Oct.	1	Balance	✔			3 4 7 9 40	

ACCOUNT Supplies—Office   ACCOUNT NO. 1150

DATE		ITEM	POST. REF.	DEBIT	CREDIT	BALANCE	
						DEBIT	CREDIT
20-- Oct.	1	Balance	✔			3 1 6 2 00	

ACCOUNT Supplies—Store   ACCOUNT NO. 1160

DATE		ITEM	POST. REF.	DEBIT	CREDIT	BALANCE	
						DEBIT	CREDIT
20-- Oct.	1	Balance	✔			2 5 9 2 00	

ACCOUNT Accounts Payable   ACCOUNT NO. 2110

DATE		ITEM	POST. REF.	DEBIT	CREDIT	BALANCE	
						DEBIT	CREDIT
20-- Oct.	1	Balance	✔				9 6 2 7 60

ACCOUNT Sales Tax Payable   ACCOUNT NO. 2120

DATE		ITEM	POST. REF.	DEBIT	CREDIT	BALANCE	
						DEBIT	CREDIT
20-- Oct.	1	Balance	✔				1 5 7 4 40

ACCOUNT Sales   ACCOUNT NO. 4110

DATE		ITEM	POST. REF.	DEBIT	CREDIT	BALANCE	
						DEBIT	CREDIT
Oct. 20--	1	Balance	✔				262 49 8 80

ACCOUNT Purchases   ACCOUNT NO. 5110

DATE		ITEM	POST. REF.	DEBIT	CREDIT	BALANCE	
						DEBIT	CREDIT
Oct. 20--	1	Balance	✔			135 0 0 0 00	

ACCOUNT Purchases Discount   ACCOUNT NO. 5120

DATE		ITEM	POST. REF.	DEBIT	CREDIT	BALANCE	
						DEBIT	CREDIT
Oct. 20--	1	Balance	✔				4 5 8 60

ACCOUNT Advertising Expense   ACCOUNT NO. 6110

DATE		ITEM	POST. REF.	DEBIT	CREDIT	BALANCE	
						DEBIT	CREDIT
Oct. 20--	1	Balance	✔			3 5 2 8 00	

ACCOUNT Miscellaneous Expense   ACCOUNT NO. 6140

DATE		ITEM	POST. REF.	DEBIT	CREDIT	BALANCE	
						DEBIT	CREDIT
Oct. 20--	1	Balance	✔			1 6 9 2 00	

11-7 CHALLENGE PROBLEM (continued)

ACCOUNT Rent Expense   ACCOUNT NO. 6160

DATE		ITEM	POST. REF.	DEBIT	CREDIT	BALANCE	
						DEBIT	CREDIT
20-- Oct.	1	Balance	✔			10 3 5 0 00	

ACCOUNT Utilities Expense   ACCOUNT NO. 6190

DATE		ITEM	POST. REF.	DEBIT	CREDIT	BALANCE	
						DEBIT	CREDIT
20-- Oct.	1	Balance	✔			2 1 4 2 00	

1.   **ACCOUNTS PAYABLE LEDGER**

VENDOR Design Golf   VENDOR NO. 210

DATE		ITEM	POST. REF.	DEBIT	CREDIT	CREDIT BALANCE
20-- Oct.	1	Balance	✔			2 9 1 6 00

VENDOR Eagle Golf Equipment   VENDOR NO. 220

DATE		ITEM	POST. REF.	DEBIT	CREDIT	CREDIT BALANCE
20-- Oct.	1	Balance	✔			2 3 5 8 00

VENDOR Golf Source   VENDOR NO. 230

DATE		ITEM	POST. REF.	DEBIT	CREDIT	CREDIT BALANCE

VENDOR Pro Golf Supply   VENDOR NO. 240

DATE		ITEM	POST. REF.	DEBIT	CREDIT	CREDIT BALANCE
20-- Oct.	1	Balance	✔			1 1 3 7 60

1.

ACCOUNTS PAYABLE LEDGER

VENDOR Vista Golf Co.   VENDOR NO. 250

DATE		ITEM	POST. REF.	DEBIT	CREDIT	CREDIT BALANCE
20-- Oct.	1	Balance	✔			3 2 1 6 00

ACCOUNTS RECEIVABLE LEDGER

CUSTOMER David Bench   CUSTOMER NO. 110

DATE		ITEM	POST. REF.	DEBIT	CREDIT	DEBIT BALANCE
20-- Oct.	1	Balance	✔			9 7 2 00

CUSTOMER Viola Davis   CUSTOMER NO. 120

DATE		ITEM	POST. REF.	DEBIT	CREDIT	DEBIT BALANCE
20-- Oct.	1	Balance	✔			8 2 9 44

CUSTOMER Barry Fuller   CUSTOMER NO. 130

DATE		ITEM	POST. REF.	DEBIT	CREDIT	DEBIT BALANCE

CUSTOMER Doris McCarley   CUSTOMER NO. 140

DATE		ITEM	POST. REF.	DEBIT	CREDIT	DEBIT BALANCE
20-- Oct.	1	Balance	✔			1 3 9 2 84

CUSTOMER Leona Silva   CUSTOMER NO. 150

DATE		ITEM	POST. REF.	DEBIT	CREDIT	DEBIT BALANCE
20-- Oct.	1	Balance	✔			2 8 5 12

11-7 CHALLENGE PROBLEM (concluded)

9. Approaches to Collecting and Paying Sales Taxes

_____

_____

_____

_____

_____

_____

_____

_____

_____

_____

_____

_____

_____

_____

_____

_____

_____

_____

_____

_____

_____

_____

_____

_____

_____

_____

_____

_____

_____

_____

_____

_____

_____

_____

_____

_____

_____

Study Guide 12

Part One—Identifying Accounting Terms

Directions: Select the one term in Column I that best fits each definition in Column II. Print the letter identifying your choice in the Answers column.

Column I	Column II	Answers
A. employee earnings record	**1.** The money paid for employee services. (p. 340)	1. _____
B. Medicare tax	**2.** The period covered by a salary payment. (p. 340)	2. _____
C. net pay	**3.** The total amount earned by all employees for a pay period. (p. 340)	3. _____
D. pay period	**4.** The total pay due for a pay period before deductions. (p. 343)	4. _____
E. payroll	**5.** Taxes based on the payroll of a business. (p. 345)	5. _____
F. payroll register	**6.** A deduction from total earnings for each person legally supported by a taxpayer, including the employee. (p. 346)	6. _____
G. payroll taxes	**7.** A federal tax paid for old-age, survivors, and disability insurance. (p. 349)	7. _____
H. salary	**8.** A federal tax paid for hospital insurance. (p. 349)	8. _____
I. social security tax	**9.** The maximum amount of earnings on which a tax is calculated. (p. 349)	9. _____
J. tax base	**10.** A business form used to record payroll information. (p. 351)	10. _____
K. total earnings	**11.** The total earnings paid to an employee after payroll taxes and other deductions. (p. 352)	11. _____
L. withholding allowance	**12.** A business form used to record details affecting payments made to an employee. (p. 353)	12. _____

Part Two—Analyzing Payroll Procedures

Directions: For each of the following items, select the choice that best completes the statement. Print the letter of your choice in the Answers column.

Answers

1. How many hours were worked by an employee who arrived at 8:10 a.m. and departed at 12:10 p.m.? (A) 4 hours (B) 5 hours (C) 4 hours and 10 minutes (D) none of these. (p. 342)

   1. _____

2. How many hours were worked by an employee who arrived at 7:05 a.m. and departed at 6:05 p.m. with one hour off for lunch? (A) 11 hours (B) 10 hours (C) 12 hours (D) none of these. (p. 342)

   2. _____

3. Employee regular earnings are calculated as (A) regular hours times regular rate (B) total hours divided by regular rate (C) total hours plus overtime rate (D) overtime hours minus overtime rate. (p. 343)

   3. _____

4. Social security tax is calculated on (A) total earnings and marital status (B) number of withholding allowances (C) total earnings and number of withholding allowances (D) employee earnings up to a maximum paid in a calendar year. (p. 349)

   4. _____

5. A separate payroll checking account is used primarily to (A) simplify the payroll accounting system (B) help reduce the cost of preparing a payroll (C) provide additional protection and control payroll payments (D) eliminate employer earnings records. (p. 356)

   5. _____

Part Three—Identifying Accounting Practices

Directions: Place a *T* for True or an *F* for False in the Answers column to
show whether each of the following statements is true or false.

Answers

1. A business may decide to pay employee salaries every week, every two weeks, twice a month, or once a month. (p. 340)

1. _____

2. Payroll time cards can be used as the basic source of information to prepare a payroll. (p. 341)

2. _____

3. Total earnings are sometimes referred to as net pay or net earnings. (p. 343)

3. _____

4. Employee total earnings are calculated as regular hours × regular rate, plus overtime hours × overtime rate. (p. 343)

4. _____

5. Payroll taxes withheld represent a liability for an employer until payment is made to the government. (p. 345)

5. _____

6. Employers in many states are required to withhold state, city, or county income tax from employee earnings. (p. 345)

6. _____

7. Employers are required to have a current Form W-4, Employee's Withholding Allowance Certificate, for all employees. (p. 346)

7. _____

8. The amount of income tax withheld from each employee's total earnings is determined from the number of withholding allowances and by the employee's marital status. (p. 346)

8. _____

9. A single person will have less income tax withheld than a married employee. (p. 346)

9. _____

10. The larger the number of withholding allowances claimed, the larger the amount of income tax withheld. (p. 346)

10. _____

11. An employee can be exempt from having federal income tax withheld under certain conditions. (p. 346)

11. _____

12. Social security tax is paid by the employer only. (p. 349)

12. _____

13. An act of Congress can change the social security tax base and tax rate at any time. (p. 349)

13. _____

14. When an employee's earnings exceed the tax base, no more social security tax is deducted. (p. 349)

14. _____

15. All deductions from employee wages are recorded in a payroll register. (p. 351)

15. _____

16. The columns of the employee earnings record consist of the amount columns in a payroll register and an accumulated earnings column. (p. 353)

16. _____

17. A new earnings record is prepared for each employee each year. (p. 353)

17. _____

18. A check for the total net pay is written and deposited in the payroll checking account. (p. 356)

18. _____

19. When EFT is used, the employee does not receive an individual check. (p. 357)

19. _____

Name _____ Date _____ Class _____

Calculating total earnings

Employee Number	Hours Worked		Regular Rate	Earnings		Total Earnings
	Regular	Overtime		Regular	Overtime	
1	40	5	$ 9.00	_____	_____	_____
2	40	3	12.50	_____	_____	_____
3	30	0	9.75	_____	_____	_____
4	40	2	11.00	_____	_____	_____

Calculating total earnings

Employee Number	Hours Worked		Regular Rate	Earnings		Total Earnings
	Regular	Overtime		Regular	Overtime	
1	40	3	$ 8.80	_____	_____	_____
2	30	0	9.00	_____	_____	_____
3	40	3	10.70	_____	_____	_____
4	40	4	12.00	_____	_____	_____

12-2 WORK TOGETHER, p. 350

Determining payroll tax withholding

No.	Name	Marital Status	Number of Withholding Allowances	Total Earnings	Federal Income Tax Withholding	Social Security Tax Withholding	Medicare Tax Withholding
3	Bates, Eric C.	M	2	$1,090.00	____	____	____
4	Cohen, Jason K.	S	1	840.00	____	____	____
1	Grimes, Christi L.	M	3	1,020.00	____	____	____
6	Key, Sharon C.	S	2	980.00	____	____	____

12-2 ON YOUR OWN, p. 350

Determining payroll tax withholding

No.	Name	Marital Status	Number of Withholding Allowances	Total Earnings	Federal Income Tax Withholding	Social Security Tax Withholding	Medicare Tax Withholding
2	Burdine, Ralph C.	S	2	$ 875.00	____	____	____
5	Gibson, Jane L.	M	3	1,080.00	____	____	____
7	Monroy, Tom E.	S	1	1,200.00	____	____	____
9	Tiffin, Andrea P.	M	0	1,030.00	____	____	____

12-3 WORK TOGETHER, p. 355

Preparing payroll records

1., 2.

PAYROLL REGISTER

SEMIMONTHLY PERIOD ENDED _____ DATE OF PAYMENT _____

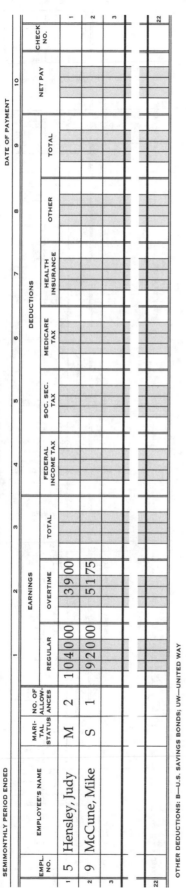

EMPL. NO.	EMPLOYEE'S NAME	MARI-TAL STATUS	NO. OF ALLOW-ANCES	EARNINGS			DEDUCTIONS						NET PAY	CHECK NO.
				REGULAR	OVERTIME	TOTAL	FEDERAL INCOME TAX	SOC. SEC. TAX	MEDICARE TAX	HEALTH INSURANCE	OTHER	TOTAL		
				1	2	3	4	5	6	7	8	9	10	
1	5	Hensley, Judy	M	2	1040 00	39 00									1
2	9	McCune, Mike	S	1	920 00	51 75									2
3															3
22															22

OTHER DEDUCTIONS: B—U.S. SAVINGS BONDS; UW—UNITED WAY

3.

EARNINGS RECORD FOR QUARTER ENDED _____

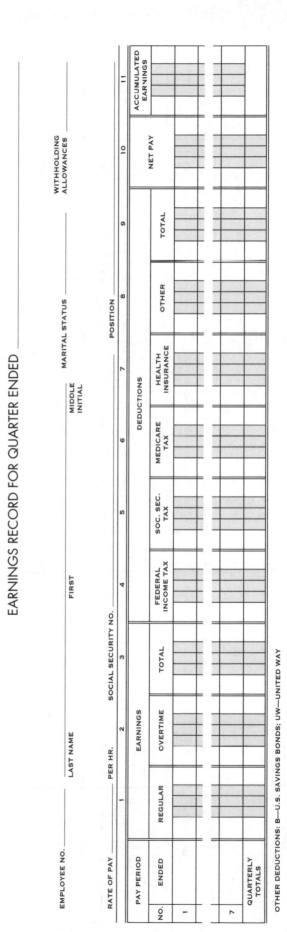

_____ _____ _____ _____
LAST NAME   FIRST   MIDDLE INITIAL   MARITAL STATUS

EMPLOYEE NO. _____

RATE OF PAY _____ PER HR. SOCIAL SECURITY NO. _____ POSITION _____ WITHHOLDING ALLOWANCES _____

PAY PERIOD		EARNINGS			DEDUCTIONS						NET PAY	ACCUMULATED EARNINGS
NO.	ENDED	REGULAR	OVERTIME	TOTAL	FEDERAL INCOME TAX	SOC. SEC. TAX	MEDICARE TAX	HEALTH INSURANCE	OTHER	TOTAL		
		1	2	3	4	5	6	7	8	9	10	11
1												
7	QUARTERLY TOTALS											

OTHER DEDUCTIONS: B—U.S. SAVINGS BONDS; UW—UNITED WAY

Preparing payroll records
1., 2.

PAYROLL REGISTER

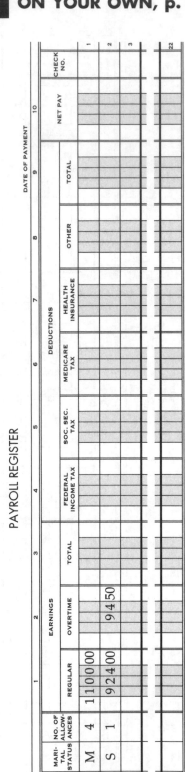

EMPL. NO.	EMPLOYEE'S NAME	MARI- TAL STATUS	NO. OF ALLOW- ANCES	EARNINGS				DEDUCTIONS					NET PAY	CHECK NO.
				REGULAR	OVERTIME	TOTAL	FEDERAL INCOME TAX	SOC. SEC. TAX	MEDICARE TAX	HEALTH INSURANCE	OTHER	TOTAL		
				1	2	3	4	5	6	7	8	9	10	
1	Best, Allen P.	M	4	1100 00										1
2	Edwards, Tammy S.	S	1	924 00	94 50									2
3														3
22														22

OTHER DEDUCTIONS: B—U.S. SAVINGS BONDS; UW—UNITED WAY

3.

EARNINGS RECORD FOR QUARTER ENDED

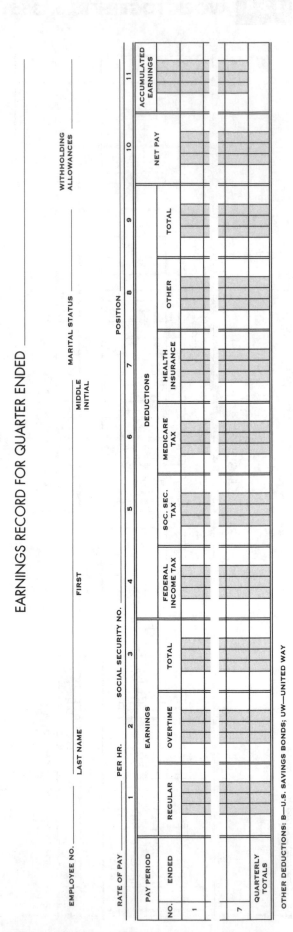

EMPLOYEE NO. _____   LAST NAME _____   FIRST _____   MIDDLE INITIAL _____   MARITAL STATUS _____   WITHHOLDING ALLOWANCES _____

RATE OF PAY _____ PER HR. _____   SOCIAL SECURITY NO. _____   POSITION _____

PAY PERIOD		EARNINGS			DEDUCTIONS					NET PAY	ACCUMULATED EARNINGS
NO.	ENDED	REGULAR	OVERTIME	TOTAL	FEDERAL INCOME TAX	SOC. SEC. TAX	MEDICARE TAX	HEALTH INSURANCE	OTHER	TOTAL		
		1	2	3	4	5	6	7	8	9	10	11
1												
7	QUARTERLY TOTALS											

OTHER DEDUCTIONS: B—U.S. SAVINGS BONDS; UW—UNITED WAY

12-4 WORK TOGETHER, p. 358

Preparing payroll checks

1., 2.

NO. **599** Date: ____ 20___ $ _____ To: _____ _____ For: _____ _____ BAL. BRO'T. FOR'D AMT. DEPOSITED TOTAL AMT. THIS CHECK BAL. CAR'D. FOR'D	**GENERAL ACCOUNT** NO. **599** 66-877 / 530 ANTIQUE SHOP _____ 20 _____ PAY TO THE ORDER OF _____ $ _____ _____ DOLLARS *For Classroom Use Only* **Peoples Bank and Trust** Charlotte, NC 28206-8444 ⑈053008774⑈ 0639580⑈ 599

CHECK NO. **186** PERIOD ENDING EARNINGS $ REG. $ O.T. $ DEDUCTIONS $ INC. TAX $ SOC. SEC. TAX $ MED. TAX $ HEALTH INS. $ OTHER $ NET PAY $	**PAYROLL ACCOUNT** 66-877 / 530 _____ 20 _____ NO. **186** PAY TO THE ORDER OF _____ $ _____ _____ DOLLARS *For Classroom Use Only* ANTIQUE SHOP **Peoples Bank and Trust** Charlotte, NC 28206-8444 ⑈053008774⑈ 0639583⑈ 186

CHECK NO. **187** PERIOD ENDING EARNINGS $ REG. $ O.T. $ DEDUCTIONS $ INC. TAX $ SOC. SEC. TAX $ MED. TAX $ HEALTH INS. $ OTHER $ NET PAY $	**PAYROLL ACCOUNT** 66-877 / 530 _____ 20 _____ NO. **187** PAY TO THE ORDER OF _____ $ _____ _____ DOLLARS *For Classroom Use Only* ANTIQUE SHOP **Peoples Bank and Trust** Charlotte, NC 28206-8444 ⑈053008774⑈ 0639583⑈ 187

Preparing payroll checks

1., 2.

NO. **824**

Date: _____ 20___ $ _____

To: _____

_____

For: _____

_____

BAL. BRO'T. FOR'D		
AMT. DEPOSITED		
TOTAL		
AMT. THIS CHECK		
BAL. CAR'D. FOR'D		

GENERAL ACCOUNT   NO. **824**   66-877 / 530

PROSSER COMPANY   _____ 20 _____

PAY TO THE
ORDER OF _____ $ _____

_____ DOLLARS

For Classroom Use Only

Peoples Bank and Trust
Charlotte, NC 28206-8444   _____

⑆053008774⑆ 196223642⑈ 824

CHECK NO. **325**

PERIOD ENDING	
EARNINGS	$
REG.	$
O.T.	$
DEDUCTIONS	$
INC. TAX	$
SOC. SEC. TAX	$
MED. TAX	$
HEALTH INS.	$
OTHER	$
NET PAY	$

PAYROLL ACCOUNT   66-877 / 530

_____ 20 _____

NO. **325**

PAY TO THE
ORDER OF _____ $ _____

_____ DOLLARS

For Classroom Use Only

THE SIGN SHOP

Peoples Bank and Trust
Charlotte, NC 28206-8444   _____

⑆053008774⑆ 1467219611⑈ 325

CHECK NO. **326**

PERIOD ENDING	
EARNINGS	$
REG.	$
O.T.	$
DEDUCTIONS	$
INC. TAX	$
SOC. SEC. TAX	$
MED. TAX	$
HEALTH INS.	$
OTHER	$
NET PAY	$

PAYROLL ACCOUNT   66-877 / 530

_____ 20 _____

NO. **326**

PAY TO THE
ORDER OF _____ $ _____

_____ DOLLARS

For Classroom Use Only

THE SIGN SHOP

Peoples Bank and Trust
Charlotte, NC 28206-8444   _____

⑆053008774⑆ 1467219611⑈ 326

12-1 APPLICATION PROBLEM, p. 360

Preparing payroll time cards
1., 2.

EMPLOYEE NO. 16 — NAME Sylvia A. Rodriguez — PERIOD ENDING April 15, 20 – –

Day	Morning IN	Morning OUT	Afternoon IN	Afternoon OUT	Overtime IN	Overtime OUT	Hours REG	Hours OT
2	758	1202	1259	503				
3	757	1203	100	500	702	832		
4	800	1200	1259	500				
5	759	1201	1258	504				
6	759	1202	1255	503				
8	758	1201	1256	502				
10	756	1200	1257	501				
11	757	1202	1257	458				
12	758	1200	1259	501				
13	759	1204	1259	500				

	HOURS	RATE	AMOUNT
REGULAR		9.20	
OVERTIME			
TOTAL HOURS		TOTAL EARNINGS	

EMPLOYEE NO. 11 — NAME Henry F. Miller — PERIOD ENDING April 15, 20 – –

Day	Morning IN	Morning OUT	Afternoon IN	Afternoon OUT	Overtime IN	Overtime OUT	Hours REG	Hours OT
2	757	1201	1259	502				
3	757	1202	1258	501				
4	756	1204	100	501	556	659		
5	757	1205	1259	500				
6	759	1205	100	502				
8	757	1204	1259	505				
10	758	1205	1256	504	600	731		
11	756	1202	1257	502				
12	756	1201	1259	501	700	932		
13	757	1200	101	500				

	HOURS	RATE	AMOUNT
REGULAR		9.80	
OVERTIME			
TOTAL HOURS		TOTAL EARNINGS	

EMPLOYEE NO. 14 — NAME Marie L. Kerns — PERIOD ENDING April 15, 20 – –

Day	Morning IN	Morning OUT	Afternoon IN	Afternoon OUT	Overtime IN	Overtime OUT	Hours REG	Hours OT
2	759	1201	1256	501				
3	757	1202	1257	502				
4	756	1201	1258	504	701	802		
5	802	1204	101	506				
6	756	1203	1259	500				
9	759	1200	1259	459	559	731		
10	800	1200	1258	501				
11	759	1202	1257	506				
12	756	1159	1256	502	558	732		
13	757	1203	1257	501				

	HOURS	RATE	AMOUNT
REGULAR		11.80	
OVERTIME			
TOTAL HOURS		TOTAL EARNINGS	

Determining payroll tax withholding

1., 2.

Employee		Marital Status	Number of Withholding Allowances	Total Earnings	Federal Income Tax Withholding	Social Security Tax Withholding	Medicare Tax Withholding
No.	Name						
2	Baird, Tony W.	M	2	$1,220.00	_____	_____	_____
6	Delgado, Rudy C.	M	3	1,090.00	_____	_____	_____
3	Garza, Kay H.	S	1	940.00	_____	_____	_____
1	Hess, Monica T.	M	5	1,060.00	_____	_____	_____
8	Levy, Irving S.	S	1	910.00	_____	_____	_____
7	Minick, Esther A.	S	2	990.00	_____	_____	_____
4	Pharr, Angela S.	S	1	900.00	_____	_____	_____
5	Reiner, Greg R.	M	3	1,250.00	_____	_____	_____

12-3 APPLICATION PROBLEM, p. 360

Preparing a payroll register

PAYROLL REGISTER

SEMIMONTHLY PERIOD ENDED _____   DATE OF PAYMENT _____

EMPL. NO.	EMPLOYEE'S NAME	MARI-TAL STATUS	NO. OF ALLOW-ANCES	EARNINGS REGULAR (1)	EARNINGS OVERTIME (2)	EARNINGS TOTAL (3)	DEDUCTIONS FEDERAL INCOME TAX (4)	DEDUCTIONS SOC. SEC. TAX (5)	DEDUCTIONS MEDICARE TAX (6)	DEDUCTIONS HEALTH INSURANCE (7)	DEDUCTIONS OTHER (8)	DEDUCTIONS TOTAL (9)	NET PAY (10)	CHECK NO.
9	Bast, John P.	S	2	1082 40						42 00	B 10 00			1
2	Clemmons, Jan C.	M	3	1134 00						60 00				2
8	Glazner, Tom S.	S	1	688 00						35 00	B 20 00			3
1	Holtman, Mark T.	M	4	959 20	65 40					90 00				4
7	Jones, John David	M	2	1364 00						42 00	B 20 00			5
10	Young, Justin L.	S	1	1040 60						35 00	B 25 00			6
3	LeBlanc, Patrick G.	M	1	1050 00						35 00				7
6	Pullen, Sharon S.	M	2	1179 20	40 20					42 00				8
11	Shappley, Mary A.	S	2	1249 60						42 00				9
4	Terrell, Terry R.	M	1	903 00						35 00				10
12	Wheat, Andrew P.	M	3	1100 00	93 75					60 00	B 20 00			11
5	Yates, Gerie V.	S	1	787 50						35 00	B 25 00			12
														13
														14
														15
														16
														17
														18
														19
														20
														21
														22
														23
														24
														25

OTHER DEDUCTIONS: B—U.S. SAVINGS BONDS; UW—UNITED WAY

Preparing an employee earnings record
1., 2., 3., 4.

EMPLOYEE NO. _____   LAST NAME _____   FIRST _____   MIDDLE INITIAL _____   MARITAL STATUS _____   WITHHOLDING ALLOWANCES _____

RATE OF PAY _____   PER HR. _____   SOCIAL SECURITY NO. _____   POSITION _____

EARNINGS RECORD FOR QUARTER ENDED _____

PAY PERIOD		EARNINGS			DEDUCTIONS						NET PAY	ACCUMULATED EARNINGS
NO.	ENDED	REGULAR	OVERTIME	TOTAL	FEDERAL INCOME TAX	SOC. SEC. TAX	MEDICARE TAX	HEALTH INSURANCE	OTHER	TOTAL		
		1	2	3	4	5	6	7	8	9	10	11
1	7/15	1320 00	45 00	1365 00	87 00	84 63	19 79	60 00	B 20 00	271 42	1093 58	
2	7/31	1200 00	90 00	1290 00	75 00	79 98	18 71	60 00	B 20 00	253 69	1036 31	
3	8/15	1320 00		1320 00	81 00	81 84	19 14	60 00	B 20 00	261 98	1058 02	
4	8/31	1020 00		1020 00	44 00	63 24	14 79	60 00	B 20 00	202 03	817 97	
5	9/15	1320 00	135 00	1455 00								
6	9/30	1200 00		1200 00								
7	QUARTERLY TOTALS											

OTHER DEDUCTIONS: B—U.S. SAVINGS BONDS; UW—UNITED WAY

Name _____ Date _____ Class _____

Preparing payroll checks

1., 2.

NO. **630**

Date: ____ 20___ $_____
To: _____
For: _____
_____

BAL. BRO'T. FOR'D		
AMT. DEPOSITED		
TOTAL		
AMT. THIS CHECK		
BAL. CAR'D. FOR'D		

GENERAL ACCOUNT   NO. **630**   66-877/530

ROYAL APPLIANCES   _____ 20 ____

PAY TO THE
ORDER OF_____ $ _____

_____ DOLLARS
For Classroom Use Only

Peoples Bank and Trust
Charlotte, NC 28206-8444   _____

⑈053008774⑈ 018654210⑈ 630

CHECK NO. **823**

PERIOD ENDING		
EARNINGS	$	
REG.	$	
O.T.	$	
DEDUCTIONS	$	
INC. TAX	$	
SOC. SEC. TAX	$	
MEDICARE TAX	$	
HEALTH INS.	$	
OTHER	$	
NET PAY	$	

PAYROLL ACCOUNT   66-877/530

_____ 20 ____   NO. **823**

PAY TO THE
ORDER OF_____ $ _____

_____ DOLLARS
For Classroom Use Only
                                        ROYAL APPLIANCES

Peoples Bank and Trust
Charlotte, NC 28206-8444   _____

⑈053008774⑈ 018654237⑈ 823

CHECK NO. **827**

PERIOD ENDING		
EARNINGS	$	
REG.	$	
O.T.	$	
DEDUCTIONS	$	
INC. TAX	$	
SOC. SEC. TAX	$	
MEDICARE TAX	$	
HEALTH INS.	$	
OTHER	$	
NET PAY	$	

PAYROLL ACCOUNT   66-877/530

_____ 20 ____   NO. **827**

PAY TO THE
ORDER OF_____ $ _____

_____ DOLLARS
For Classroom Use Only
                                        ROYAL APPLIANCES

Peoples Bank and Trust
Charlotte, NC 28206-8444   _____

⑈053008774⑈ 018654237⑈ 827

Preparing a semimonthly payroll

1.

PAYROLL REGISTER

SEMIMONTHLY PERIOD ENDED _____   DATE OF PAYMENT _____

EMPL. NO.	EMPLOYEE'S NAME	MARI-TAL STATUS	NO. OF ALLOW-ANCES	EARNINGS REGULAR	EARNINGS OVERTIME	EARNINGS TOTAL	DEDUCTIONS FEDERAL INCOME TAX	DEDUCTIONS SOC. SEC. TAX	DEDUCTIONS MEDICARE TAX	DEDUCTIONS HEALTH INSURANCE	DEDUCTIONS OTHER	DEDUCTIONS TOTAL	NET PAY	CHECK NO.
5	Acron, Peter C.	M	3	1126 40	115 20					60 00	B 10 00			
7	Barenis, Mary P.	S	1	1155 00						25 00				
6	Epps, John P.	M	2	792 00						40 00	B 10 00			
1	Goforth, Alice A.	S	2	1135 20	77 40					40 00				
8	Hiett, Franklin B.	M	3	1188 00						60 00	B 10 00			
9	Land, Keith	S	1	954 60						25 00	B 10 00			
2	Malone, Lillie L.	S	1	1083 60						25 00				
4	Rivers, Linda K.	M	2	1091 20	93 00					40 00				
10	Sowell, Jacob S.	M	2	1161 60						40 00	B 10 00			
3	Vole, Ryan V.	M	5	1075 00						80 00	B 10 00			

OTHER DEDUCTIONS: B—U.S. SAVINGS BONDS; UW—UNITED WAY

12-6   MASTERY PROBLEM (concluded)

2., 3.

NO. **928**

Date: _____ 20___ $_____

To: _____

For: _____

BAL. BRO'T. FOR'D			
AMT. DEPOSITED			
TOTAL			
AMT. THIS CHECK			
BAL. CAR'D. FOR'D			

GENERAL ACCOUNT   NO. **928**   8-8335/430

ARROW COMPANY   _____ 20 _____

PAY TO THE ORDER OF _____ $ _____

_____ DOLLARS

For Classroom Use Only

First Security Bank of Pittsburgh
Pittsburgh, PA 15210-3402

⑆043083356⑆ 005972164⑈ 928

CHECK NO. **1692**

PERIOD ENDING	
EARNINGS	$
REG.	$
O.T.	$
DEDUCTIONS	$
INC. TAX	$
SOC. SEC. TAX	$
MED. TAX	$
HEALTH INS.	$
OTHER	$
NET PAY	$

PAYROLL ACCOUNT   8-8335/430

_____ 20 _____   NO. **1692**

PAY TO THE ORDER OF _____ $ _____

_____ DOLLARS

For Classroom Use Only   ARROW COMPANY

First Security Bank of Pittsburgh
Pittsburgh, PA 15210-3402

⑆043083356⑆ 005972165⑈ 1692

CHECK NO. **1696**

PERIOD ENDING	
EARNINGS	$
REG.	$
O.T.	$
DEDUCTIONS	$
INC. TAX	$
SOC. SEC. TAX	$
MED. TAX	$
HEALTH INS.	$
OTHER	$
NET PAY	$

PAYROLL ACCOUNT   8-8335/430

_____ 20 _____   NO. **1696**

PAY TO THE ORDER OF _____ $ _____

_____ DOLLARS

For Classroom Use Only   ARROW COMPANY

First Security Bank of Pittsburgh
Pittsburgh, PA 15210-3402

⑆043083356⑆ 005972165⑈ 1696

Calculating piecework wages

PAYROLL REGISTER

SEMIMONTHLY PERIOD ENDED

DATE OF PAYMENT

EMPL. NO.	EMPLOYEE'S NAME	MARITAL STATUS	NO. OF ALLOWANCES
1	C3	Bell, Julie M.	M	4
2	C6	Hairston, Gary P.	M	2
3	C9	Reeves, John M.	S	1
4	A2	Bullock, Amy C.	S	2
5	A6	Green, Steven P.	S	1
6	A9	Prine, Jacob R.	M	4
7	F5	Gerez, Dave A.	M	2
8	F2	Kyle, Ryan G.	S	1

EARNINGS: 1 REGULAR, 2 INCENTIVE, 3 TOTAL

DEDUCTIONS: 4 FEDERAL INCOME TAX, 5 SOC. SEC. TAX, 6 MEDICARE TAX, 7 HEALTH INSURANCE, 8 OTHER, 9 TOTAL

10 NET PAY

CHECK NO.

Name	Perfect Score	Your Score
Analyzing Payroll Records	15 Pts.	
Analyzing Transactions Affecting Payroll	5 Pts.	
Analyzing Form W-2	10 Pts.	
Total	30 Pts.	

Part One—Analyzing Payroll Records

Directions: For each of the following items, select the choice that best completes the statement. Print the letter identifying your choice in the Answers column.

Answers

1. All the payroll information needed to prepare payroll and tax reports is found on (A) Form W-4 and the employee earnings record (B) Form W-4 and the payroll register (C) the payroll register and the employee earnings record (D) Form W-4. (p. 368)

1. _____

2. The payroll journal entry is based on the totals of the (A) Earnings Total column, each deduction column, and the Net Pay column (B) Earnings Total, Earnings Regular, Earnings Overtime, and Deductions Total columns (C) Earnings Regular, Earnings Overtime, and Deductions Total columns (D) Earnings Total, Earnings Regular, and Earnings Overtime Total columns. (p. 369)

2. _____

3. The Earnings Total column total is journalized as a debit to (A) Cash (B) Salary Expense (C) Employee Income Tax Payable (D) Social Security Tax Payable. (p. 370)

3. _____

4. The total of the Federal Income Tax column of a payroll register is credited to (A) a revenue account (B) an expense account (C) a liability account (D) an asset account. (p. 370)

4. _____

5. The total of the Net Pay column of the payroll register is credited to (A) a revenue account (B) an expense account (C) an asset account (D) a liability account. (p. 370)

5. _____

6. When a semimonthly payroll is paid, the credit to Cash is equal to the (A) total earnings of all employees (B) total deductions for income tax and social security tax (C) total deductions (D) net pay of all employees. (p. 370)

6. _____

7. Employer business taxes are (A) assets (B) liabilities (C) revenues (D) expenses. (p. 373)

7. _____

8. Payroll taxes that are paid by both the employer and the employee are (A) federal unemployment tax and social security tax (B) federal unemployment tax and Medicare tax (C) social security tax and Medicare tax (D) federal income tax, social security tax, and Medicare tax. (p. 373)

8. _____

9. A federal tax used for state and federal administrative expenses of the unemployment program is the (A) social security tax (B) Medicare tax (C) federal unemployment tax (D) state unemployment tax. (p. 375)

9. _____

10. A state tax used to pay benefits to unemployed workers is the (A) social security tax (B) Medicare tax (C) unemployment tax (D) state unemployment tax. (p. 375)

10. _____

11. To record the employer payroll taxes expense, the following accounts are credited: (A) Payroll Taxes Expense and Employee Income Tax Payable (B) Employee Income Tax Payable, Social Security Tax Payable, Medicare Tax Payable, Unemployment Tax Payable—Federal, and Unemployment Tax Payable—State (C) Social Security Tax Payable, Medicare Tax Payable, Unemployment Tax Payable—Federal, and Unemployment Tax Payable—State (D) none of these. (p. 376)

11. _____

12. Each employer who withholds income tax, social security tax, and Medicare tax from employee earnings must furnish each employee an (A) IRS Form W-4 (B) IRS Form W-2 (C) IRS Form W-3 (D) IRS Form 941. (p. 378)

12. _____

13. Each employer is required by law to report payroll taxes on an (A) IRS Form W-4 (B) IRS Form 941 (C) IRS Form W-2 (D) IRS Form W-3. (p. 380)

13. _____

14. To record the total federal tax payment for employee income tax, social security tax, and Medicare tax, the account credited is (A) Cash (B) Employee Income Tax Payable (C) Social Security Tax Payable (D) Medicare Tax Payable. (p. 385)

14. _____

15. To record the payment of federal unemployment tax, the account debited is (A) a revenue account (B) an expense account (C) a liability account (D) an asset account. (p. 387)

15. _____

Part Two—Analyzing Transactions Affecting Payroll

Directions: Analyze each of the following transactions into debit and credit parts. Print the letters identifying your choices in the proper Answers column.

Account Title	Transaction	Answers Debit	Credit

Account Title

A. Cash

B. Employee Income Tax Payable

C. Health Insurance Premiums Payable

D. Medicare Tax Payable

E. Payroll Taxes Expense

F. Salary Expense

G. Social Security Tax Payable

H. U.S. Savings Bonds Payable

I. Unemployment Tax Payable—Federal

J. Unemployment Tax Payable—State

K. United Way Donations Payable

Transaction

1. Paid cash for semimonthly payroll. (p. 371) _____ _____

2. Recorded employer payroll taxes expense. (p. 376) _____ _____

3. Paid cash for liability for employee income tax, social security tax, and Medicare tax. (p. 385) _____ _____

4. Paid cash for federal unemployment tax liability. (p. 387) _____ _____

5. Paid cash for state unemployment tax liability. (p. 387) _____ _____

Name _____ Date _____ Class _____

Part Three—Analyzing Form W-2

Directions: Analyze the following statements about a Form W-2, Wage and Tax Statement. Use the Form W-2 below to answer the specific questions about Rick Selby. Place a *T* for True or an *F* for False in the Answers column to show whether each of the following statements is true or false. (p. 378)

a Control number	22222	Void ☐	For Official Use Only OMB No. 1545-0008		
b Employer identification number 31-0429632				1 Wages, tips, other compensation 24,843.00	2 Federal income tax withheld 648.00
c Employer's name, address, and ZIP code Hobby Shack, Inc. 1420 College Plaza Atlanta, GA 30337-1726				3 Social security wages 24,843.00	4 Social security tax withheld 1,540.27
				5 Medicare wages and tips 24,843.00	6 Medicare tax withheld 360.22
				7 Social security tips	8 Allocated tips
d Employee's social security number 450-70-6432				9 Advance EIC payment	10 Dependent care benefits
e Employee's first name and initial Rick E. Last name Selby				11 Nonqualified plans	12a See instructions for box 12
1625 Northland Drive Clarkdale, GA 30020-6523				13 Statutory employee ☐ Retirement plan ☐ Third-party sick pay ☐	12b
				14 Other	12c
					12d
f Employee's address and ZIP code					
15 State Employer's state ID number	16 State wages, tips, etc.	17 State income tax	18 Local wages, tips, etc.	19 Local income tax	20 Locality name

Form **W-2** Wage and Tax Statement   20- -
Copy A For Social Security Administration — Send this entire page with Form W-3 to the Social Security Administration; photocopies are **not** acceptable.
Cat. No. 10134D
Department of the Treasury—Internal Revenue Service
For Privacy Act and Paperwork Reduction Act Notice, see back of Copy D.

Answers

1. Rick Selby's total salary is more than his total social security salary.   1. _____

2. This Form W-2 shows Rick Selby's net pay for the entire year.   2. _____

3. The amount withheld for Mr. Selby's social security and Medicare tax was more than the amount withheld for his federal income tax.   3. _____

4. State income tax was withheld from Mr. Selby's salary.   4. _____

5. All deductions from Mr. Selby's salary are shown on his Form W-2.   5. _____

6. This Form W-2 would indicate whether Mr. Selby had more than one employer during the year.   6. _____

7. If an employee works for several employers during the year, that employee must receive a Form W-2 from each employer.   7. _____

8. An employer is required to provide employees with a Form W-2 no later than January 31 of the year following the one for which the report has been completed.   8. _____

9. When Rick Selby files his federal income tax return, he must attach Copy A of Form W-2 to his return.   9. _____

10. Businesses in states with state income tax must prepare additional copies of Form W-2.   10. _____

COPYRIGHT © SOUTH-WESTERN CENGAGE LEARNING

Chapter 13 • **325**

Study Skills

Improving Your Ability to Remember

Do you sometimes find it difficult to remember things? Do you occasionally forget important points in a lesson? Most of us do. It is very common to forget things, but we must make a special effort to remember important things. What can we do to improve our memory? There are a number of things we can do to help us remember.

Grouping

Grouping is a technique that makes learning easier. If we group similar information, we will be able to remember it better. For example, suppose you are studying geography and want to learn each of the states in the United States. You can group the New England states, the Middle Atlantic states, or the Southwestern states. This will help you to remember them more easily.

A similar principle works when we try to remember other types of information. Let's suppose we want to remember a string of numbers like a Social Security number, 142869426. If we try to remember each single number, it is quite difficult. However, if we group the numbers, it becomes easier: 142-86-9426. It is easier to remember three groups of numbers rather than nine individual numbers.

Practice and Reinforcement

Suppose that you want to call a friend on the phone. You look up the number in the directory, and find that it is 453-1191. By grouping the first three numbers and the last four, you will be able to remember it for a short time. However, if you try to recall the number later, you will likely not be able to do so.

To remember a number or a fact for a long period of time, you must practice using it. You should repeat it silently as well as aloud and practice using it in as many ways as possible. The more you use information, the more likely you will remember it.

Your learning practice sessions should not be too long, and they should be spaced over a number of days. Spaced practice is less tiring, and the frequent review helps to decrease forgetting. A great deal of practice at one time is much less useful than spaced practice. This is why it is so difficult to learn material if you leave all your work to be done on the night before an exam.

Work to Remember Better

To remember better, work every day in sessions of a reasonable length. Make your study personal and meaningful. If you do, you will be able to remember facts much more easily, and your grades will very likely improve.

13-1 WORK TOGETHER, p. 372

Recording a payroll

1.

Salary Expense

Employee Income Tax Payable

Social Security Tax Payable

Medicare Tax Payable

Cash

2.

CASH PAYMENTS JOURNAL PAGE 15

				GENERAL		ACCOUNTS PAYABLE	CASH	
DATE	ACCOUNT TITLE	CK. NO.	POST. REF.	DEBIT	CREDIT	DEBIT	CREDIT	
				1	2	3	4	
1								1
2								2
3								3
4								4
5								5
6								6
7								7
8								8
9								9

Recording a payroll

1.

| Salary Expense |
| Employee Income Tax Payable |
| Social Security Tax Payable |
| Medicare Tax Payable |
| Cash |

2.

CASH PAYMENTS JOURNAL

PAGE 16

| | | | | GENERAL | | ACCOUNTS PAYABLE | CASH |
DATE	ACCOUNT TITLE	CK. NO.	POST. REF.	DEBIT	CREDIT	DEBIT	CREDIT
				1	2	3	4

Name _____ Date _____ Class _____

13-2 WORK TOGETHER, p. 377

Recording employer payroll taxes

1., 2.

Employee Name	Accumulated Earnings, April 30	Total Earnings for May 1–15 Pay Period	Unemployment Taxable Earnings
Beltran, Tamela C.	$5,100.00	$ 637.50	_____
Cintron, Irma V.	7,350.00	920.00	_____
	Totals	_____	_____

Social Security Tax Payable, 6.2% _____
Medicare Tax Payable, 1.45% _____
Unemployment Tax Payable—Federal, 0.8% _____
Unemployment Tax Payable—State, 5.4% _____
    Total Payroll Taxes _____

3.

GENERAL JOURNAL   PAGE 10

	DATE	ACCOUNT TITLE	DOC. NO.	POST. REF.	DEBIT	CREDIT	
1							1
2							2
3							3
4							4
5							5
6							6
7							7
8							8
9							9
10							10

Recording employer payroll taxes

1., 2.

Employee Name	Accumulated Earnings, May 31	Total Earnings for June 1–15 Pay Period	Unemployment Taxable Earnings
Caldwell, Sarah H.	$6,020.00	$ 580.00	_____
Easley, Benjamin P.	5,450.00	620.00	_____
Franks, John J.	8,420.00	1,000.00	_____
Totals		_____	_____

Social Security Tax Payable, 6.2%	_____
Medicare Tax Payable, 1.45%	_____
Unemployment Tax Payable—Federal, 0.8%	_____
Unemployment Tax Payable—State, 5.4%	_____
Total Payroll Taxes	_____

3.

GENERAL JOURNAL   PAGE 12

	DATE	ACCOUNT TITLE	DOC. NO.	POST. REF.	DEBIT	CREDIT	
1							1
2							2
3							3
4							4
5							5
6							6
7							7
8							8
9							9
10							10

13-3 WORK TOGETHER, p. 382

Reporting withholding and payroll taxes

1.

Form **941**

Employer's Quarterly Federal Tax Return

▶ See separate instructions revised January 20-- for information on completing this return.

Department of the Treasury
Internal Revenue Service (99)

Please type or print.

Enter state code for state in which deposits were made **only** if different from state in address to the right ▶ ☐ (see page 2 of separate instructions).

Name (as distinguished from trade name)	Date quarter ended
Trade name, if any	Employer identification number
Address (number and street)	City, state, and ZIP code

OMB No. 1545-0029

T
FF
FD
FP
I
T

If address is different from prior return, check here ▶ ☐

IRS Use

1	1	1	1	1	1	1	1	1	1	2	3	3	3	3	3	3	3	4	4	4	5	5	5

6 7 8 8 8 8 8 8 8 9 9 9 9 9 10 10 10 10 10 10 10 10 10 10

A If you **do not have to file** returns in the future, check here ▶ ☐ and enter date final wages paid ▶ _____
B If you are a seasonal employer, see **Seasonal employers** on page 1 of the instructions and check here ▶ ☐ _____

1	Number of employees in the pay period that includes March 12th . ▶	1		
2	Total wages and tips, plus other compensation (see separate instructions)		**2**	
3	Total income tax withheld from wages, tips, and sick pay		**3**	
4	Adjustment of withheld income tax for preceding quarters of **this calendar year**		**4**	
5	Adjusted total of income tax withheld (line 3 as adjusted by line 4)		**5**	

6	Taxable social security wages	**6a**		. 12.4% (.124) =	**6b**	
	Taxable social security tips	**6c**		. 12.4% (.124) =	**6d**	
7	Taxable Medicare wages and tips . . .	**7a**		. 2.9% (.029) =	**7b**	

8	Total social security and Medicare taxes (add lines 6b, 6d, and 7b). **Check here if wages are not subject to social security and/or Medicare tax** . . . . ▶ ☐	**8**	
9	Adjustment of social security and Medicare taxes (see instructions for required explanation) Sick Pay $ _____ ± Fractions of Cents $ _____ ± Other $ _____ =	**9**	
10	Adjusted total of social security and Medicare taxes (line 8 as adjusted by line 9)	**10**	
11	**Total taxes** (add lines 5 and 10)	**11**	
12	Advance earned income credit (EIC) payments made to employees (see instructions) . . .	**12**	
13	Net taxes (subtract line 12 from line 11). **If $2,500 or more, this must equal line 17, column (d) below (or line D of Schedule B (Form 941))**	**13**	
14	Total deposits for quarter, including overpayment applied from a prior quarter	**14**	
15	**Balance due** (subtract line 14 from line 13). See instructions	**15**	
16	**Overpayment.** If line 14 is more than line 13, enter excess here ▶ $ _____		

and check if to be: ☐ Applied to next return   **or**   ☐ Refunded.

● **All filers:** If line 13 is less than $2,500, **do not** complete line 17 or Schedule B (Form 941).
● **Semiweekly schedule depositors:** Complete Schedule B (Form 941) and check here . . . . ▶ ☐
● **Monthly schedule depositors:** Complete line 17, columns (a) through (d), and check here. . . . . ▶ ☐

17	Monthly Summary of Federal Tax Liability. (Complete **Schedule B (Form 941)** instead, if you were a semiweekly schedule depositor.)			
	(a) First month liability	**(b)** Second month liability	**(c)** Third month liability	**(d)** Total liability for quarter

Third Party Designee

Do you want to allow another person to discuss this return with the IRS (see separate instructions)?   ☐ **Yes.** Complete the following.   ☐ **No**

Designee's name ▶ _____   Phone no. ▶ ( )   Personal identification number (PIN) ▶ ☐☐☐☐☐

Sign Here

Under penalties of perjury, I declare that I have examined this return, including accompanying schedules and statements, and to the best of my knowledge and belief, it is true, correct, and complete.

Signature ▶ _____   Print Your Name and Title ▶ _____   Date ▶ _____

For Privacy Act and Paperwork Reduction Act Notice, see back of Payment Voucher.   Cat. No. 17001Z   Form **941**

Reporting withholding and payroll taxes

1.

Form **941**

Department of the Treasury
Internal Revenue Service (99)

Employer's Quarterly Federal Tax Return

▶ See separate instructions revised January 20-- for information on completing this return.

Please type or print.

OMB No. 1545-0029

Enter state code for state in which deposits were made **only** if different from state in address to the right ▶ (see page 2 of separate instructions).

Name (as distinguished from trade name)	Date quarter ended
Trade name, if any	Employer identification number
Address (number and street)	City, state, and ZIP code

T	
FF	
FD	
FP	
I	
T	

If address is different from prior return, check here ▶

IRS Use

1 1 1 1 1 1 1 1 1	2	3 3 3 3 3 3 3	4 4 4	5 5 5

6   7   8 8 8 8 8 8 8   9 9 9 9   10 10 10 10 10 10 10 10 10 10

A If you **do not have to file** returns in the future, check here ▶ ☐ and enter date final wages paid ▶

B If you are a seasonal employer, see **Seasonal employers** on page 1 of the instructions and check here ▶ ☐

1	Number of employees in the pay period that includes March 12th . ▶	**1**	
2	Total wages and tips, plus other compensation (see separate instructions)	**2**	
3	Total income tax withheld from wages, tips, and sick pay	**3**	
4	Adjustment of withheld income tax for preceding quarters of **this calendar year**	**4**	
5	Adjusted total of income tax withheld (line 3 as adjusted by line 4)	**5**	

6	Taxable social security wages	**6a**		· 12.4% (.124) =	**6b**	
	Taxable social security tips	**6c**		· 12.4% (.124) =	**6d**	
7	Taxable Medicare wages and tips	**7a**		2.9% (.029) =	**7b**	

8	Total social security and Medicare taxes (add lines 6b, 6d, and 7b). **Check here if wages are not subject to social security and/or Medicare tax** . . . . ▶ ☐	**8**	
9	Adjustment of social security and Medicare taxes (see instructions for required explanation) Sick Pay $ _____ ± Fractions of Cents $ _____ ± Other $ _____ =	**9**	
10	Adjusted total of social security and Medicare taxes (line 8 as adjusted by line 9) . . .	**10**	
11	**Total taxes** (add lines 5 and 10)	**11**	
12	Advance earned income credit (EIC) payments made to employees (see instructions) . . .	**12**	
13	Net taxes (subtract line 12 from line 11). **If $2,500 or more, this must equal line 17, column (d) below (or line D of Schedule B (Form 941))**	**13**	
14	Total deposits for quarter, including overpayment applied from a prior quarter	**14**	
15	**Balance due** (subtract line 14 from line 13). See instructions	**15**	

16 **Overpayment.** If line 14 is more than line 13, enter excess here ▶ $ _____

and check if to be: ☐ Applied to next return **or** ☐ Refunded.

• **All filers:** If line 13 is less than $2,500, **do not** complete line 17 **or** Schedule B (Form 941).

• **Semiweekly schedule depositors:** Complete Schedule B (Form 941) and check here . . . . ▶ ☐

• **Monthly schedule depositors:** Complete line 17, columns (a) through (d), and check here . . . . . . ▶ ☐

17	**Monthly Summary of Federal Tax Liability.** (Complete **Schedule B (Form 941)** instead, if you were a semiweekly schedule depositor.)		
(a) First month liability	**(b)** Second month liability	**(c)** Third month liability	**(d)** Total liability for quarter

Third Party Designee

Do you want to allow another person to discuss this return with the IRS (see separate instructions)? ☐ **Yes.** Complete the following. ☐ **No**

Designee's name ▶

Phone no. ▶ ( )

Personal identification number (PIN) ▶

Sign Here

Under penalties of perjury, I declare that I have examined this return, including accompanying schedules and statements, and to the best of my knowledge and belief, it is true, correct, and complete.

Signature ▶

Print Your Name and Title ▶

Date ▶

For Privacy Act and Paperwork Reduction Act Notice, see back of Payment Voucher.   Cat. No. 17001Z   Form **941**

13-4 **WORK TOGETHER, p. 389**

Paying withholding and payroll taxes

1., 2.

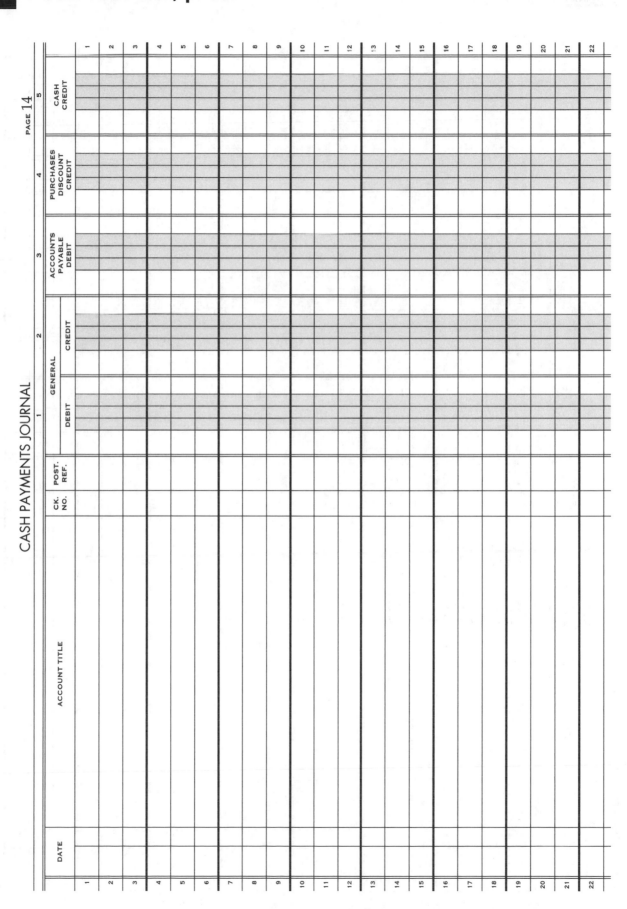

CASH PAYMENTS JOURNAL

PAGE 14

Paying withholding and payroll taxes

1., 2.

CASH PAYMENTS JOURNAL

PAGE 19

				GENERAL		ACCOUNTS PAYABLE DEBIT	PURCHASES DISCOUNT CREDIT	CASH CREDIT
DATE	ACCOUNT TITLE	CK. NO.	POST. REF.	DEBIT	CREDIT			
				1	2	3	4	5

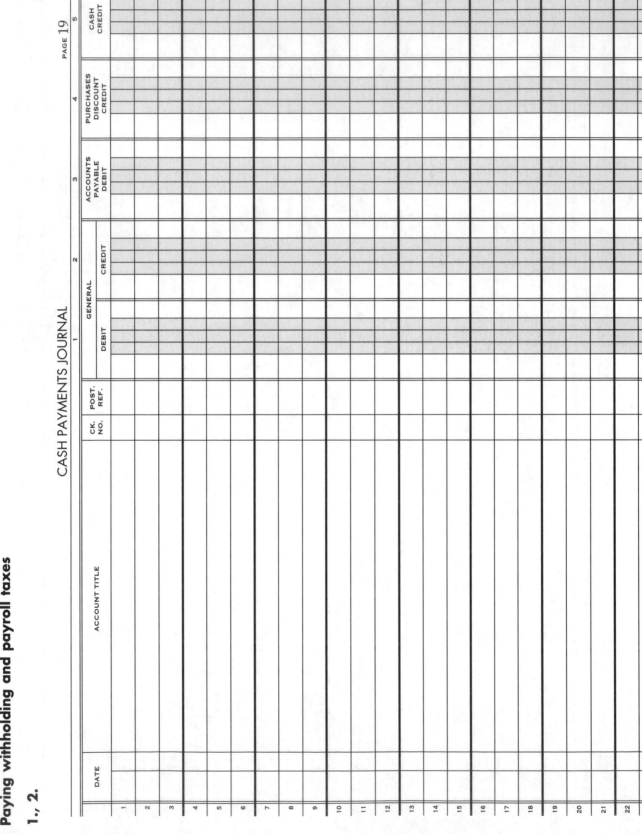

13-1 **APPLICATION PROBLEM, p. 391**

Recording a payroll

CASH PAYMENTS JOURNAL

PAGE 15

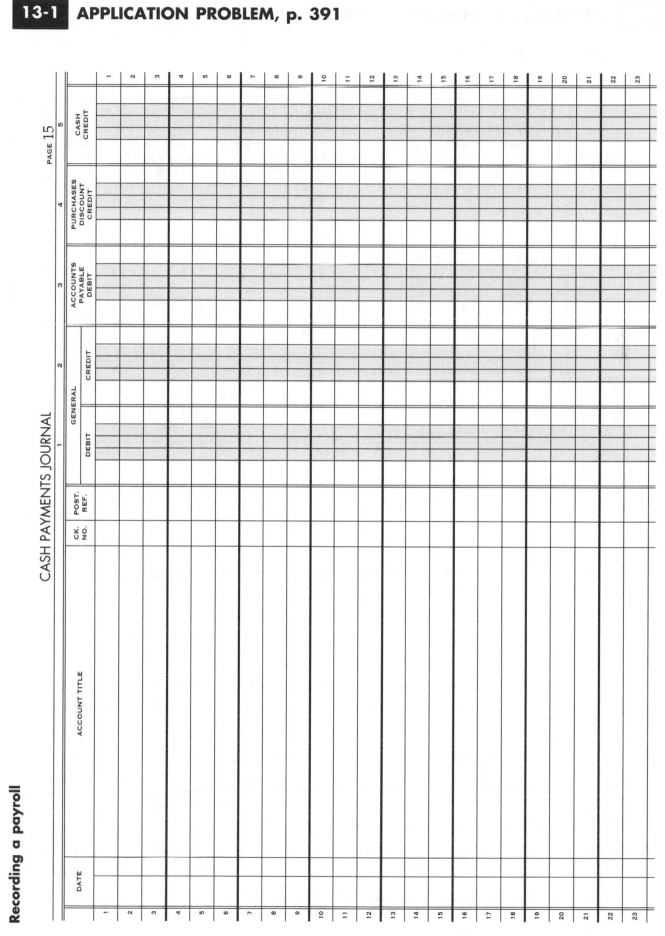

	DATE	ACCOUNT TITLE	CK. NO.	POST. REF.	GENERAL DEBIT 1	GENERAL CREDIT 2	ACCOUNTS PAYABLE DEBIT 3	PURCHASES DISCOUNT CREDIT 4	CASH CREDIT 5
1									
2									
3									
4									
5									
6									
7									
8									
9									
10									
11									
12									
13									
14									
15									
16									
17									
18									
19									
20									
21									
22									
23									

13-2 APPLICATION PROBLEM, pp. 391, 392

Recording employer payroll taxes

1., 2., 4.

Employee Name	Accumulated Earnings, March 31	Total Earnings for April 1–15 Pay Period	Unemployment Taxable Earnings, April 15	Accumulated Earnings, April 15	Total Earnings for April 16–30 Pay Period	Unemployment Taxable Earnings, April 30
Bolser, Frank T.	$4,860.00	$ 810.00	_____	_____	$ 795.00	_____
Denham, Beth R.	5,670.00	945.00	_____	_____	980.00	_____
Harjo, Teresa S.	7,500.00	1,250.00	_____	_____	1,250.00	_____
Knutzen, John L.	3,720.00	620.00	_____	_____	635.00	_____
Prescott, Laura F.	4,560.00	760.00	_____	_____	740.00	_____
Schmidt, Ian T.	6,900.00	1,150.00	_____	_____	1,125.00	_____
	Totals	_____	_____	Totals	_____	_____

Social Security Tax Payable	_____		Social Security Tax Payable	_____
Medicare Tax Payable	_____		Medicare Tax Payable	_____
Unemployment Tax Payable—Federal	_____		Unemployment Tax Payable—Federal	_____
Unemployment Tax Payable—State	_____		Unemployment Tax Payable—State	_____

3., 5.

GENERAL JOURNAL

	DATE	ACCOUNT TITLE	DOC. NO.	POST. REF.	DEBIT	CREDIT	
1							1
2							2
3							3
4							4
5							5
6							6
7							7
8							8
9							9
10							10
11							11
12							12

13-3 APPLICATION PROBLEM, p. 392

Reporting withholding and payroll taxes

Form **941**

Department of the Treasury
Internal Revenue Service (99)

Employer's Quarterly Federal Tax Return

▶ See separate instructions revised January 20-- for information on completing this return.

Please type or print.

Enter state code for state in which deposits were made **only** if different from state in address to the right ▶ ⬚
(see page 2 of separate instructions).

Name (as distinguished from trade name)

Trade name, if any

Address (number and street)

Date quarter ended

Employer identification number

City, state, and ZIP code

OMB No. 1545-0029

T	
FF	
FD	
FP	
I	
T	

If address is different from prior return, check here ▶ ⬚

IRS Use

1 1 1 1 1 1 1 1 1 1 2 3 3 3 3 3 3 3 4 4 4 5 5 5

6 7 8 8 8 8 8 8 8 9 9 9 9 9 10 10 10 10 10 10 10 10 10

A If you **do not have to file** returns in the future, check here ▶ ⬚ and enter date final wages paid ▶
B If you are a seasonal employer, see **Seasonal employers** on page 1 of the instructions and check here ▶ ⬚

1	Number of employees in the pay period that includes March 12th ▶	1
2	Total wages and tips, plus other compensation (see separate instructions)	2
3	Total income tax withheld from wages, tips, and sick pay	3
4	Adjustment of withheld income tax for preceding quarters of **this calendar year**	4
5	Adjusted total of income tax withheld (line 3 as adjusted by line 4)	5

6 Taxable social security wages . . . . . | 6a | | · 12.4% (.124) = | 6b |
Taxable social security tips . . . . . . | 6c | | · 12.4% (.124) = | 6d |
7 Taxable Medicare wages and tips . . . | 7a | | · 2.9% (.029) = | 7b |

8	Total social security and Medicare taxes (add lines 6b, 6d, and 7b). **Check here if wages are not subject to social security and/or Medicare tax** . . . . ▶ ⬚	8
9	Adjustment of social security and Medicare taxes (see instructions for required explanation) Sick Pay $ _____ ± Fractions of Cents $ _____ ± Other $ _____ =	9
10	Adjusted total of social security and Medicare taxes (line 8 as adjusted by line 9)	10
11	**Total taxes** (add lines 5 and 10)	11
12	Advance earned income credit (EIC) payments made to employees (see instructions) . . .	12
13	Net taxes (subtract line 12 from line 11). **If $2,500 or more, this must equal line 17, column (d) below (or line D of Schedule B (Form 941))**	13
14	Total deposits for quarter, including overpayment applied from a prior quarter	14
15	**Balance due** (subtract line 14 from line 13). See instructions	15
16	**Overpayment.** If line 14 is more than line 13, enter excess here ▶ $ _____	

and check if to be: ⬚ Applied to next return **or** ⬚ Refunded.

- **All filers:** If line 13 is less than $2,500, **do not** complete line 17 or Schedule B (Form 941).
- **Semiweekly schedule depositors:** Complete Schedule B (Form 941) and check here . . . . ▶ ⬚
- **Monthly schedule depositors:** Complete line 17, columns (a) through (d), and check here. . . . . ▶ ⬚

17	**Monthly Summary of Federal Tax Liability.** (Complete **Schedule B (Form 941)** instead, if you were a semiweekly schedule depositor.)			
	(a) First month liability	**(b)** Second month liability	**(c)** Third month liability	**(d)** Total liability for quarter

Third Party Designee

Do you want to allow another person to discuss this return with the IRS (see separate instructions)? ⬚ **Yes.** Complete the following. ⬚ **No**

Designee's name ▶ _____   Phone no. ▶ ( ) _____   Personal identification number (PIN) ▶ ⬚⬚⬚⬚⬚

Sign Here

Under penalties of perjury, I declare that I have examined this return, including accompanying schedules and statements, and to the best of my knowledge and belief, it is true, correct, and complete.

Signature ▶ _____   Print Your Name and Title ▶ _____   Date ▶ _____

For Privacy Act and Paperwork Reduction Act Notice, see back of Payment Voucher.   Cat. No. 17001Z   Form **941**

Paying withholding and payroll taxes
1., 2., 3.

CASH PAYMENTS JOURNAL

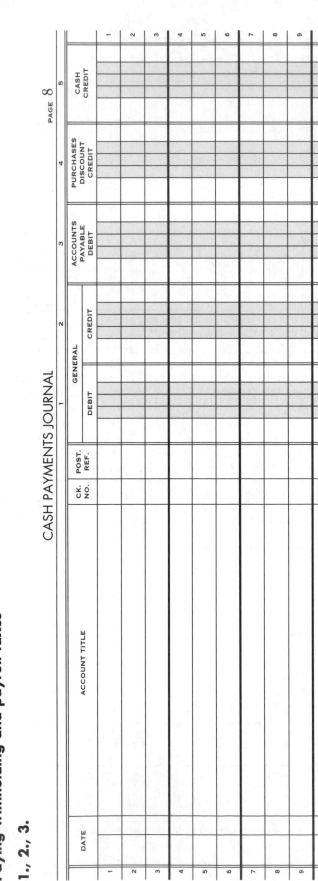

PAGE 8

13-5 MASTERY PROBLEM, p. 393

Journalizing payroll transactions

1., 2.

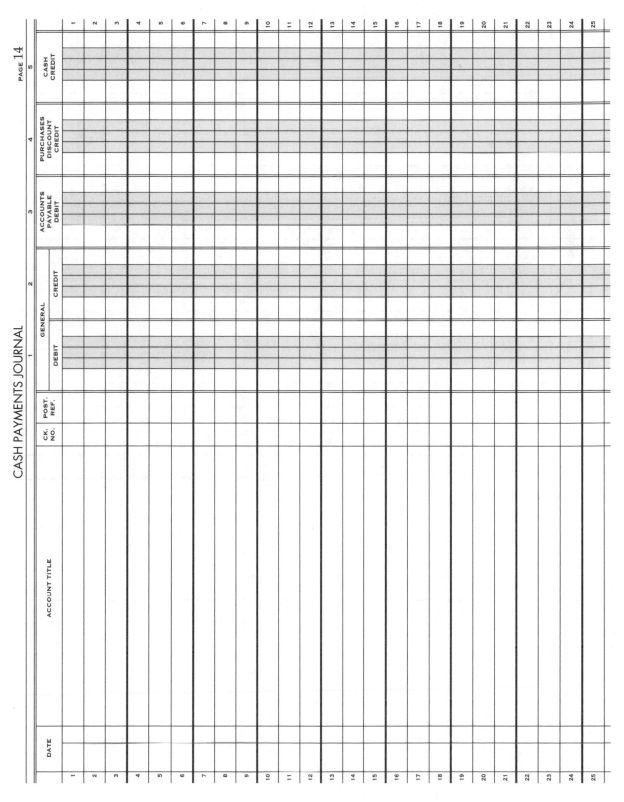

CASH PAYMENTS JOURNAL

PAGE 14

1.

GENERAL JOURNAL   PAGE 10

	DATE		ACCOUNT TITLE	DOC. NO.	POST. REF.	DEBIT	CREDIT	
1								1
2								2
3								3
4								4
5								5
6								6
7								7
8								8
9								9
10								10
11								11
12								12
13								13
14								14
15								15
16								16
17								17
18								18
19								19
20								20
21								21
22								22
23								23
24								24
25								25

13-6 CHALLENGE PROBLEM, pp. 393, 394

Journalizing and posting payroll transactions

1., 2.

CASH PAYMENTS JOURNAL

PAGE 1

DATE	ACCOUNT TITLE	CK. NO.	POST. REF.	GENERAL DEBIT	GENERAL CREDIT	ACCOUNTS PAYABLE DEBIT	PURCHASES DISCOUNT CREDIT	CASH CREDIT	
				1	2	3	4	5	
									1
									2
									3
									4
									5
									6
									7
									8
									9
									10
									11
									12
									13
									14
									15
									16
									17
									18
									19
									20

1., 3.

GENERAL JOURNAL

PAGE 1

	DATE	ACCOUNT TITLE	DOC. NO.	POST. REF.	DEBIT	CREDIT	
1							1
2							2
3							3
4							4
5							5
6							6
7							7
8							8
9							9
10							10
11							11
12							12
13							13
14							14
15							15
16							16
17							17
18							18
19							19
20							20
21							21
22							22
23							23
24							24
25							25

13-6 **CHALLENGE PROBLEM (continued)**

2., 3., 4.

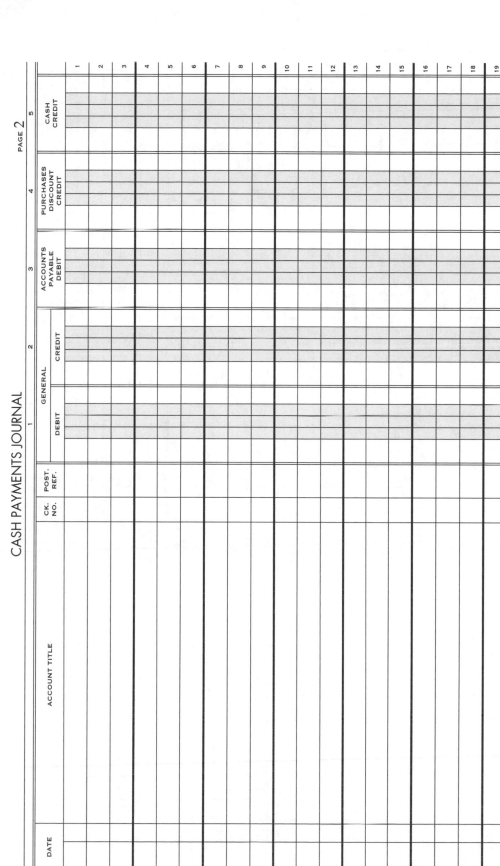

1., 3. GENERAL LEDGER

ACCOUNT Employee Income Tax Payable   ACCOUNT NO. 2120

DATE		ITEM	POST. REF.	DEBIT	CREDIT	BALANCE	
						DEBIT	CREDIT
20-- Jan.	1	Balance	✔				1 2 9 2 00

ACCOUNT Social Security Tax Payable   ACCOUNT NO. 2130

DATE		ITEM	POST. REF.	DEBIT	CREDIT	BALANCE	
						DEBIT	CREDIT
20-- Jan.	1	Balance	✔				1 5 2 7 50

ACCOUNT Medicare Tax Payable   ACCOUNT NO. 2140

DATE		ITEM	POST. REF.	DEBIT	CREDIT	BALANCE	
						DEBIT	CREDIT
20-- Jan.	1	Balance	✔				1 7 6 25

13-6 CHALLENGE PROBLEM (concluded)

ACCOUNT Unemployment Tax Payable—Federal   ACCOUNT NO. 2150

DATE		ITEM	POST. REF.	DEBIT	CREDIT	BALANCE DEBIT	BALANCE CREDIT
20-- Jan.	1	Balance	✔				2 6 4 00

ACCOUNT Unemployment Tax Payable—State   ACCOUNT NO. 2160

DATE		ITEM	POST. REF.	DEBIT	CREDIT	BALANCE DEBIT	BALANCE CREDIT
20-- Jan.	1	Balance	✔				1 7 8 2 00

ACCOUNT U.S. Savings Bonds Payable   ACCOUNT NO. 2180

DATE		ITEM	POST. REF.	DEBIT	CREDIT	BALANCE DEBIT	BALANCE CREDIT
20-- Jan.	1	Balance	✔				3 7 5 00

ACCOUNT Payroll Taxes Expense   ACCOUNT NO. 6150

DATE	ITEM	POST. REF.	DEBIT	CREDIT	BALANCE DEBIT	BALANCE CREDIT

ACCOUNT Salary Expense   ACCOUNT NO. 6170

DATE	ITEM	POST. REF.	DEBIT	CREDIT	BALANCE DEBIT	BALANCE CREDIT

REINFORCEMENT ACTIVITY 2

PART A, p. 398

An Accounting Cycle for a Corporation: Journalizing and Posting Transactions

1., 4., 5.

SALES JOURNAL

PAGE 12

	DATE		ACCOUNT DEBITED	SALE NO.	POST. REF.	ACCOUNTS RECEIVABLE DEBIT 1	SALES CREDIT 2	SALES TAX PAYABLE CREDIT 3	
1									1
2									2
3									3
4									4
5									5
6									6
7									7
8									8
9									9
10									10
11									11
12									12
13									13
14									14
15									15
16									16
17									17
18									18
19									19

REINFORCEMENT ACTIVITY 2

PART A (continued)

1., 4., 6.

PURCHASES JOURNAL   PAGE 12

	DATE		ACCOUNT CREDITED	PURCH. NO.	POST. REF.	PURCHASES DR. ACCTS. PAY. CR.	
1							1
2							2
3							3
4							4
5							5
6							6
7							7
8							8
9							9
10							10
11							11
12							12
13							13
14							14
15							15
16							16
17							17
18							18
19							19
20							20
21							21
22							22
23							23
24							24
25							25

REINFORCEMENT ACTIVITY 2

PART A (continued)

1., 4.

GENERAL JOURNAL

	DATE		ACCOUNT TITLE	DOC. NO.	POST. REF.	DEBIT	CREDIT	
1								1
2								2
3								3
4								4
5								5
6								6
7								7
8								8
9								9
10								10
11								11
12								12
13								13
14								14
15								15
16								16
17								17
18								18
19								19
20								20
21								21
22								22
23								23
24								24
25								25
26								26
27								27
28								28
29								29
30								30
31								31
32								32

1., 4., 7., 9.

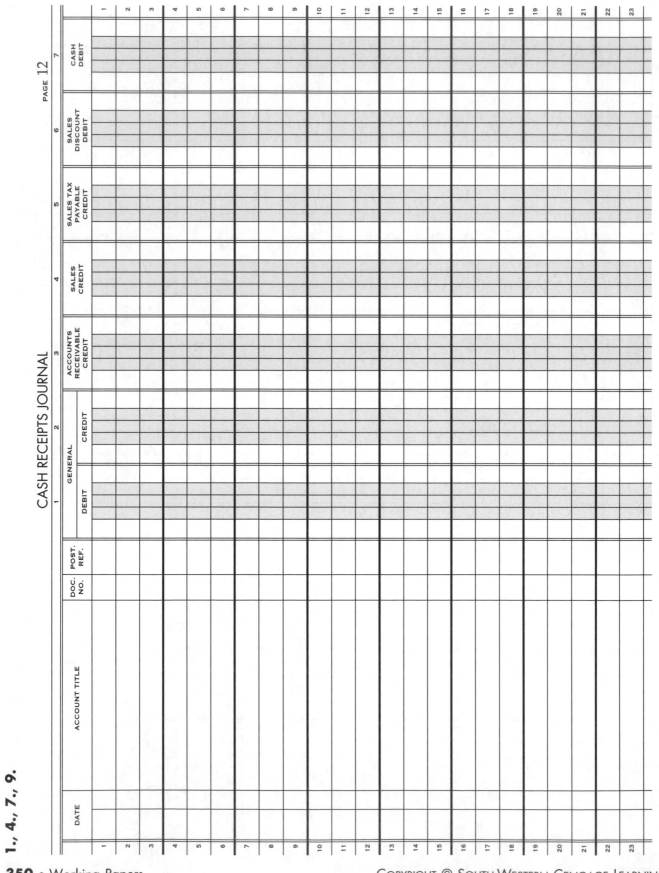

CASH RECEIPTS JOURNAL

PAGE 12

DATE	ACCOUNT TITLE	DOC. NO.	POST. REF.	GENERAL DEBIT (1)	GENERAL CREDIT (2)	ACCOUNTS RECEIVABLE CREDIT (3)	SALES CREDIT (4)	SALES TAX PAYABLE CREDIT (5)	SALES DISCOUNT DEBIT (6)	CASH DEBIT (7)

REINFORCEMENT ACTIVITY 2

PART A (continued)

1., 2.

CASH PAYMENTS JOURNAL

PAGE 23

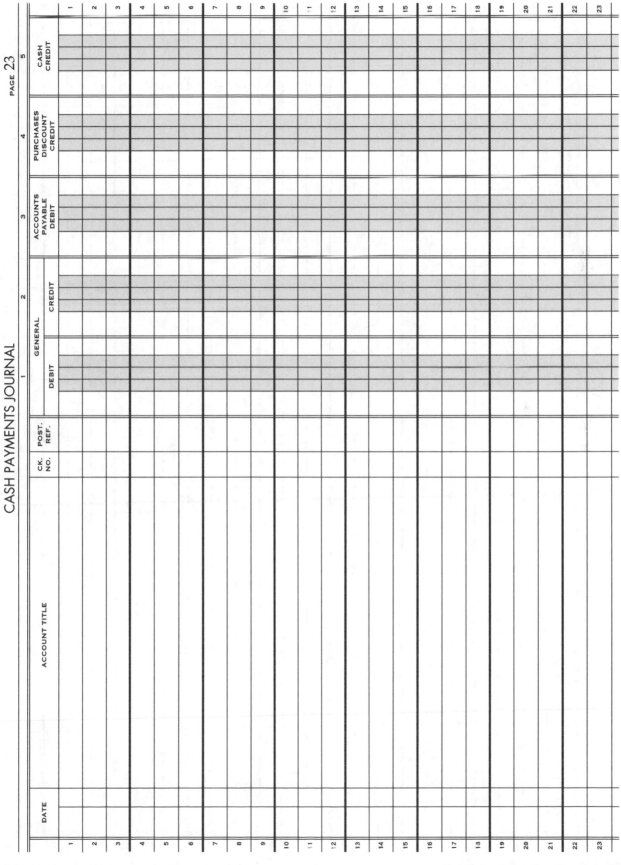

3., 4., 7., 10.

CASH PAYMENTS JOURNAL

PAGE 24

DATE	ACCOUNT TITLE	CK. NO.	POST. REF.	GENERAL DEBIT	GENERAL CREDIT	ACCOUNTS PAYABLE DEBIT	PURCHASES DISCOUNT CREDIT	CASH CREDIT

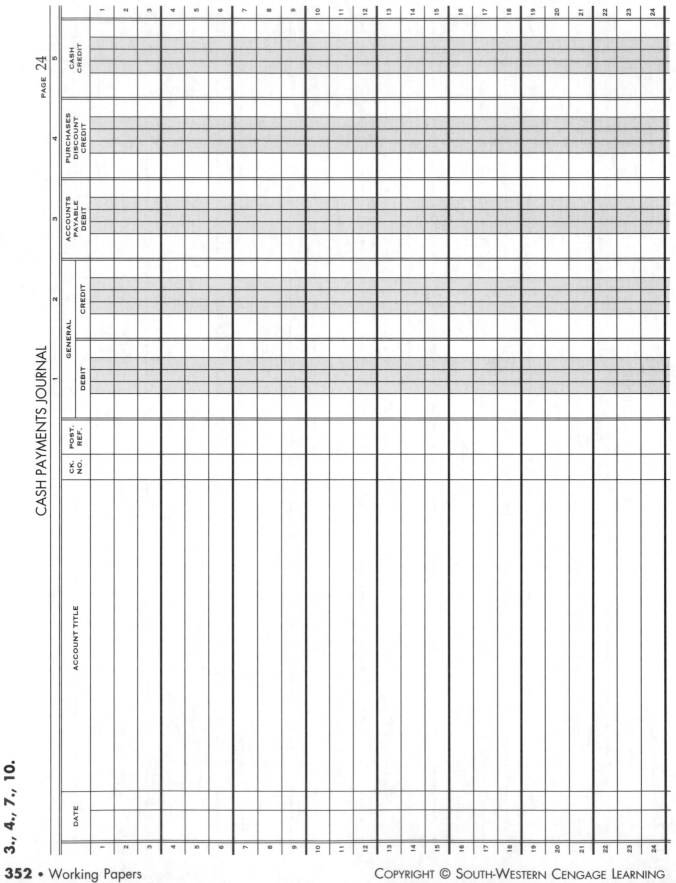

REINFORCEMENT ACTIVITY 2

PART A (continued)

1., 4.   **ACCOUNTS RECEIVABLE LEDGER**

CUSTOMER Bratton Clinic   CUSTOMER NO. 110

DATE	ITEM	POST. REF.	DEBIT	CREDIT	DEBIT BALANCE
20-- Dec. 1	Balance	✔			4 9 6 7 60

CUSTOMER Clegg Medical Center   CUSTOMER NO. 120

DATE	ITEM	POST. REF.	DEBIT	CREDIT	DEBIT BALANCE
20-- Dec. 1	Balance	✔			4 1 3 40

CUSTOMER Glenmore School   CUSTOMER NO. 130

DATE	ITEM	POST. REF.	DEBIT	CREDIT	DEBIT BALANCE

CUSTOMER Jamacus Clinic   CUSTOMER NO. 140

DATE	ITEM	POST. REF.	DEBIT	CREDIT	DEBIT BALANCE
20-- Dec. 1	Balance	✔			1 6 4 3 00

CUSTOMER Odom Daycare   CUSTOMER NO. 150

DATE	ITEM	POST. REF.	DEBIT	CREDIT	DEBIT BALANCE

CUSTOMER Treet Retirement Home   CUSTOMER NO. 160

DATE	ITEM	POST. REF.	DEBIT	CREDIT	DEBIT BALANCE
20-- Dec. 1	Balance	✔			8 0 0 1 52

REINFORCEMENT ACTIVITY 2

PART A (continued)

1., 4.   ACCOUNTS PAYABLE LEDGER

VENDOR Armstrong Medical   VENDOR NO. 210

DATE		ITEM	POST. REF.	DEBIT	CREDIT	CREDIT BALANCE
20-- Dec.	1	Balance	✔			1 2 7 2 00

VENDOR Cross Office Supply   VENDOR NO. 220

DATE		ITEM	POST. REF.	DEBIT	CREDIT	CREDIT BALANCE
20-- Dec.	1	Balance	✔			1 4 1 7 25

VENDOR Evans Supply   VENDOR NO. 230

DATE		ITEM	POST. REF.	DEBIT	CREDIT	CREDIT BALANCE
20-- Dec.	1	Balance	✔			1 3 9 6 00

VENDOR Ogden Instruments   VENDOR NO. 240

DATE		ITEM	POST. REF.	DEBIT	CREDIT	CREDIT BALANCE
20-- Dec.	1	Balance	✔			2 2 0 0 00

VENDOR Spencer Industries   VENDOR NO. 250

DATE		ITEM	POST. REF.	DEBIT	CREDIT	CREDIT BALANCE
20-- Dec.	1	Balance	✔			5 8 0 00

VENDOR Ziegler, Inc.   VENDOR NO. 260

DATE		ITEM	POST. REF.	DEBIT	CREDIT	CREDIT BALANCE

REINFORCEMENT ACTIVITY 2

PART A (continued)

11.

GENERAL LEDGER

ACCOUNT Cash   ACCOUNT NO. 1110

DATE		ITEM	POST. REF.	DEBIT	CREDIT	BALANCE DEBIT	BALANCE CREDIT
20-- Dec.	1	Balance	✔			1 9 9 6 4 82	

ACCOUNT Petty Cash   ACCOUNT NO. 1120

DATE		ITEM	POST. REF.	DEBIT	CREDIT	BALANCE DEBIT	BALANCE CREDIT
20-- Dec.	1	Balance	✔			2 5 0 00	

ACCOUNT Accounts Receivable   ACCOUNT NO. 1130

DATE		ITEM	POST. REF.	DEBIT	CREDIT	BALANCE DEBIT	BALANCE CREDIT
20-- Dec.	1	Balance	✔			1 5 0 2 5 52	

ACCOUNT Allowance for Uncollectible Accounts   ACCOUNT NO. 1135

DATE		ITEM	POST. REF.	DEBIT	CREDIT	BALANCE DEBIT	BALANCE CREDIT
20-- Dec.	1	Balance	✔				1 0 2 12

ACCOUNT Merchandise Inventory   ACCOUNT NO. 1140

DATE		ITEM	POST. REF.	DEBIT	CREDIT	BALANCE DEBIT	BALANCE CREDIT
20-- Dec.	1	Balance	✔			3 4 5 2 1 56	

REINFORCEMENT ACTIVITY 2

PART A (continued)

ACCOUNT Supplies—Office   ACCOUNT NO. 1145

DATE	ITEM	POST. REF.	DEBIT	CREDIT	BALANCE DEBIT	BALANCE CREDIT
20-- Dec. 1	Balance	✔			3 7 5 6 00	

ACCOUNT Supplies—Store   ACCOUNT NO. 1150

DATE	ITEM	POST. REF.	DEBIT	CREDIT	BALANCE DEBIT	BALANCE CREDIT
20-- Dec. 1	Balance	✔			4 2 1 0 00	

ACCOUNT Prepaid Insurance   ACCOUNT NO. 1160

DATE	ITEM	POST. REF.	DEBIT	CREDIT	BALANCE DEBIT	BALANCE CREDIT
20-- Dec. 1	Balance	✔			8 0 0 0 00	

ACCOUNT Office Equipment   ACCOUNT NO. 1210

DATE	ITEM	POST. REF.	DEBIT	CREDIT	BALANCE DEBIT	BALANCE CREDIT
20-- Dec. 1	Balance	✔			1 3 7 5 2 00	

ACCOUNT Accumulated Depreciation—Office Equipment   ACCOUNT NO. 1220

DATE	ITEM	POST. REF.	DEBIT	CREDIT	BALANCE DEBIT	BALANCE CREDIT
20-- Dec. 1	Balance	✔				2 2 1 0 00

ACCOUNT Store Equipment   ACCOUNT NO. 1230

DATE	ITEM	POST. REF.	DEBIT	CREDIT	BALANCE DEBIT	BALANCE CREDIT
20-- Dec. 1	Balance	✔			10 259 00	

ACCOUNT Accumulated Depreciation—Store Equipment   ACCOUNT NO. 1240

DATE	ITEM	POST. REF.	DEBIT	CREDIT	BALANCE DEBIT	BALANCE CREDIT
20-- Dec. 1	Balance	✔				5 844 00

ACCOUNT Accounts Payable   ACCOUNT NO. 2110

DATE	ITEM	POST. REF.	DEBIT	CREDIT	BALANCE DEBIT	BALANCE CREDIT
20-- Dec. 1	Balance	✔				6 865 25

ACCOUNT Federal Income Tax Payable   ACCOUNT NO. 2115

DATE	ITEM	POST. REF.	DEBIT	CREDIT	BALANCE DEBIT	BALANCE CREDIT

ACCOUNT Employee Income Tax Payable   ACCOUNT NO. 2120

DATE	ITEM	POST. REF.	DEBIT	CREDIT	BALANCE DEBIT	BALANCE CREDIT
20-- Dec. 1	Balance	✔				342 00

REINFORCEMENT ACTIVITY 2

PART A (continued)

ACCOUNT Social Security Tax Payable   ACCOUNT NO. 2130

DATE		ITEM	POST. REF.	DEBIT	CREDIT	BALANCE	
						DEBIT	CREDIT
20-- Dec.	1	Balance	✔				7 6 7 00

ACCOUNT Medicare Tax Payable   ACCOUNT NO. 2135

DATE		ITEM	POST. REF.	DEBIT	CREDIT	BALANCE	
						DEBIT	CREDIT
20-- Dec.	1	Balance	✔				1 7 9 38

ACCOUNT Sales Tax Payable   ACCOUNT NO. 2140

DATE		ITEM	POST. REF.	DEBIT	CREDIT	BALANCE	
						DEBIT	CREDIT
20-- Dec.	1	Balance	✔				1 5 9 25

ACCOUNT Unemployment Tax Payable—Federal   ACCOUNT NO. 2150

DATE		ITEM	POST. REF.	DEBIT	CREDIT	BALANCE	
						DEBIT	CREDIT
20-- Dec.	1	Balance	✔				1 2 00

ACCOUNT Unemployment Tax Payable—State   ACCOUNT NO. 2160

DATE		ITEM	POST. REF.	DEBIT	CREDIT	BALANCE	
						DEBIT	CREDIT
20-- Dec.	1	Balance	✔				8 1 00

ACCOUNT Health Insurance Premiums Payable ACCOUNT NO. 2170

DATE	ITEM	POST. REF.	DEBIT	CREDIT	BALANCE DEBIT	BALANCE CREDIT

ACCOUNT U.S. Savings Bonds Payable ACCOUNT NO. 2180

DATE	ITEM	POST. REF.	DEBIT	CREDIT	BALANCE DEBIT	BALANCE CREDIT

ACCOUNT United Way Donations Payable ACCOUNT NO. 2190

DATE	ITEM	POST. REF.	DEBIT	CREDIT	BALANCE DEBIT	BALANCE CREDIT

ACCOUNT Dividends Payable ACCOUNT NO. 2195

DATE	ITEM	POST. REF.	DEBIT	CREDIT	BALANCE DEBIT	BALANCE CREDIT
20-- Dec. 1	Balance	✔				7 500 00

ACCOUNT Capital Stock ACCOUNT NO. 3110

DATE	ITEM	POST. REF.	DEBIT	CREDIT	BALANCE DEBIT	BALANCE CREDIT
20-- Dec. 1	Balance	✔				1 0 000 00

ACCOUNT Retained Earnings ACCOUNT NO. 3120

DATE	ITEM	POST. REF.	DEBIT	CREDIT	BALANCE DEBIT	BALANCE CREDIT
20-- Dec. 1	Balance	✔				3 8 718 01

REINFORCEMENT ACTIVITY 2

PART A (continued)

ACCOUNT Dividends — ACCOUNT NO. 3130

DATE	ITEM	POST. REF.	DEBIT	CREDIT	BALANCE DEBIT	BALANCE CREDIT
Dec. 1	Balance	✔			3 0 0 0 00	

ACCOUNT Income Summary — ACCOUNT NO. 3140

DATE	ITEM	POST. REF.	DEBIT	CREDIT	BALANCE DEBIT	BALANCE CREDIT

ACCOUNT Sales — ACCOUNT NO. 4110

DATE	ITEM	POST. REF.	DEBIT	CREDIT	BALANCE DEBIT	BALANCE CREDIT
Dec. 1	Balance	✔				310 1 5 9 00

ACCOUNT Sales Discount — ACCOUNT NO. 4120

DATE	ITEM	POST. REF.	DEBIT	CREDIT	BALANCE DEBIT	BALANCE CREDIT
Dec. 1	Balance	✔			2 5 3 00	

ACCOUNT Sales Returns and Allowances — ACCOUNT NO. 4130

DATE	ITEM	POST. REF.	DEBIT	CREDIT	BALANCE DEBIT	BALANCE CREDIT
Dec. 1	Balance	✔			1 5 6 0 00	

ACCOUNT Purchases — ACCOUNT NO. 5110

DATE	ITEM	POST. REF.	DEBIT	CREDIT	BALANCE DEBIT	BALANCE CREDIT
Dec. 1	Balance	✔			123 5 7 8 10	

REINFORCEMENT ACTIVITY 2

PART A (continued)

ACCOUNT Purchases Discount   ACCOUNT NO. 5120

DATE	ITEM	POST. REF.	DEBIT	CREDIT	BALANCE DEBIT	BALANCE CREDIT
20-- Dec. 1	Balance	✔				1 8 9 7 35

ACCOUNT Purchases Returns and Allowances   ACCOUNT NO. 5130

DATE	ITEM	POST. REF.	DEBIT	CREDIT	BALANCE DEBIT	BALANCE CREDIT
20-- Dec. 1	Balance	✔				2 2 8 4 50

ACCOUNT Advertising Expense   ACCOUNT NO. 6110

DATE	ITEM	POST. REF.	DEBIT	CREDIT	BALANCE DEBIT	BALANCE CREDIT
20-- Dec. 1	Balance	✔			1 6 5 2 3 00	

ACCOUNT Cash Short and Over   ACCOUNT NO. 6115

DATE	ITEM	POST. REF.	DEBIT	CREDIT	BALANCE DEBIT	BALANCE CREDIT
20-- Dec. 1	Balance	✔			8 43	

ACCOUNT Credit Card Fee Expense   ACCOUNT NO. 6120

DATE	ITEM	POST. REF.	DEBIT	CREDIT	BALANCE DEBIT	BALANCE CREDIT
20-- Dec. 1	Balance	✔			1 9 8 2 55	

ACCOUNT Depreciation Expense—Office Equipment   ACCOUNT NO. 6125

DATE	ITEM	POST. REF.	DEBIT	CREDIT	BALANCE DEBIT	BALANCE CREDIT

REINFORCEMENT ACTIVITY 2

PART A (continued)

ACCOUNT Depreciation Expense—Store Equipment ACCOUNT NO. 6130

DATE	ITEM	POST. REF.	DEBIT	CREDIT	BALANCE DEBIT	BALANCE CREDIT

ACCOUNT Insurance Expense ACCOUNT NO. 6135

DATE	ITEM	POST. REF.	DEBIT	CREDIT	BALANCE DEBIT	BALANCE CREDIT

ACCOUNT Miscellaneous Expense ACCOUNT NO. 6140

DATE	ITEM	POST. REF.	DEBIT	CREDIT	BALANCE DEBIT	BALANCE CREDIT
20-- Dec. 1	Balance	✔			1 5 3 8 00	

ACCOUNT Payroll Taxes Expense ACCOUNT NO. 6150

DATE	ITEM	POST. REF.	DEBIT	CREDIT	BALANCE DEBIT	BALANCE CREDIT
20-- Dec. 1	Balance	✔			6 5 8 7 43	

ACCOUNT Rent Expense ACCOUNT NO. 6160

DATE	ITEM	POST. REF.	DEBIT	CREDIT	BALANCE DEBIT	BALANCE CREDIT
20-- Dec. 1	Balance	✔			10 8 0 0 00	

ACCOUNT Repairs Expense ACCOUNT NO. 6165

DATE	ITEM	POST. REF.	DEBIT	CREDIT	BALANCE DEBIT	BALANCE CREDIT
20-- Dec. 1	Balance	✔			2 4 4 6 00	

ACCOUNT Salary Expense   ACCOUNT NO. 6170

DATE	ITEM	POST. REF.	DEBIT	CREDIT	BALANCE DEBIT	BALANCE CREDIT
20-- Dec. 1	Balance	✔			63 3 6 0 00	

ACCOUNT Supplies Expense—Office   ACCOUNT NO. 6175

DATE	ITEM	POST. REF.	DEBIT	CREDIT	BALANCE DEBIT	BALANCE CREDIT

ACCOUNT Supplies Expense—Store   ACCOUNT NO. 6180

DATE	ITEM	POST. REF.	DEBIT	CREDIT	BALANCE DEBIT	BALANCE CREDIT

ACCOUNT Uncollectible Accounts Expense   ACCOUNT NO. 6185

DATE	ITEM	POST. REF.	DEBIT	CREDIT	BALANCE DEBIT	BALANCE CREDIT

ACCOUNT Utilities Expense   ACCOUNT NO. 6190

DATE	ITEM	POST. REF.	DEBIT	CREDIT	BALANCE DEBIT	BALANCE CREDIT
20-- Dec. 1	Balance	✔			8 7 4 5 45	

ACCOUNT Federal Income Tax Expense   ACCOUNT NO. 7105

DATE	ITEM	POST. REF.	DEBIT	CREDIT	BALANCE DEBIT	BALANCE CREDIT
20-- Dec. 1	Balance	✔			10 0 0 0 00	

Study Guide 14

Name	Perfect Score	Your Score
Identifying Accounting Concepts and Practices	20 Pts.	
Analyzing Adjustments on a Work Sheet	12 Pts.	
Analyzing Work Sheet Extensions	38 Pts.	
Total	70 Pts.	

Part One—Identifying Accounting Concepts and Practices

Directions: Place a *T* for True or an *F* for False in the Answers column to show whether each of the following statements is true or false.

Answers

1. A stockholder is an owner of one of more shares of a corporation. (p. 405) 1. _____

2. Owners' equity accounts for a corporation normally are listed under a major chart of accounts division titled Capital Stock. (p. 405) 2. _____

3. Retained earnings are earnings distributed to stockholders. (p. 405) 3. _____

4. A dividend is an amount earned by a corporation and not yet distributed to stockholders. (p. 405) 4. _____

5. A dividends account has a normal debit balance and is increased by a debit. (p. 405) 5. _____

6. A group of persons elected by the stockholders to manage a corporation is called a board of directors. (p. 406) 6. _____

7. A board of directors distributes earnings of a corporation to stockholders by declaring a dividend. (p. 406) 7. _____

8. A declared dividend is classified as an expense. (p. 406) 8. _____

9. The accounts used to record the declaration of a dividend are Dividends Payable and Dividends Expense. (p. 406) 9. _____

10. When a declared dividend is paid, Dividends Payable is debited. (p. 407) 10. _____

11. The purpose of a work sheet is to plan adjustments and summarize the information necessary to prepare financial statements. (p. 409) 11. _____

12. The Prepaid Insurance account is adjusted to show the value of insurance that has been used. (p. 413) 12. _____

13. During a fiscal period, the amount of merchandise on hand increases and decreases. (p. 415) 13. _____

14. Most accounts needing adjustment at the end of a fiscal period have a related temporary account. (p. 416) 14. _____

15. The risk of uncollectible accounts should be recorded as an expense in the same accounting period that the revenue is earned. (p. 419) 15. _____

16. The account Allowance for Uncollectible Accounts is a contra account. (p. 419) 16. _____

17. Many businesses use a percentage of total sales on account to estimate uncollectible accounts expense. (p. 420) 17. _____

18. Assets that will be used for a number of years in the operation of a business are called current assets. (p. 423) 18. _____

19. Accumulated depreciation is the depreciation expense that has been recorded since the purchase of a plant asset. (p. 424) 19. _____

20. Federal income tax is an expense of a corporation. (p. 427) 20. _____

Part Two—Analyzing Adjustments on a Work Sheet

Directions: For each of the following items, select the choice that best completes the statement. Print the letter identifying your choice in the Answers column.

1. The Supplies—Office amount in a work sheet's Trial Balance Debit column represents the value of supplies (A) at the beginning of a fiscal period (B) used during a fiscal period (C) at the beginning of a fiscal period plus office supplies bought during the fiscal period (D) bought during a fiscal period. (p. 411)

   1. _____

2. The two accounts used to adjust the Office Supplies account are (A) Supplies and Purchases (B) Supplies—Office and Income Summary (C) Supplies—Office and Supplies Expense—Office (D) Supplies Expense—Office and Income Summary. (p. 411)

   2. _____

3. The portion of the insurance premiums that has expired during a fiscal period is classified as (A) a liability (B) an asset (C) an expense (D) capital. (p. 413)

   3. _____

4. The two accounts used to adjust the Prepaid Insurance account are (A) Insurance Expense and Income Summary (B) Prepaid Insurance and Insurance Expense (C) Prepaid Insurance and Income Summary (D) Prepaid Insurance Expense and Income Summary. (p. 413)

   4. _____

5. The amount of goods on hand for sale to customers is called (A) supplies inventory (B) purchases (C) sales (D) merchandise inventory. (p. 415)

   5. _____

6. The Merchandise Inventory amount in a work sheet's Trial Balance Debit column represents the merchandise inventory (A) at the end of a fiscal period (B) at the beginning of a fiscal period (C) purchased during a fiscal period (D) available during a fiscal period. (p. 416)

   6. _____

7. The two accounts used to adjust the Merchandise Inventory account are (A) Merchandise Inventory and Supplies (B) Merchandise Inventory and Purchases (C) Merchandise Inventory and Income Summary (D) Merchandise Inventory and Sales. (p. 416)

   7. _____

8. The Income Summary amount in a work sheet's Adjustments Debit column represents the (A) decrease in Merchandise Inventory (B) increase in Merchandise Inventory (C) beginning Merchandise Inventory (D) ending Merchandise Inventory. (p. 416)

   8. _____

9. Recording expenses in the accounting period in which the expenses contribute to earning revenue is an application of the accounting concept (A) Matching Expenses with Revenue (B) Consistent Reporting (C) Historical Cost (D) Adequate Disclosure. (p. 419)

   9. _____

10. The two accounts used to adjust the uncollectible accounts are (A) Uncollectible Accounts Expense and Allowance for Uncollectible Accounts (B) Accounts Receivable and Uncollectible Accounts Expense (C) Accounts Receivable and Allowance for Uncollectible Accounts (D) Accounts Receivable and Accounts Receivable Expense. (p. 421)

    10. _____

11. The two accounts used to adjust the depreciation of store equipment are (A) Store Equipment and Store Equipment Expense (B) Accumulated Depreciation—Store Equipment and Accumulated Depreciation Expense (C) Accumulated Depreciation—Store Equipment and Store Equipment Expense (D) Accumulated Depreciation—Store Equipment and Depreciation Expense—Store Equipment. (p. 425)

    11. _____

12. The two accounts used to record the adjustment for federal income tax are (A) Federal Income Tax Expense and Prepaid Taxes (B) Federal Income Tax Payable and Federal Income Tax Expense (C) Federal Income Tax Expense and Allowance for Federal Tax Expense (D) Federal Income Tax Expense and Federal Income Tax Adjustments. (p. 429)

    12. _____

Part Three—Analyzing Work Sheet Extensions (pp. 432–433)

Directions: For each account listed below, place a check mark in the column to which amounts are extended on a work sheet.

Account Title	Income Statement Debit	Income Statement Credit	Balance Sheet Debit	Balance Sheet Credit
1. Accounts Payable				
2. Accounts Receivable				
3. Accumulated Depreciation—Office Equipment				
4. Accumulated Depreciation—Store Equipment				
5. Advertising Expense				
6. Allowance for Uncollectible Accounts				
7. Capital Stock				
8. Cash				
9. Credit Card Fee Expense				
10. Dividends				
11. Employee Income Tax Payable				
12. Health Insurance Premiums Payable				
13. Income Summary (ending inventory smaller than beginning inventory)				
14. Insurance Expense				
15. Medicare Tax Payable				
16. Merchandise Inventory				
17. Miscellaneous Expense				
18. Office Equipment				
19. Payroll Taxes Expense				
20. Petty Cash				
21. Prepaid Insurance				
22. Purchases				
23. Rent Expense				
24. Retained Earnings				
25. Salary Expense				
26. Sales				
27. Sales Tax Payable				
28. Social Security Tax Payable				
29. Store Equipment				
30. Supplies Expense—Office				
31. Supplies Expense—Store				
32. Supplies—Office				
33. Supplies—Store				
34. Unemployment Tax Payable—Federal				
35. Unemployment Tax Payable—State				
36. United Way Donations Payable				
37. U.S. Savings Bonds Payable				
38. Utilities Expense				

14-1 WORK TOGETHER, p. 408

Journalizing dividends

1.

GENERAL JOURNAL   PAGE 14

	DATE	ACCOUNT TITLE	DOC. NO.	POST. REF.	DEBIT	CREDIT	
1							1
2							2
3							3
4							4
5							5

2.

CASH PAYMENTS JOURNAL

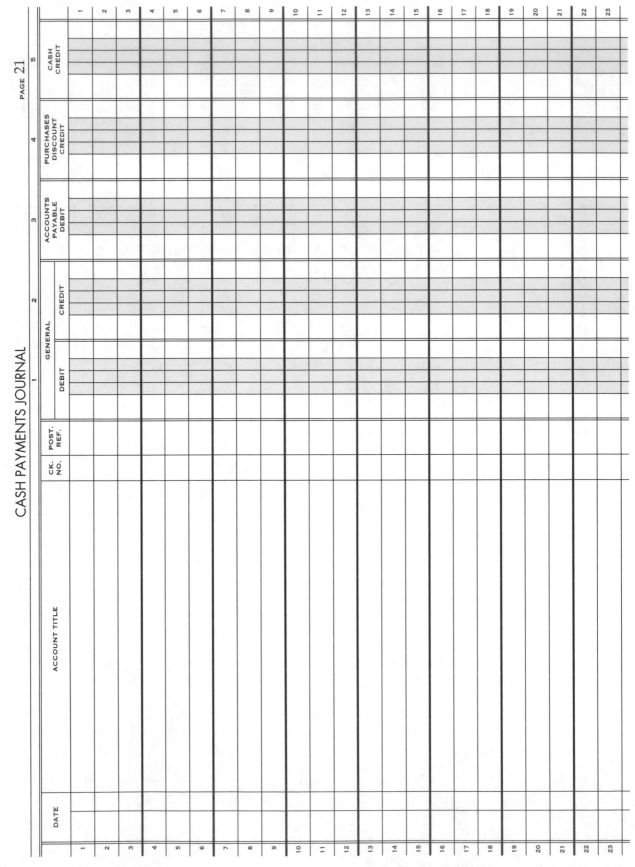

DATE	ACCOUNT TITLE	CK. NO.	POST. REF.	GENERAL DEBIT	GENERAL CREDIT	ACCOUNTS PAYABLE DEBIT	PURCHASES DISCOUNT CREDIT	CASH CREDIT
								1
								2
								3
								4
								5
								6
								7
								8
								9
								10
								11
								12
								13
								14
								15
								16
								17
								18
								19
								20
								21
								22
								23

14-1 ON YOUR OWN, p. 408

Journalizing dividends

1.

GENERAL JOURNAL

	DATE	ACCOUNT TITLE	DOC. NO.	POST. REF.	DEBIT	CREDIT	
1							1
2							2
3							3
4							4
5							5
6							6
7							7
8							8
9							9
10							10
11							11
12							12
13							13
14							14
15							15
16							16
17							17
18							18
19							19
20							20
21							21
22							22
23							23
24							24
25							25
26							26
27							27
28							28
29							29
30							30
31							31
32							32

2.

CASH PAYMENTS JOURNAL

PAGE 24

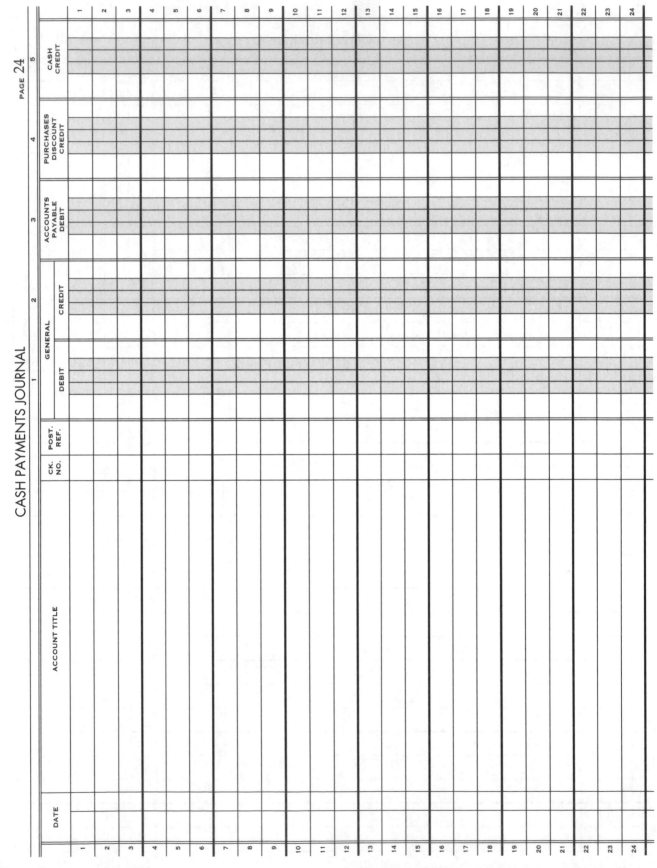

14-2 Beginning an 8-column work sheet for a merchandising business
14-3 Analyzing and recording an adjustment for merchandise inventory
14-4 Analyzing and recording an adjustment for uncollectible accounts expense
14-5 Planning and recording adjustments for depreciation
14-6 Completing an 8-column work sheet for a merchandising business organized as a corporation

Coastal Aquatics
Work Sheet
For Year Ended December 31, 20 - -

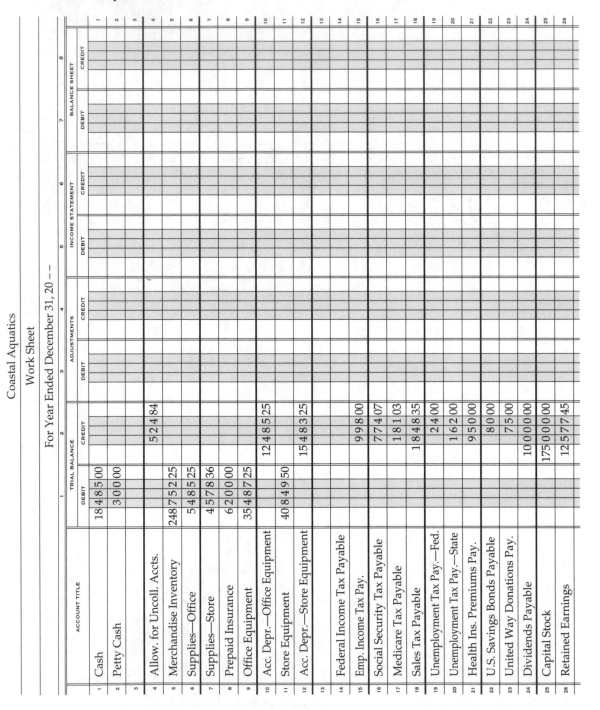

	ACCOUNT TITLE	TRIAL BALANCE DEBIT	TRIAL BALANCE CREDIT
1	Cash	18 485 00	
2	Petty Cash	300 00	
3			
4	Allow. for Uncoll. Accts.		5 24 84
5	Merchandise Inventory	248 752 25	
6	Supplies—Office	5 485 25	
7	Supplies—Store	4 578 36	
8	Prepaid Insurance	6 200 00	
9	Office Equipment	35 487 25	
10	Acc. Depr.—Office Equipment		12 485 25
11	Store Equipment	40 849 50	
12	Acc. Depr.—Store Equipment		15 483 25
13			
14	Federal Income Tax Payable		
15	Emp. Income Tax Pay.		998 00
16	Social Security Tax Payable		774 07
17	Medicare Tax Payable		181 03
18	Sales Tax Payable		1 848 35
19	Unemployment Tax Pay.—Fed.		24 00
20	Unemployment Tax Pay.—State		162 00
21	Health Ins. Premiums Pay.		950 00
22	U.S. Savings Bonds Payable		80 00
23	United Way Donations Pay.		75 00
24	Dividends Payable		10 000 00
25	Capital Stock		175 000 00
26	Retained Earnings		125 774 45

Before Federal Income Tax

Total of Income Statement Credit column _____

Total of Income Statement Debit column _____

Net Income Before Federal Income Tax _____

Coastal Aquatics

Work Sheet

For Year Ended December 31, 20 - -

	ACCOUNT TITLE	1 TRIAL BALANCE DEBIT	2 TRIAL BALANCE CREDIT	3 ADJUSTMENTS DEBIT	4 ADJUSTMENTS CREDIT	5 INCOME STATEMENT DEBIT	6 INCOME STATEMENT CREDIT	7 BALANCE SHEET DEBIT	8 BALANCE SHEET CREDIT	
27	Dividends	21 0 0 0 00								27
28	Income Summary									28
29										29
30	Sales Discount	6 4 8 25								30
31	Sales Returns and Allowances	8 1 5 7 27								31
32										32
33	Purchases Discount		4 6 1 5 25							33
34	Purch. Returns and Allowances		9 4 9 7 00							34
35	Advertising Expense	15 2 8 0 00								35
36	Cash Short and Over	1 2 85								36
37	Credit Card Fee Expense	6 4 8 2 27								37
38	Depr. Exp.—Office Equipment									38
39	Depr. Exp.—Store Equipment									39
40	Insurance Expense									40
41	Miscellaneous Expense	4 5 6 8 97								41
42	Payroll Taxes Expense	16 1 8 4 25								42
43	Rent Expense	24 0 0 0 00								43
44	Salary Expense	204 1 8 0 85								44
45	Supplies Expense—Office									45
46	Supplies Expense—Store									46
47	Uncollectible Accounts Exp.									47
48	Utilities Expense	4 2 6 4 28								48
49	Fed. Income Tax Expense	40 0 0 0 00								49
50										50
51										51
52										52

Federal Income Tax   Rate   Tax

First $50,000   ____   _____

Next $25,000   ____   _____

Next $25,000

_____ − $100,000.00 = _____   ____   _____

Total Federal Income Tax   _____

14-2 Beginning an 8-column work sheet for a merchandising business
14-3 Analyzing and recording an adjustment for merchandise inventory
14-4 Analyzing and recording an adjustment for uncollectible accounts expense
14-5 Planning and recording adjustments for depreciation
14-6 Completing an 8-column work sheet for a merchandising business organized as a corporation

Sonoma Treasures
Work Sheet
For Year Ended December 31, 20 – –

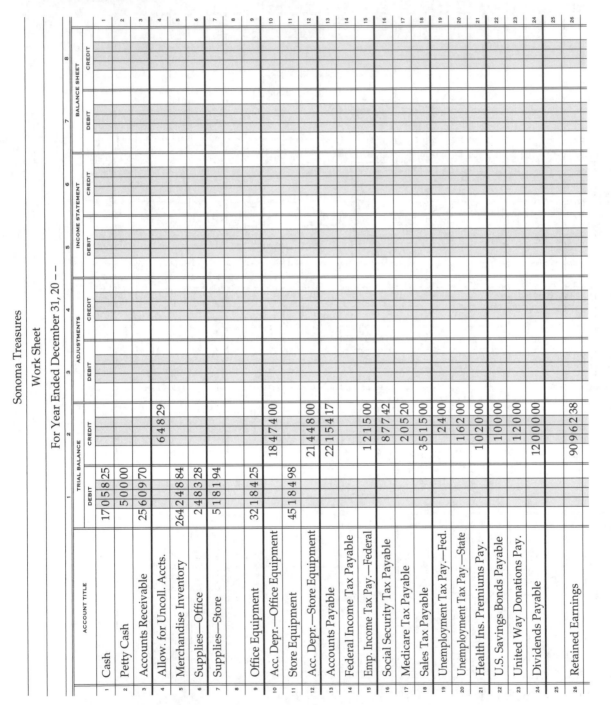

	ACCOUNT TITLE	TRIAL BALANCE DEBIT	TRIAL BALANCE CREDIT	ADJUSTMENTS DEBIT	ADJUSTMENTS CREDIT	INCOME STATEMENT DEBIT	INCOME STATEMENT CREDIT	BALANCE SHEET DEBIT	BALANCE SHEET CREDIT
1	Cash	17 058 25							
2	Petty Cash	500 00							
3	Accounts Receivable	25 609 70							
4	Allow. for Uncoll. Accts.		648 29						
5	Merchandise Inventory	264 248 84							
6	Supplies—Office	2 483 28							
7	Supplies—Store	5 181 94							
8									
9	Office Equipment	32 184 25							
10	Acc. Depr.—Office Equipment		18 474 00						
11	Store Equipment	45 184 98							
12	Acc. Depr.—Store Equipment		21 448 00						
13	Accounts Payable		22 154 17						
14	Federal Income Tax Payable								
15	Emp. Income Tax Pay.—Federal		1 215 00						
16	Social Security Tax Payable		877 42						
17	Medicare Tax Payable		205 20						
18	Sales Tax Payable		3 515 00						
19	Unemployment Tax Pay.—Fed.		24 00						
20	Unemployment Tax Pay.—State		162 00						
21	Health Ins. Premiums Pay.		1 020 00						
22	U.S. Savings Bonds Payable		100 00						
23	United Way Donations Pay.		120 00						
24	Dividends Payable		1 200 00						
25									
26	Retained Earnings		90 962 38						

Before Federal Income Tax
Total of Income Statement Credit column _____
Total of Income Statement Debit column _____
Net Income Before Federal Income Tax _____

14-2, 14-3, 14-4, 14-5, and 14-6 ON YOUR OWN (concluded)

Sonoma Treasures

Work Sheet

For Year Ended December 31, 20 – –

	ACCOUNT TITLE	TRIAL BALANCE		ADJUSTMENTS		INCOME STATEMENT		BALANCE SHEET	
		DEBIT	CREDIT	DEBIT	CREDIT	DEBIT	CREDIT	DEBIT	CREDIT
27	Dividends	84 000 00							
28	Income Summary								
29	Sales		925 183 20						
30									
31	Sales Returns and Allowances	6 942 28							
32	Purchases	482 101 66							
33	Purchases Discount		4 215 35						
34	Purch. Returns and Allowances		8 148 99						
35	Advertising Expense	13 250 00							
36	Cash Short and Over	1 11 18							
37	Credit Card Fee Expense	12 451 27							
38	Depr. Exp.—Office Equipment								
39	Depr. Exp.—Store Equipment								
40	Insurance Expense								
41	Miscellaneous Expense	8 402 00							
42	Payroll Taxes Expense	21 482 88							
43									
44	Salary Expense	234 182 25							
45	Supplies Expense—Office								
46	Supplies Expense—Store								
47	Uncollectible Accounts Exp.								
48	Utilities Expense	6 482 99							
49	Fed. Income Tax Expense	16 000 00							
50									
51									
52									

Federal Income Tax	Rate	Tax
First $50,000	____	_____
Next $25,000	____	_____
_____ − $75,000.00 = _____	____	_____
Total Federal Income Tax		_____

Planning and recording adjustments for depreciation

1.

Original Cost _____
Estimated Salvage Value _____
Estimated Total Depreciation Expense _____ $\div$ ____ Years of Estimated Useful Life = _____ Annual Depreciation Expense

2.

Original Cost _____
Depreciation: Year 1 _____
Year 2 _____
Book Value _____

Planning and recording adjustments for depreciation

1.

Original Cost _____
Estimated Salvage Value _____
Estimated Total Depreciation Expense _____ $\div$ ____ Years of Estimated Useful Life = _____ Annual Depreciation Expense

2.

Original Cost _____
Depreciation: Year 1 _____
Year 2 _____
Year 3 _____
Book Value _____

Name _____ Date _____ Class _____

Journalizing dividends

1.

GENERAL JOURNAL

PAGE 17

	DATE		ACCOUNT TITLE	DOC. NO.	POST. REF.	DEBIT	CREDIT	
1								1
2								2
3								3
4								4
5								5
6								6
7								7

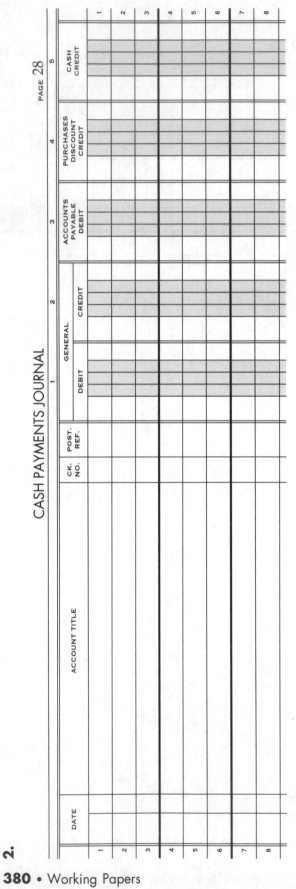

2.

14-2 Beginning an 8-column work sheet for a merchandising business

14-3 Analyzing and recording a merchandise inventory adjustment on a work sheet

14-4 Analyzing and recording an allowance for uncollectible accounts adjustment on a work sheet

14-5 Planning and recording adjustments for depreciation

14-6 Calculating federal income tax and completing an 8-column work sheet for a merchandising business

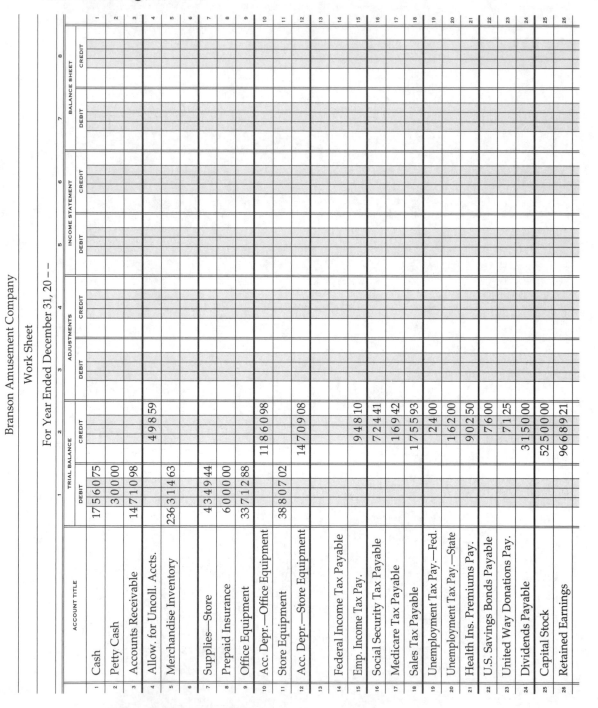

Branson Amusement Company
Work Sheet
For Year Ended December 31, 20 - -

	ACCOUNT TITLE	TRIAL BALANCE DEBIT	TRIAL BALANCE CREDIT
1	Cash	17 5 6 0 75	
2	Petty Cash	3 0 0 00	
3	Accounts Receivable	14 7 1 0 98	
4	Allow. for Uncoll. Accts.		4 9 8 59
5	Merchandise Inventory	236 3 1 4 63	
6			
7	Supplies—Store	4 3 4 9 44	
8	Prepaid Insurance	6 0 0 0 00	
9	Office Equipment	33 7 1 2 88	
10	Acc. Depr.—Office Equipment		11 8 6 0 98
11	Store Equipment	38 8 0 7 02	
12	Acc. Depr.—Store Equipment		14 7 0 9 08
13			
14	Federal Income Tax Payable		
15	Emp. Income Tax Pay.		9 4 8 10
16	Social Security Tax Payable		7 2 4 41
17	Medicare Tax Payable		1 6 9 42
18	Sales Tax Payable		17 5 5 93
19	Unemployment Tax Pay.—Fed.		2 4 00
20	Unemployment Tax Pay.—State		1 6 2 00
21	Health Ins. Premiums Pay.		9 0 2 50
22	U.S. Savings Bonds Payable		7 6 00
23	United Way Donations Pay.		7 1 25
24	Dividends Payable		3 1 5 0 00
25	Capital Stock		52 5 0 0 00
26	Retained Earnings		96 6 8 9 21

Before Federal Income Tax

Total of Income Statement Credit column _____

Total of Income Statement Debit column _____

Net Income Before Federal Income Tax _____

14-2, 14-3, 14-4, 14-5, and 14-6 APPLICATION PROBLEMS (concluded)

Branson Amusement Company

Work Sheet

For Year Ended December 31, 20 – –

	TRIAL BALANCE		ADJUSTMENTS		INCOME STATEMENT		BALANCE SHEET	
ACCOUNT TITLE	DEBIT	CREDIT	DEBIT	CREDIT	DEBIT	CREDIT	DEBIT	CREDIT
27 Dividends	12 6 0 0 00							
28 Income Summary								
29 Sales		843 5 3 6 68						
30 Sales Discount	25 1 5 25							
31 Sales Returns and Allowances	8 4 8 2 25							
32 Purchases	369 7 2 4 80							
33								
34 Purch. Returns and Allowances		9 0 2 2 15						
35 Advertising Expense	14 5 1 6 00							
36 Cash Short and Over	7 72							
37 Credit Card Fee Expense	6 1 5 8 15							
38 Depr. Exp.—Office Equipment								
39 Depr. Exp.—Store Equipment								
40 Insurance Expense								
41 Miscellaneous Expense	4 3 4 5 00							
42 Payroll Taxes Expense	15 3 7 5 03							
43 Rent Expense	22 8 0 0 00							
44								
45 Supplies Expense—Office								
46 Supplies Expense—Store								
47 Uncollectible Accounts Exp.								
48 Utilities Expense	4 0 5 1 06							
49 Fed. Income Tax Expense	48 0 0 0 00							
50								
51								
52								

Federal Income Tax	Rate	Tax
First $50,000	_____	_____
Next $25,000	_____	_____
Next $25,000	_____	_____
_____ − $100,000.00 = _____	_____	_____
Total Federal Income Tax		_____

APPLICATION PROBLEM, p. 439

Planning and recording adjustments for depreciation

Wave Diving Company scuba testing equipment:

1.

Original Cost   _____
Estimated Salvage Value   _____
Estimated Total Depreciation Expense   _____ ÷ _____ Years of Estimated Useful Life = _____ Annual Depreciation Expense

2.

Original Cost   _____
Depreciation: Year 1   _____
                Year 2   _____
Book Value   _____

Preparing an 8-column work sheet for a merchandising business

Carol's Closet

Work Sheet

For Year Ended December 31, 20 – –

	ACCOUNT TITLE	TRIAL BALANCE DEBIT	TRIAL BALANCE CREDIT	ADJUSTMENTS DEBIT	ADJUSTMENTS CREDIT	INCOME STATEMENT DEBIT	INCOME STATEMENT CREDIT	BALANCE SHEET DEBIT	BALANCE SHEET CREDIT
1	Cash	28 548 25							
2	Petty Cash	50 0 00							
3	Accounts Receivable	32 518 28							
4	Allow. for Uncoll. Accts.		1 55 25						
5	Merchandise Inventory	229 282 36							
6	Supplies—Office	6 128 25							
7	Supplies—Store	4 218 36							
8	Prepaid Insurance	12 000 00							
9	Office Equipment	28 187 25							
10	Acc. Depr.—Office Equipment		5 158 25						
11	Store Equipment	42 841 05							
12	Acc. Depr.—Store Equipment		12 483 25						
13	Accounts Payable		21 543 20						
14	Federal Income Tax Payable								
15	Emp. Income Tax Pay.		1 248 25						
16	Social Security Tax Payable		8 22 00						
17	Medicare Tax Payable		1 92 24						
18	Sales Tax Payable		2 415 25						
19	Unemployment Tax Pay.—Fed.		33 60						
20	Unemployment Tax Pay.—State		2 26 80						
21	Health Ins. Premiums Pay.		9 60 00						
22	U.S. Savings Bonds Payable		75 00						
23	United Way Donations Pay.		1 00 00						
24	Dividends Payable		11 000 00						
25	Capital Stock		55 000 00						
26	Retained Earnings		172 980 13						

Before Federal Income Tax

Total of Income Statement Credit column _____

Total of Income Statement Debit column _____

Net Income Before Federal Income Tax _____

14-7 MASTERY PROBLEM (concluded)

Carol's Closet

Work Sheet

For Year Ended December 31, 20 - -

	ACCOUNT TITLE	TRIAL BALANCE DEBIT	TRIAL BALANCE CREDIT	ADJUSTMENTS DEBIT	ADJUSTMENTS CREDIT	INCOME STATEMENT DEBIT	INCOME STATEMENT CREDIT	BALANCE SHEET DEBIT	BALANCE SHEET CREDIT
27	Dividends	44 0 0 0 00							
28	Income Summary								
29	Sales		948 4 8 4 25						
30	Sales Discount	3 1 5 4 15							
31	Sales Returns and Allowances	7 1 4 8 15							
32	Purchases	489 3 3 5 54							
33	Purchases Discount		5 0 1 5 25						
34	Purch. Returns and Allowances		7 0 5 8 05						
35	Advertising Expense	16 0 2 5 00							
36	Cash Short and Over	7 25							
37	Credit Card Fee Expense	7 0 1 5 95							
38	Depr. Exp.—Office Equipment								
39	Depr. Exp.—Store Equipment								
40	Insurance Expense								
41	Miscellaneous Expense	5 0 9 8 00							
42	Payroll Taxes Expense	18 1 5 2 25							
43	Rent Expense	28 0 0 0 00							
44	Salary Expense	193 9 7 1 80							
45	Supplies Expense—Office								
46	Supplies Expense—Store								
47	Uncollectible Accounts Exp.								
48	Utilities Expense	4 8 1 8 88							
49	Fed. Income Tax Expense	44 0 0 0 00							
50									
51									
52									

Federal Income Tax	Rate	Tax
First $50,000	____	_____
Next $25,000	____	_____
Next $25,000	____	_____
_____ − $100,000.00 = _____	____	_____
Total Federal Income Tax		_____

Preparing a 10-column work sheet for a merchandising business

Hillside Ski Shop

Work Sheet

For Year Ended December 31, 20– –

	ACCOUNT TITLE	TRIAL BALANCE DEBIT	TRIAL BALANCE CREDIT	ADJUSTMENTS DEBIT	ADJUSTMENTS CREDIT
1	Cash	14 2 5 8 25			
2	Petty Cash	2 5 0 00			
3	Accounts Receivable	16 4 8 5 25			
4	Allow. for Uncoll. Accts.		2 5 1 25		
5	Merchandise Inventory	169 1 5 8 66			
6	Supplies—Office	3 1 8 4 67			
7	Supplies—Store	2 4 1 5 29			
8	Prepaid Insurance	12 0 0 0 00			
9	Office Equipment	28 1 8 7 25			
10	Acc. Depr.—Office Equipment		12 1 8 2 00		
11	Store Equipment	32 1 8 4 84			
12	Acc. Depr.—Store Equipment		16 1 8 4 00		
13	Accounts Payable		12 4 8 2 36		
14	Federal Income Tax Payable				
15	Emp. Income Tax Pay.—Federal		1 2 4 8 25		
16	Social Security Tax Payable		5 1 1 83		
17	Medicare Tax Payable		1 1 9 70		
18	Sales Tax Payable		1 2 1 5 25		
19	Unemployment Tax Pay.—Fed.		2 5 60		
20	Unemployment Tax Pay.—State		1 7 2 80		
21	Health Ins. Premiums Pay.		5 6 0 00		
22	U.S. Savings Bonds Payable		2 0 00		
23	United Way Donations Pay.		6 0 00		
24	Dividends Payable		12 0 0 0 00		
25	Capital Stock		150 0 0 0 00		
26	Retained Earnings		22 1 0 8 43		

Before Federal Income Tax
Total of Income Statement Credit column _____
Total of Income Statement Debit column _____
Net Income Before Federal Income Tax _____

14-8 CHALLENGE PROBLEM (continued)

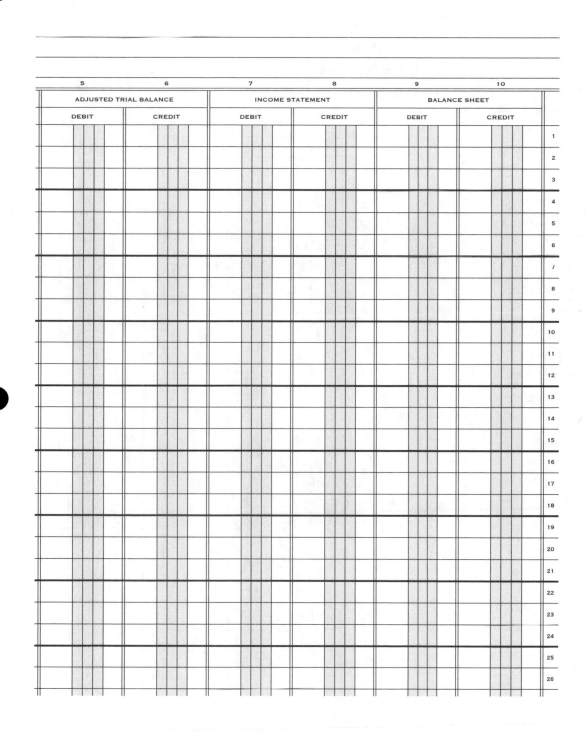

Hillside Ski Shop

Work Sheet

For Year Ended December 31, 20 – –

	ACCOUNT TITLE	TRIAL BALANCE		ADJUSTMENTS	
		DEBIT	CREDIT	DEBIT	CREDIT
27	Dividends	48 0 0 0 00			
28	Income Summary				
29	Sales		508 2 1 8 88		
30	Sales Discount	1 5 4 8 81			
31	Sales Returns and Allowances	2 1 8 4 94			
32	Purchases	204 8 4 0 10			
33	Purchases Discount		2 4 8 9 05		
34	Purch. Returns and Allowances		3 1 4 8 08		
35	Advertising Expense	12 5 0 0 00			
36	Cash Short and Over	8 04			
37	Credit Card Fee Expense	2 4 8 4 10			
38	Depr. Exp.—Office Equipment				
39	Depr. Exp.—Store Equipment				
40	Insurance Expense				
41	Miscellaneous Expense	4 1 5 0 00			
42	Payroll Taxes Expense	12 1 8 4 20			
43	Rent Expense	24 0 0 0 00			
44	Salary Expense	130 1 5 4 20			
45	Supplies Expense—Office				
46	Supplies Expense—Store				
47	Uncollectible Accounts Exp.				
48	Utilities Expense	4 8 1 8 88			
49	Fed. Income Tax Expense	18 0 0 0 00			
50					
51					
52					

Federal Income Tax	Rate	Tax
First $50,000	____	_____
Next $25,000	____	_____
_____ – $75,000.00 = _____	____	_____
Total Federal Income Tax		_____

14-8 CHALLENGE PROBLEM (concluded)

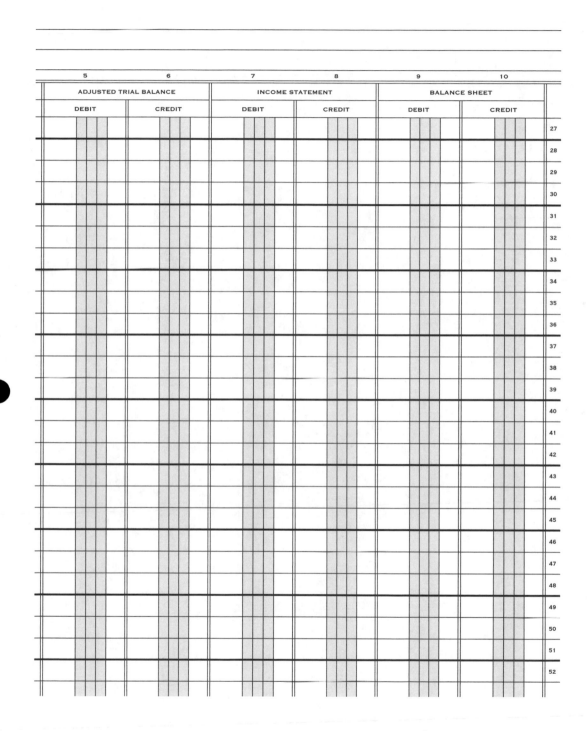

	5	6	7	8	9	10	
	ADJUSTED TRIAL BALANCE		INCOME STATEMENT		BALANCE SHEET		
	DEBIT	CREDIT	DEBIT	CREDIT	DEBIT	CREDIT	
							27
							28
							29
							30
							31
							32
							33
							34
							35
							36
							37
							38
							39
							40
							41
							42
							43
							44
							45
							46
							47
							48
							49
							50
							51
							52

Study Guide 15

Name	Perfect Score	Your Score
Identifying Accounting Terms	11 Pts.	
Analyzing Acceptable Component Percentages	8 Pts.	
Analyzing Financial Statements for a Merchandising Business	20 Pts.	
Total	39 Pts.	

Part One—Identifying Accounting Terms

Directions: Select the one term in Column I that best fits each definition in Column II. Print the letter identifying your choice in the Answers column.

Column I	Column II	Answers
A. cost of merchandise sold	**1.** Total sales less sales discount and sales returns and allowances. (p. 449)	1. _____
B. current liabilities	**2.** The original price of all merchandise sold during a fiscal period. (p. 450)	2. _____
C. earnings per share	**3.** The revenue remaining after cost of merchandise sold has been deducted. (p. 452)	3. _____
D. financial ratio	**4.** A comparison between two items of financial information. (p. 459)	4. _____
E. gross profit on sales	**5.** The amount of net income after federal income tax belonging to a single share of stock. (p. 459)	5. _____
F. long-term liabilities	**6.** The relationship between the market value per share and earnings per share of a stock. (p. 459)	6. _____
G. net sales	**7.** A financial statement that shows changes in a corporation's ownership for a fiscal period. (p. 461)	7. _____
H. par value	**8.** A value assigned to a share of stock and printed on the stock certificate. (p. 461)	8. _____
I. price-earnings ratio	**9.** Liabilities due within a short time, usually within a year. (p. 467)	9. _____
J. statement of stockholders' equity	**10.** Liabilities owed for more than a year. (p. 467)	10. _____
K. supporting schedule	**11.** A report prepared to give details about an item on a principal financial statement. (p. 470)	11. _____

Part Two—Analyzing Acceptable Component Percentages

Directions: For each of the income statement component percentages given, write a *U* in the Answers column if it is Unacceptable and write an *A* in the Answers column if it is Acceptable. (pp. 455–456)

Acceptable Component Percentages	
Sales	100%
Cost of merchandise sold	Not more than 48.6%
Gross profit on sales	Not less than 51.4%
Total expenses	Not more than 34.9%
Net income	Not less than 16.5%

Answers

1. The component percentage for total expenses is 42.8% this year.

1. _____

2. The component percentage for cost of merchandise sold is 51.0% this year.

2. _____

3. The component percentage for gross profit on sales is 52.8% this year.

3. _____

4. The component percentage for total expenses is 34.3% this year.

4. _____

5. The component percentage for gross profit on sales is 51.4% this year.

5. _____

6. The component percentage for net income is 17.0% this year.

6. _____

7. The component percentage for cost of merchandise sold is 48.7% this year.

7. _____

8. The component percentage for net income is 10.4% this year.

8. _____

Part Three—Analyzing Financial Statements for a Merchandising Business

Directions: Place a *T* for True or an *F* for False in the Answers column to show whether each of the following statements is true or false.

Answers

1. Financial statements provide the primary source of information needed by owners and managers to make decisions on the future activity of a business. (p. 446)

   1. _____

2. Reporting financial information the same way from one fiscal period to the next is an application of the accounting concept Adequate Disclosure. (p. 446)

   2. _____

3. An income statement is used to report a business's financial progress. (p. 448)

   3. _____

4. An income statement for a merchandising business has three main sections: revenue section, cost of merchandise sold section, and expenses section. (p. 448)

   4. _____

5. Cost of merchandise sold is also known as cost of goods sold. (p. 450)

   5. _____

6. Revenue less cost of merchandise sold equals net income. (p. 452)

   6. _____

7. Calculating a ratio between gross profit on sales and net sales enables management to compare its performance to prior fiscal periods. (p. 452)

   7. _____

8. Total expenses on an income statement are deducted from the gross profit on sales to find net income before federal income tax. (p. 453)

   8. _____

9. For a merchandising business, every sales dollar reported on the income statement includes only three components: gross profit on sales, total expenses, and net income. (p. 455)

   9. _____

10. When a business's expenses are less than the gross profit on sales, the difference is known as a net loss. (p. 457)

   10. _____

11. Increasing sales revenue while keeping cost of merchandise sold the same will increase gross profit on sales. (p. 458)

   11. _____

12. Most businesses correct an unacceptable component percentage for gross profit by simply increasing the markup on merchandise purchased for sale because an increased selling price will always increase profit. (p. 458)

   12. _____

13. Individual amounts reported on an income statement have little meaning without being compared to another amount. (p. 459)

   13. _____

14. A statement of stockholders' equity contains two major sections: (1) capital stock and (2) retained earnings. (p. 461)

   14. _____

15. The beginning balance of the capital stock account is the amount of capital stock issued at the beginning of the year. (p. 461)

   15. _____

16. The amounts in the capital stock section of the statement of stockholders' equity are obtained from the general ledger account, Capital Stock. (p. 461)

   16. _____

17. Net income is shown on the last line of a statement of stockholders' equity. (p. 462)

   17. _____

18. Some income may be distributed as dividends to provide stockholders with a return on their investments. (p. 462)

   18. _____

19. Data needed to prepare the liabilities section of a balance sheet are obtained from a work sheet. (p. 467)

   19. _____

20. Ruled double lines across both amount columns below the Assets section and below the Stockholders' Equity section show that the assets equal liabilities plus owners' equity. (p. 468)

   20. _____

Memory Hooks

We learned a number of things we can do to improve our ability to remember. When we concentrate on several specific memory techniques, we call them *memory hooks*.

Acronyms

You may wish to remember a list of items from a textbook. One way to remember names or words is to use an acronym, a word formed by using the first letter or so of each of the words you want to remember.

For example, you may want to remember the names of the five Great Lakes—Huron, Ontario, Michigan, Erie, and Superior. The first letter of each of their names spells the word *homes*. By remembering this word, you will be able to remember the names of the lakes.

You may also use the first letter or so of the word you want to remember as the first letter of each word in a phrase or sentence. For example, you might be required to remember the Seven Wonders of the Ancient World: the *P*yramids, the *H*anging Gardens, the statue of *Z*eus, the *M*ausoleum, the *C*olossus, the Temple of *D*iana, and the *L*ighthouse. It might be difficult to remember all of them, but you can probably recall them if you remember a short, absurd sentence: *Please Hand Zeek My Cat's Dog License*. The first letter of each word is the same as a key word in each of the seven wonders.

Chaining

You can use a memory technique called *chaining* to link isolated items. To chain, you should make a mental connection between the first item and the second, between the second item and the third, and so on. For example, you might want to remember to make an appointment with the doctor, schedule an auto repair, and buy tickets for the theater. To connect the first two, you could visualize your doctor operating on your car. To connect the second and third, you could visualize your car parked in the theater lobby. When you remember one item in the chain, the next item will be cued.

Personalize Your Memory Hooks

You may be able to use these techniques just as they are, or you may wish to change them or develop new ones to meet your own personal needs. Employ any device that makes remembering easier for you. It is fun, and it will help you in your work now and in the future.

15-1 WORK TOGETHER, p. 454

Preparing an income statement for a merchandising business

Interstate Tires, Inc.

Work Sheet

For Year Ended December 31, 20 – –

	ACCOUNT TITLE	TRIAL BALANCE DEBIT	TRIAL BALANCE CREDIT	ADJUSTMENTS DEBIT	ADJUSTMENTS CREDIT	INCOME STATEMENT DEBIT	INCOME STATEMENT CREDIT	BALANCE SHEET DEBIT	BALANCE SHEET CREDIT	
1	Cash	12848 00						12848 00		1
2	Petty Cash	300 00						300 00		2
3	Accounts Receivable	18438 90						18438 90		3
4	Allow. for Uncoll. Accts.		847 29		(e) 1680 00				2527 29	4
5	Merchandise Inventory	198480 33			(d) 9481 08			188999 25		5
6	Supplies—Office	3341 58			(a) 2486 99			854 59		6
7	Supplies—Store	4248 96			(b) 2948 28			1300 68		7
8	Prepaid Insurance	9000 00			(c) 6000 00			3000 00		8
9	Office Equipment	18486 38						18486 38		9
10	Acc. Depr.—Office Equip.		9485 25		(f) 4260 00				13745 25	10
11	Store Equipment	32184 07						32184 07		11
12	Acc. Depr.—Store Equip.		18486 45		(g) 5750 00				24236 45	12
13	Accounts Payable		16107 08						16107 08	13
14	Federal Income Tax Payable				(h) 2603 79				2603 79	14
15	Emp. Income Tax Payable		840 00						840 00	15
16	Social Security Tax Payable		529 98						529 98	16
17	Medicare Tax Payable		123 95						123 95	17
18	Sales Tax Payable		1848 25						1848 25	18
19	Unemploy. Tax Payable—Fed.		32 00						32 00	19
20	Unemploy. Tax Payable—State		216 00						216 00	20
21	Health Insur. Premiums Payable		620 00						620 00	21
22	U.S. Savings Bonds Payable		35 00						35 00	22
23	United Way Donations Payable		40 00						40 00	23
24	Dividends Payable		2200 00						2200 00	24
25	Capital Stock		110000 00						110000 00	25
26	Retained Earnings		46599 48						46599 48	26

(Note: Work sheet is continued on next page.)

Interstate Tires, Inc.

Work Sheet

For Year Ended December 31, 20 - -

	ACCOUNT TITLE	TRIAL BALANCE DEBIT	TRIAL BALANCE CREDIT	ADJUSTMENTS DEBIT	ADJUSTMENTS CREDIT	INCOME STATEMENT DEBIT	INCOME STATEMENT CREDIT	BALANCE SHEET DEBIT	BALANCE SHEET CREDIT	
27	Dividends	8 8 0 0 00						8 8 0 0 00		27
28	Income Summary			(d) 9 4 8 1 08		9 4 8 1 08				28
29	Sales		5 4 8 9 8 9 25				5 4 8 9 8 9 25			29
30	Sales Discount	6 6 1 69				6 6 1 69				30
31	Sales Returns and Allowances	3 5 1 2 84				3 5 1 2 84				31
32	Purchases	2 7 8 4 5 2 39				2 7 8 4 5 2 39				32
33	Purchases Discount		1 8 4 5 78				1 8 4 5 78			33
34	Purch. Returns and Allowances		3 5 4 8 65				3 5 4 8 65			34
35	Advertising Expense	9 3 2 0 00				9 3 2 0 00				35
36	Cash Short and Over	5 27				5 27				36
37	Credit Card Fee Expense	9 4 5 4 45				9 4 5 4 45				37
38	Depr. Exp.—Office Equipment			(f) 4 2 6 0 00		4 2 6 0 00				38
39	Depr. Exp.—Store Equipment			(g) 5 7 5 0 00		5 7 5 0 00				39
40	Insurance Expense			(c) 6 0 0 0 00		6 0 0 0 00				40
41	Miscellaneous Expense	6 4 8 0 00				6 4 8 0 00				41
42	Payroll Taxes Expense	9 3 1 5 66				9 3 1 5 66				42
43	Rent Expense	1 8 0 0 0 00				1 8 0 0 0 00				43
44	Salary Expense	1 0 2 5 7 6 00				1 0 2 5 7 6 00				44
45	Supplies Expense—Office			(a) 2 4 8 6 99		2 4 8 6 99				45
46	Supplies Expense—Store			(b) 2 9 4 8 28		2 9 4 8 28				46
47	Uncollectible Accounts Expense			(e) 1 6 8 0 00		1 6 8 0 00				47
48	Utilities Expense	6 4 8 7 89				6 4 8 7 89				48
49	Federal Income Tax Expense	1 2 0 0 0 00		(h) 2 6 0 3 79		1 4 6 0 3 79				49
50		7 6 2 3 9 4 41	7 6 2 3 9 4 41	3 5 2 1 0 14	3 5 2 1 0 14	4 9 1 4 7 6 33	5 5 4 3 8 3 68	2 8 5 2 1 1 87	2 2 2 3 0 4 52	50
51	Net Income after Fed. Income Tax					6 2 9 0 7 35			6 2 9 0 7 35	51
52						5 5 4 3 8 3 68	5 5 4 3 8 3 68	2 8 5 2 1 1 87	2 8 5 2 1 1 87	52
53										53

WORK TOGETHER (concluded)

1., 2.

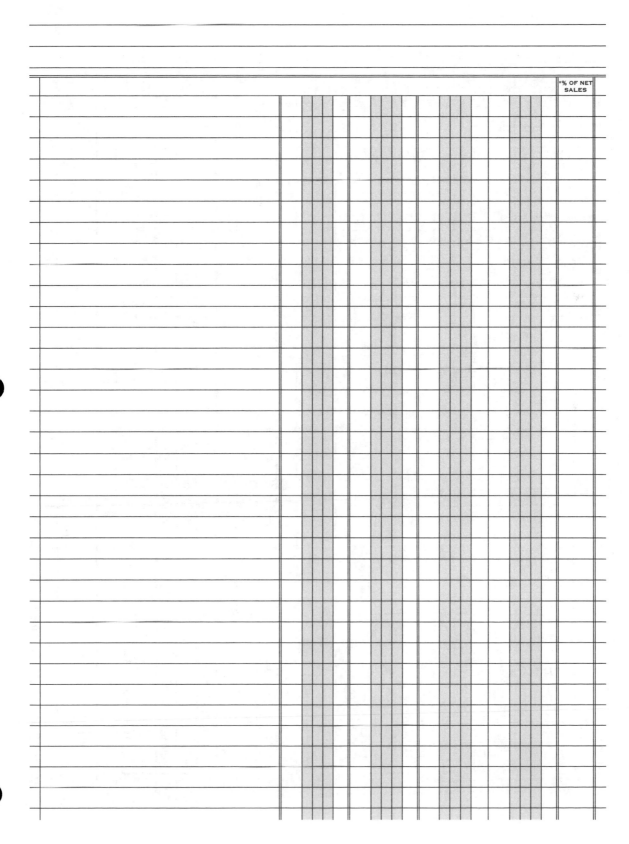

*Rounded to the nearest 0.1%

Preparing an income statement for a merchandising business

Osborn Corporation

Work Sheet

For Year Ended December 31, 20 - -

	ACCOUNT TITLE	TRIAL BALANCE DEBIT	TRIAL BALANCE CREDIT	ADJUSTMENTS DEBIT	ADJUSTMENTS CREDIT	INCOME STATEMENT DEBIT	INCOME STATEMENT CREDIT	BALANCE SHEET DEBIT	BALANCE SHEET CREDIT
1	Cash	15 218 25						15 218 25	
2	Petty Cash	2 500 00						2 500 00	
3	Accounts Receivable	22 485 28						22 485 28	
4	Allow. for Uncoll. Accts.		1 052 05		(e) 1 720 00				2 772 05
5	Merchandise Inventory	228 189 80			(d) 8 424 00			219 765 80	
6	Supplies—Office	3 158 15			(a) 2 749 00			409 15	
7	Supplies—Store	3 819 74			(b) 3 043 35			776 39	
8	Prepaid Insurance	8 000 00			(c) 7 200 00			800 00	
9	Office Equipment	22 183 08						22 183 08	
10	Acc. Depr.—Office Equip.		8 483 00		(f) 4 580 00				13 063 00
11	Store Equipment	45 184 98						45 184 98	
12	Acc. Depr.—Store Equip.		11 250 00		(g) 4 890 00				16 140 00
13	Accounts Payable		22 154 17						22 154 17
14	Federal Income Tax Payable				(h) 1 541 19				1 541 19
15	Emp. Income Tax Payable		1 025 00						1 025 00
16	Social Security Tax Payable		753 80						753 80
17	Medicare Tax Payable		176 29						176 29
18	Sales Tax Payable		2 487 00						2 487 00
19	Unemploy. Tax Payable—Fed.		24 00						24 00
20	Unemploy. Tax Payable—State		162 00						162 00
21	Health Insur. Premiums Payable		800 00						800 00
22	U.S. Savings Bonds Payable		60 00						60 00
23	United Way Donations Payable		70 00						70 00
24	Dividends Payable		7 500 00						7 500 00
25	Capital Stock		200 000 00						200 000 00
26	Retained Earnings		19 735 06						19 735 06

(Note: Work sheet is continued on next page.)

15-1 ON YOUR OWN (continued)

Osborn Corporation

Work Sheet

For Year Ended December 31, 20 - -

| | TRIAL BALANCE | | ADJUSTMENTS | | INCOME STATEMENT | | BALANCE SHEET | |
ACCOUNT TITLE	DEBIT	CREDIT	DEBIT	CREDIT	DEBIT	CREDIT	DEBIT	CREDIT
27 Dividends	30 000 00						30 000 00	
28 Income Summary			(d) 8 424 00		8 424 00			
29 Sales		704 809 54				704 809 54		
30 Sales Discount	6 15 25				6 15 25			
31 Sales Returns and Allowances	4 789 84				4 789 84			
32 Purchases	369 485 04				369 485 04			
33 Purchases Discount		3 05 89				3 05 89		
34 Purch. Returns and Allowances		4 800 85				4 800 85		
35 Advertising Expense	8 500 00				8 500 00			
36 Cash Short and Over	9 33				9 33			
37 Credit Card Fee Expense	12 458 22				12 458 22			
38 Depr. Exp.—Office Equipment			(f) 4 580 00		4 580 00			
39 Depr. Exp.—Store Equipment			(g) 4 890 00		4 890 00			
40 Insurance Expense			(c) 7 200 00		7 200 00			
41 Miscellaneous Expense	7 480 00				7 480 00			
42 Payroll Taxes Expense	13 130 64				13 130 64			
43 Rent Expense	24 000 00				24 000 00			
44 Salary Expense	145 896 00				145 896 00			
45 Supplies Expense—Office			(a) 2 749 00		2 749 00			
46 Supplies Expense—Store			(b) 3 043 35		3 043 35			
47 Uncollectible Accounts Expense			(e) 1 720 00		1 720 00			
48 Utilities Expense	7 548 05				7 548 05			
49 Federal Income Tax Expense	16 000 00		(h) 1 541 19		17 541 19			
50	988 401 65	988 401 65	34 147 54	34 147 54	644 059 91	712 669 28	357 072 93	288 463 56
51 Net Income after Fed. Income Tax					68 609 37			68 609 37
52					712 669 28	712 669 28	357 072 93	357 072 93
53								

1., 2.

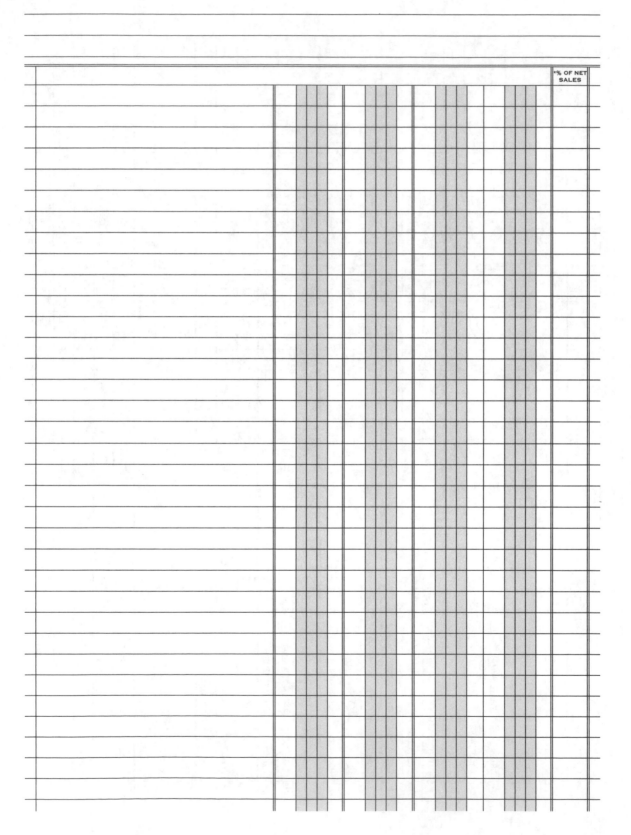

									*% OF NET SALES

*Rounded to the nearest 0.1%

15-2 WORK TOGETHER, p. 460

Analyzing an income statement

1., 2., 3.

Component	Acceptable Percentage	Actual Percentage	Acceptable Result		Recommended Action If Needed
			Yes	No	
Cost of merchandise sold	No more than 53.0%				
Gross profit on sales	No less than 47.0%				

Earnings per Share

Net Income after Federal Income Tax		Number of Shares Outstanding		Earnings per Share
$	÷		=	$

Price-Earnings Ratio

Market Price per Share		Earnings per Share		Price-Earnings Ratio
$	÷	$	=	

Analyzing an income statement

1., 2., 3.

Component	Acceptable Percentage	Actual Percentage	Acceptable Result Yes	Acceptable Result No	Recommended Action If Needed
Total expenses	No more than 30.0%				
Net income before federal income tax	No less than 15.0%				

Earnings per Share

Net Income after Federal Income Tax		Number of Shares Outstanding		Earnings per Share
$	÷		=	$
	÷		=	

Price-Earnings Ratio

Market Price per Share		Earnings per Share		Price-Earnings Ratio
$	÷		=	
	÷	$	=	

15-3 WORK TOGETHER, p. 463

Preparing a statement of stockholders' equity

1.

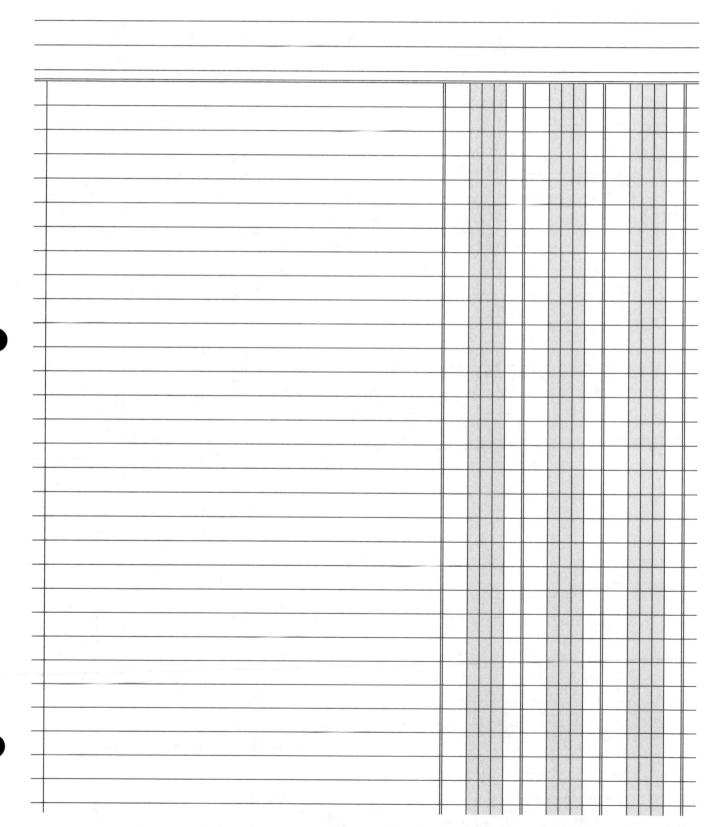

Preparing a statement of stockholders' equity

1.

15-4 **WORK TOGETHER, p. 471**

Preparing a balance sheet for a corporation

1.

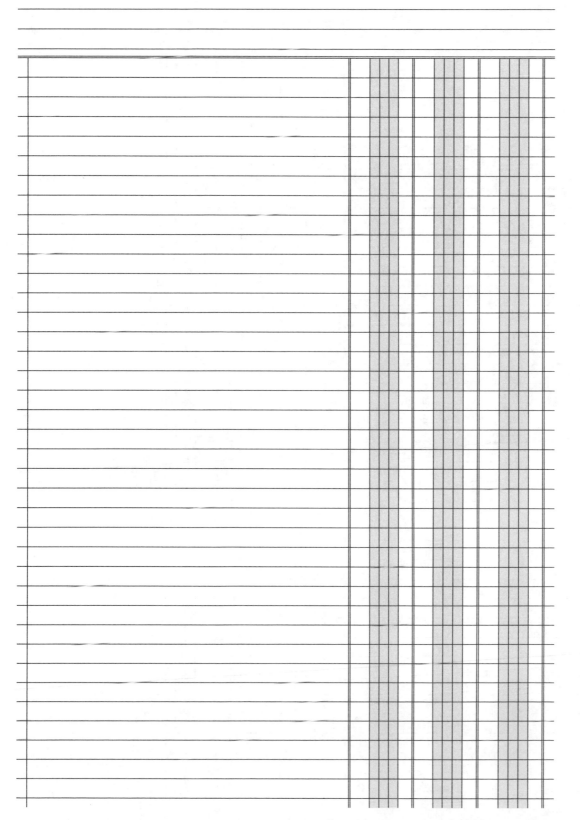

Preparing a balance sheet for a corporation

1.

Preparing an income statement for a merchandising business

15-1 APPLICATION PROBLEM, p. 473

Historic Doors, Inc.

Work Sheet

For Year Ended December 31, 20 --

| | TRIAL BALANCE | | ADJUSTMENTS | | INCOME STATEMENT | | BALANCE SHEET | |
ACCOUNT TITLE	DEBIT	CREDIT	DEBIT	CREDIT	DEBIT	CREDIT	DEBIT	CREDIT
	1	2	3	4	5	6	7	8
5 Merchandise Inventory	201 184 25			(d) 2 548 25			198 636 00	
29 Sales		615 258 25				615 258 25		
30 Sales Discount	1 184 25				1 184 25			
31 Sales Returns and Allowances	4 152 88				4 152 88			
32 Purchases	301 525 80				301 525 80			
33 Purchases Discount		2 151 81				2 151 81		
34 Purch. Returns and Allowances		4 150 08				4 150 08		
35 Advertising Expense	12 500 00				12 500 00			
36 Cash Short and Over	2 88				2 88			
37 Credit Card Fee Expense	8 428 25				8 428 25			
38 Depr. Exp.—Office Equipment			(f) 4 515 00		4 515 00			
39 Depr. Exp.—Store Equipment			(g) 2 815 00		2 815 00			
40 Insurance Expense			(c) 8 000 00		8 000 00			
41 Miscellaneous Expense	7 450 00				7 450 00			
42 Payroll Taxes Expense	9 415 25				9 415 25			
43 Rent Expense	24 000 00				24 000 00			
44 Salary Expense	108 482 25				108 482 25			
45 Supplies Expense—Office			(a) 1 482 25		1 482 25			
46 Supplies Expense—Store			(b) 3 018 28		3 018 28			
47 Uncollectible Accounts Expense			(e) 1 720 00		1 720 00			
48 Utilities Expense	7 158 22				7 158 22			
49 Federal Income Tax Expense	26 000 00		(h) 1 383 02		27 383 02			
50	819 131 92	819 131 92	25 481 80	25 481 80	535 781 58	621 560 14	208 004 80	208 004 80
51 Net Income after Fed. Income Tax					85 778 56			85 778 56
52					621 560 14	621 560 14	293 783 36	293 783 36

1., 2.

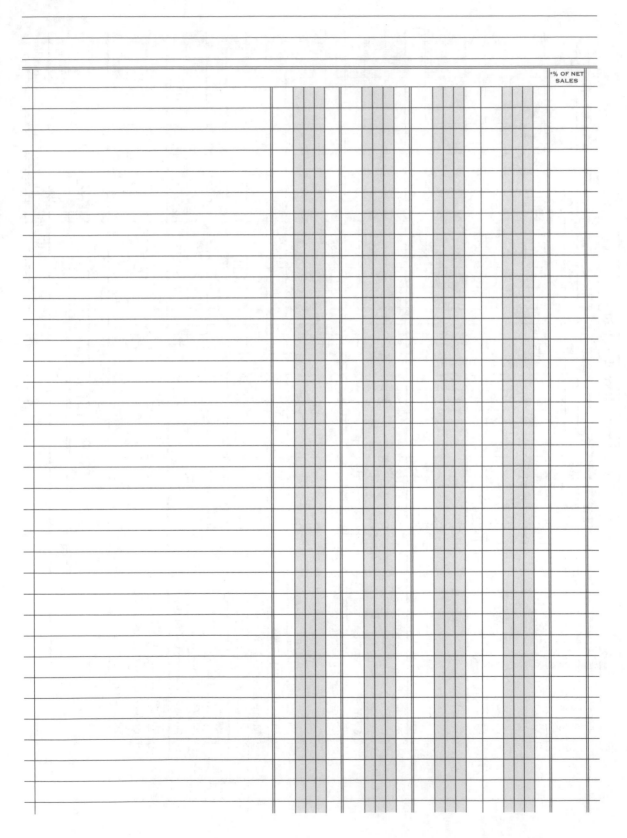

							*% OF NET SALES

*Rounded to the nearest 0.1%

15-2 APPLICATION PROBLEM, p. 473

Analyzing component percentages and financial ratios

Custom Jewelry, Inc.

Income Statement

For Year Ended December 31, 20 – –

					*% OF NET SALES
Revenue:					
Sales				915 48 2 15	
Less: Sales Discount		2 15 8 28			
Sales Ret. and Allow.		6 14 8 25	8 30 6 53		
Net Sales				907 1 7 5 62	100.0
Cost of Merchandise Sold:					
Merchandise Inventory, January 1, 20 – –			201 1 8 4 25		
Purchases		331 2 5 8 25			
Less: Purchases Discount	4 15 8 25				
Purch. Ret. and Allow.	2 41 8 29	6 57 6 54			
Net Purchases			324 6 8 1 71		
Total Cost of Mdse. Avail. for Sale			525 8 6 5 96		
Less Mdse. Inventory, Dec. 31, 20 – –			198 6 3 6 00		
Cost of Merchandise Sold				327 2 2 9 96	36.1
Gross Profit on Sales				579 9 4 5 66	63.9
Expenses:					
Advertising Expense			52 4 0 0 00		
Credit Card Fee Expense			12 4 8 2 88		
Depr. Exp.—Office Equipment			3 4 8 5 00		
Depr. Exp.—Store Equipment			8 4 5 0 00		
Insurance Expense			12 0 0 0 00		
Miscellaneous Expense			14 1 8 4 29		
Payroll Taxes Expense			21 4 8 2 27		
Rent Expense			36 0 0 0 00		
Salary Expense			201 4 8 2 80		
Supplies Expense—Office			2 4 8 1 05		
Supplies Expense—Store			6 0 8 1 80		
Uncollectible Accounts Expense			5 8 4 0 00		
Utilities Expense			8 4 0 8 09		
Total Expenses				384 7 7 8 18	42.4
Net Income before Federal Income Tax				195 1 6 7 48	21.5
Less Federal Income Tax Expense				59 3 6 5 32	
Net Income after Federal Income Tax				135 8 0 2 16	

*Rounded to the nearest 0.1%

1.

Component	Acceptable Percentage	Actual Percentage	Acceptable Result		Recommended Action If Needed
			Yes	No	
Cost of merchandise sold	No more than 35.0%				
Gross profit on sales	No less than 65.0%				
Total expenses	No more than 40.0%				
Net income before federal income tax	No less than 25.0%				

2.

Earnings per Share

Net Income after Federal Income Tax		Number of Shares Outstanding		Earnings per Share
$	÷		=	
	÷		=	$

Price-Earnings Ratio

Market Price per Share		Earnings per Share		Price-Earnings Ratio
$	÷		=	
	÷	$	=	

15-3 APPLICATION PROBLEM, p. 473

Preparing a statement of stockholders' equity

Preparing a balance sheet for a corporation

Henderson Corporation

Work Sheet

For Year Ended December 31, 20 − −

	TRIAL BALANCE		ADJUSTMENTS		INCOME STATEMENT		BALANCE SHEET	
ACCOUNT TITLE	DEBIT	CREDIT	DEBIT	CREDIT	DEBIT	CREDIT	DEBIT	CREDIT
1 Cash	22 154 00						22 154 00	
2 Petty Cash	3 000 00						3 000 00	
3 Accounts Receivable	35 158 25						35 158 25	
4 Allow. for Uncoll. Accts.		91 25		(e) 4 150 00				4 241 25
5 Merchandise Inventory	251 018 80			(d) 1 548 25			249 470 55	
6 Supplies—Office	4 215 89			(a) 3 818 04			397 85	
7 Supplies—Store	5 184 69			(b) 4 818 77			365 92	
8 Prepaid Insurance	14 000 00			(c) 12 000 00			2 000 00	
9 Office Equipment	19 485 28						19 485 28	
10 Acc. Depr.—Office Equip.		4 185 00		(f) 4 260 00				8 445 00
11 Store Equipment	38 481 50						38 481 50	
12 Acc. Depr.—Store Equip.		12 158 00		(g) 5 750 00				17 908 00
13 Accounts Payable		23 154 50						23 154 50
14 Federal Income Tax Payable				(h) 881 17				881 17
15 Emp. Income Tax Payable		1 548 00						1 548 00
16 Social Security Tax Payable		815 30						815 30
17 Medicare Tax Payable		190 68						190 68
18 Sales Tax Payable		3 154 20						3 154 20
19 Unemploy. Tax Payable—Fed.		33 60						33 60
20 Unemploy. Tax Payable—State		226 80						226 80
21 Health Insur. Premiums Payable		750 00						750 00
22 U.S. Savings Bonds Payable		100 00						100 00
23 United Way Donations Payable		70 00						70 00
24 Dividends Payable		9 000 00						9 000 00
25 Capital Stock		200 000 00						200 000 00
26 Retained Earnings		57 966 71						57 966 71
27 Dividends	28 000 00						28 000 00	
28 Income Summary			(d) 1 548 25		1 548 25			

15-4 **APPLICATION PROBLEM (concluded)**

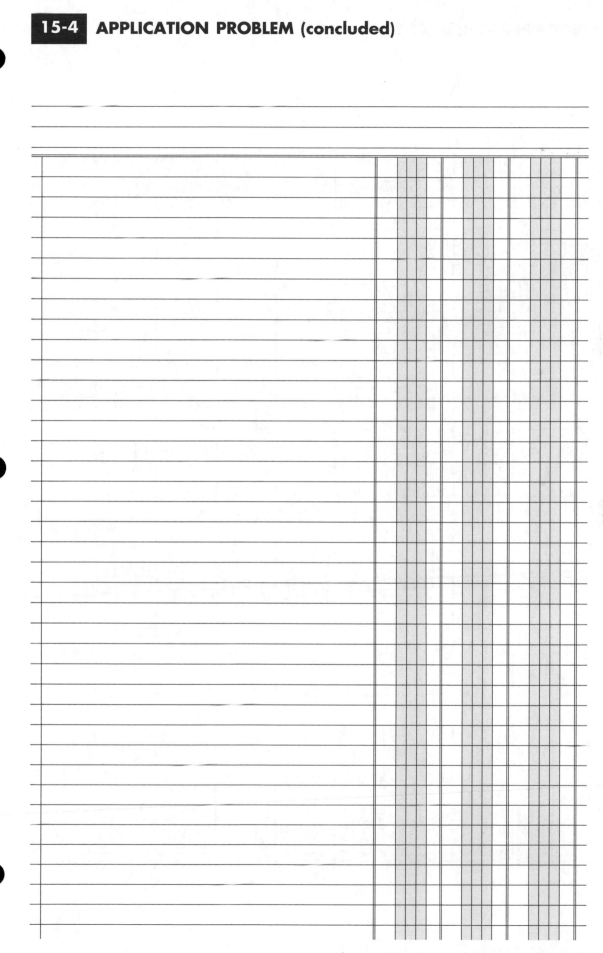

Preparing financial statements

Lighting Center, Inc.

Work Sheet

For Year Ended December 31, 20 — —

	ACCOUNT TITLE	TRIAL BALANCE DEBIT	TRIAL BALANCE CREDIT	ADJUSTMENTS DEBIT	ADJUSTMENTS CREDIT	INCOME STATEMENT DEBIT	INCOME STATEMENT CREDIT	BALANCE SHEET DEBIT	BALANCE SHEET CREDIT	
1	Cash	14 258 00						14 258 00		1
2	Petty Cash	500 00						500 00		2
3	Accounts Receivable	22 318 25						22 318 25		3
4	Allow. for Uncoll. Accts.		1 088 80		(e) 1 525 00				2 613 80	4
5	Merchandise Inventory	219 248 25			(d) 2 154 25			217 094 00		5
6	Supplies—Office	3 510 15			(a) 3 015 12			495 03		6
7	Supplies—Store	4 828 19			(b) 3 815 32			1 012 87		7
8	Prepaid Insurance	12 000 00			(c) 10 000 00			2 000 00		8
9	Office Equipment	23 185 00						23 185 00		9
10	Acc. Depr.—Office Equip.		8 450 00		(f) 4 050 00				12 500 00	10
11	Store Equipment	46 184 00						46 184 00		11
12	Acc. Depr.—Store Equip.		12 280 00		(g) 6 025 00				18 305 00	12
13	Accounts Payable		24 158 20						24 158 20	13
14	Federal Income Tax Payable				(h) 52 86				52 86	14
15	Emp. Income Tax Payable		1 055 00						1 055 00	15
16	Social Security Tax Payable		747 60						747 60	16
17	Medicare Tax Payable		174 84						174 84	17
18	Sales Tax Payable		2 248 25						2 248 25	18
19	Unemploy. Tax Payable—Fed.		25 60						25 60	19
20	Unemploy. Tax Payable—State		172 80						172 80	20
21	Health Insur. Premiums Payable		750 00						750 00	21
22	U.S. Savings Bonds Payable		100 00						100 00	22
23	United Way Donations Payable		70 00						70 00	23
24	Dividends Payable									24
25	Capital Stock		100 000 00						100 000 00	25
26	Retained Earnings		107 246 92						107 246 92	26

(Note: Work sheet is continued on next page.)

15-5 MASTERY PROBLEM (continued)

Lighting Center, Inc.

Work Sheet

For Year Ended December 31, 20 - -

| | TRIAL BALANCE | | ADJUSTMENTS | | INCOME STATEMENT | | BALANCE SHEET | |
ACCOUNT TITLE	DEBIT	CREDIT	DEBIT	CREDIT	DEBIT	CREDIT	DEBIT	CREDIT
27 Dividends	40 000 00						40 000 00	
28 Income Summary			(d) 2 154 25		2 154 25			
29 Sales		745 824 50				745 824 50		
30 Sales Discount	1 154 25				1 154 25			
31 Sales Returns and Allowances	3 481 25				3 481 25			
32 Purchases	368 482 22				368 482 22			
33 Purchases Discount		1 548 00				1 548 00		
34 Purch. Returns and Allowances		3 848 77				3 848 77		
35 Advertising Expense	12 510 00				12 510 00			
36 Cash Short and Over	14 02				14 02			
37 Credit Card Fee Expense	9 182 22				9 182 22			
38 Depr. Exp.—Office Equipment			(f) 4 050 00		4 050 00			
39 Depr. Exp.—Store Equipment			(g) 6 025 00		6 025 00			
40 Insurance Expense			(c) 10 000 00		10 000 00			
41 Miscellaneous Expense	12 140 00				12 140 00			
42 Payroll Taxes Expense	15 482 98				15 482 98			
43 Rent Expense	36 000 00				36 000 00			
44 Salary Expense	139 158 47				139 158 47			
45 Supplies Expense—Office			(a) 3 015 12		3 015 12			
46 Supplies Expense—Store			(b) 3 815 32		3 815 32			
47 Uncollectible Accounts Expense			(e) 1 525 00		1 525 00			
48 Utilities Expense	8 152 03				8 152 03			
49 Federal Income Tax Expense	28 000 00		(h) 5 2 86		28 052 86			
50	1019 789 28	1019 789 28	30 637 55	30 637 55	664 394 99	751 221 27	367 047 15	280 220 87
51 Net Income after Fed. Income Tax					86 826 28			86 826 28
52					751 221 27	751 221 27	367 047 15	367 047 15

1.

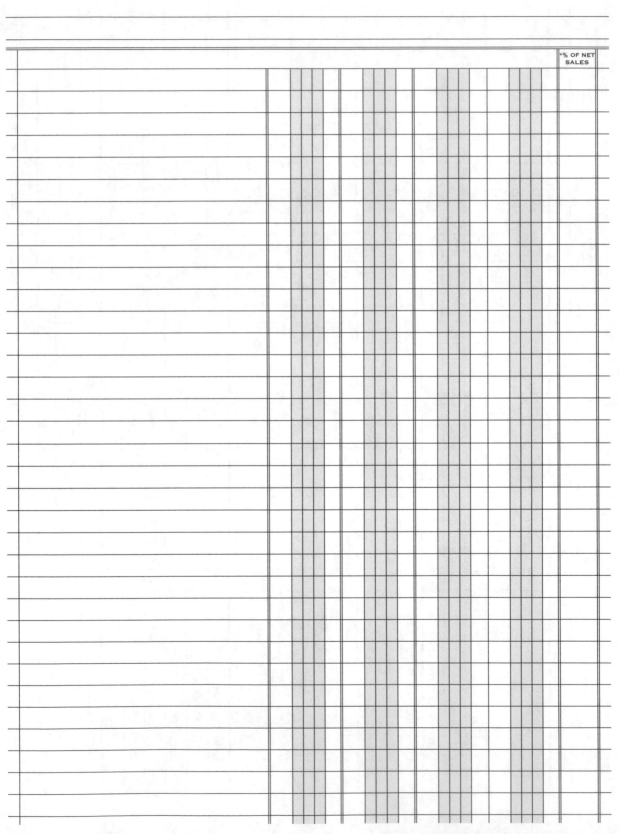

					*% OF NET SALES

15-5 MASTERY PROBLEM (continued)

2.

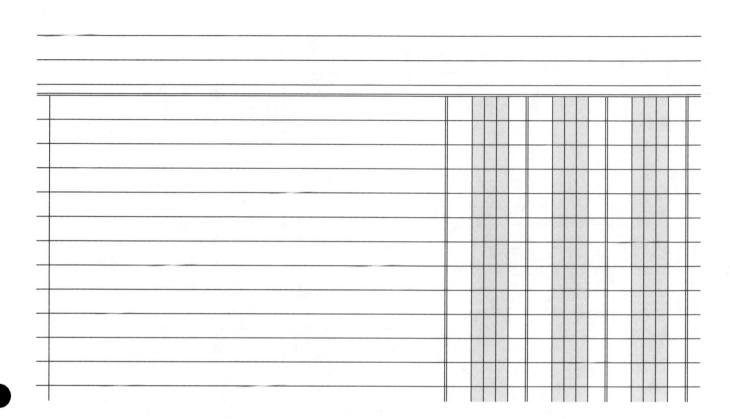

4.

Earnings per Share

Net Income after Federal Income Tax	÷	Number of Shares Outstanding	=	Earnings per Share
$	÷		=	$

Price-Earnings Ratio

Market Price per Share	÷	Earnings per Share	=	Price-Earnings Ratio
$	÷	$	=	

3.

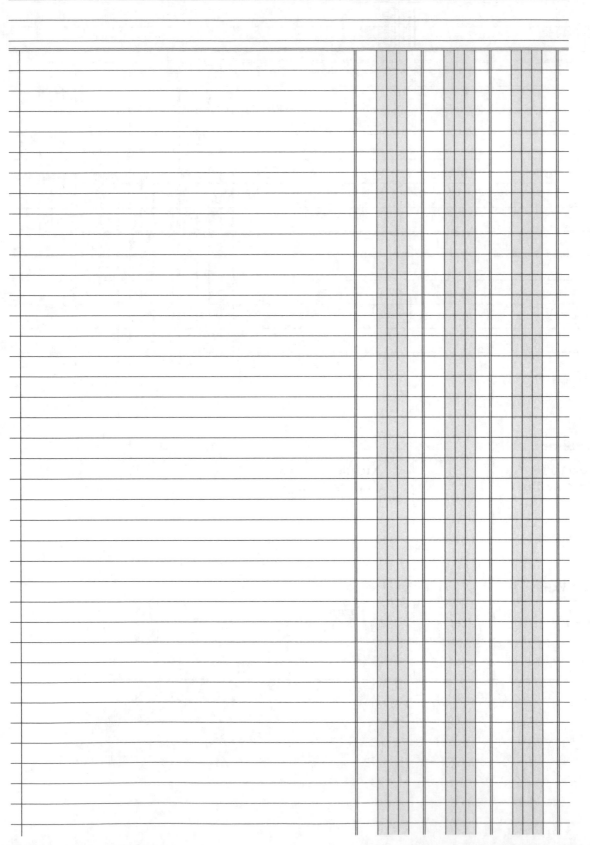

Study Guide 16

Name		Perfect Score	Your Score
Analyzing Accounts Affected by Adjusting and Closing Entries		24 Pts.	
Examining Adjusting and Closing Entries		18 Pts.	
Analyzing the Accounting Cycle for a Merchandising Business Organized as a Corporation		9 Pts.	
	Total	51 Pts.	

Part One—Analyzing Accounts Affected by Adjusting and Closing Entries

Directions: For each adjusting or closing entry described, decide which accounts are debited and credited. Print the letter identifying your choice in the proper Answers column.

Accounts to Be

Account Title	Transaction	Debited	Credited
A. Accumulated Depreciation—Office Equipment	1–2. Adjusting entry for allowance for uncollectible accounts. (p. 482)		
B. Accumulated Depreciation—Store Equipment	3–4. Adjusting entry for a decrease in merchandise inventory. (p. 482)		
C. Allowance for Uncollectible Accounts	5–6. Adjusting entry for office supplies. (p. 483)		
D. Dividends	7–8. Adjusting entry for store supplies. (p. 483)		
E. Depreciation Expense—Office Equipment	9–10. Adjusting entry for prepaid insurance. (p. 484)		
F. Depreciation Expense—Store Equipment	11–12. Adjusting entry for depreciation of office equipment. (p. 484)		
G. Federal Income Tax Expense	13–14. Adjusting entry for depreciation of store equipment. (p. 485)		
H. Federal Income Tax Payable	15–16. Adjusting entry for federal income taxes. (p. 485)		
I. Income Summary	17–18. Closing entry for the sales account. (p. 488)		
J. Insurance Expense	19–20. Closing entry for the purchases account. (p. 490)		
K. Merchandise Inventory	21–22. Closing entry for the income summary account with a net income. (p. 491)		
L. Prepaid Insurance	23–24. Closing entry for dividends. (p. 491)		
M. Purchases			
N. Retained Earnings			
O. Sales			
P. Supplies—Office			
Q. Supplies—Store			
R. Supplies Expense—Office			
S. Supplies Expense—Store			
T. Uncollectible Accounts Expense			

Part Two—Examining Adjusting and Closing Entries

Directions: Place a *T* for True or an *F* for False in the Answers column to show whether each of the following statements is true or false.

Answers

1. General ledger account balances are changed only by posting journal entries. (p. 481)   1. _____

2. Adjusting entries bring subsidiary ledger accounts up to date. (p. 481)   2. _____

3. Hobby Shack records the adjusting entries in the general journal on the next line following the last daily transaction. (p. 481)   3. _____

4. Indicating a source document is not necessary when journalizing adjusting entries. (p. 481)   4. _____

5. Temporary accounts are closed at the end of a fiscal period to prepare the general ledger for the next fiscal period. (p. 487)   5. _____

6. Closing the temporary accounts at the end of a fiscal period is an application of the accounting concept Matching Expenses with Revenue. (p. 487)   6. _____

7. A temporary account is closed by recording an equal amount on the side opposite the balance. (p. 487)   7. _____

8. The Trial Balance columns of a work sheet and an income statement contain the information needed to journalize closing entries. (p. 487)   8. _____

9. Permanent accounts are sometimes referred to as nominal accounts. (p. 487)   9. _____

10. The ending account balances of permanent accounts for one fiscal period are the beginning account balances for the next fiscal period. (p. 487)   10. _____

11. Contra accounts with credit balances are closed by debiting the accounts and crediting Income Summary. (p. 488)   11. _____

12. Expense accounts are closed by debiting the expense accounts and crediting Income Summary. (p. 489)   12. _____

13. The Income Summary account is closed into the Retained Earnings account. (p. 491)   13. _____

14. Dividends increase the earnings retained by a corporation. (p. 491)   14. _____

15. After the closing entry for the Dividends account is posted, the Dividends account has a zero balance. (p. 491)   15. _____

16. After all closing entries are posted, the income statement accounts are the only general ledger accounts that have balances. (p. 494)   16. _____

17. When the general ledger is ready for the next fiscal period, this is an application of the Business Entity accounting concept. (p. 494)   17. _____

18. The purpose of the post-closing trial balance is to prove the general ledger equality of debits and credits. (p. 496)   18. _____

Part Three—Analyzing the Accounting Cycle for a Merchandising Business Organized as a Corporation

Directions: Write a number from 1 to 9 to the left of each step to indicate the correct sequence of all the steps in the accounting cycle. (p. 497)

Answers

1. _____ Post journal entries to the subsidiary ledgers and the general ledger.

2. _____ Check source documents for accuracy, and analyze transactions into debit and credit parts.

3. _____ Journalize adjusting and closing entries from the work sheet.

4. _____ Record transactions in journals, using information on source documents.

5. _____ Prepare the schedules of accounts payable and accounts receivable, using information from the subsidiary ledgers.

6. _____ Prepare a post-closing trial balance of the general ledger.

7. _____ Prepare financial statements from the work sheet.

8. _____ Post adjusting and closing entries to the general ledger.

9. _____ Prepare a work sheet, including a trial balance, from the general ledger.

Study Skills

Making a Speech

You will often be responsible for making a speech or presentation while you are in school and after school as well. Many people fear speaking in front of others, but it is actually very easy if you are well prepared.

Choosing Your Topic

Your topic must be of interest to your audience and one that you can cover adequately in the time available. A common error that students make is to pick a topic that is so broad that they cannot really cover the topic in a short speech. The result is that the speech may ramble and not make any real points. Another error students sometimes make is that they use only one idea. In this case, they may simply make the same point over and over.

Practicing Your Talk

You should always practice giving your speech before you actually make it before the group. Practicing will help you work out any rough spots, and it will make you feel much more at ease when you make the actual presentation.

A good technique is to give the talk in front of a mirror. Watching yourself while speaking can be very distracting, but it will give you valuable practice in keeping on the subject and avoiding distractions.

Your Appearance

On the day you are to give your talk, be sure to be well rested, and be sure to dress appropriately. When you are introduced, walk directly to the platform. Stand straight without slouching or leaning on the desk or lectern. A sloppy appearance will detract from your talk.

Giving Your Speech

In most cases you should not read a speech. You should talk to the members of the audience, following the ideas from notes that you have made.

When you begin your talk, start with a point that will gain the attention of the group. It is not necessary to try to tell a joke. If you do not get the attention of the group at the outset, however, you may have trouble maintaining their interest.

Each point should be easy to understand, and you may illustrate it with examples that are clearly related and support the point. When you proceed to the next point, you should make it clear to the group that you are moving to the next item of interest.

A common error is to direct your talk to only one person in the audience, particularly someone who agrees with your points. However, you are speaking to all members of the audience and you should look at all of them.

After you have made your major points, you should summarize briefly. Your conclusions should be based on the material that you have presented and should be easy to follow. Your talk should end on a strong note, and you should then stop. A common error is for a speaker to repeat the conclusion several times, allowing the speech to end on a low note.

Keep on Time

Keep your speech to the allotted time. If you have 20 minutes, be sure that you do not take 25 minutes. Pace yourself so that you will finish all points on time. Do not go too slowly at first and then rush at the end. This can make your talk dull at the beginning and hard to follow at the end.

With proper planning and practice, you will soon be making excellent talks.

16-1 WORK TOGETHER, p. 486

Journalizing adjusting entries

Discount Books, Inc.

Work Sheet

For Year Ended December 31, 20 - -

	Trial Balance Debit	Trial Balance Credit	Adjustments Debit	Adjustments Credit	Income Statement Debit	Income Statement Credit	Balance Sheet Debit	Balance Sheet Credit
1 Cash	5 1 4 8 25						5 1 4 8 25	
2 Petty Cash	2 0 0 00						2 0 0 00	
3 Accounts Receivable	14 1 5 8 22						14 1 5 8 22	
4 Allow. for Uncoll. Accts.		2 1 20		(e) 1 5 0 0 00				1 5 2 1 20
5 Merchandise Inventory	84 8 1 5 20		(d) 1 8 4 8 25				86 6 6 3 45	
6 Supplies—Office	1 6 4 8 85			(a) 1 4 4 8 55			2 0 0 30	
7 Supplies—Store	3 4 8 1 12			(b) 3 2 4 8 11			2 3 3 01	
8 Prepaid Insurance	12 0 0 0 00			(c) 1 1 0 0 0 00			1 0 0 0 00	
9 Office Equipment	14 1 5 4 55						14 1 5 4 55	
10 Acc. Depr.—Office Equipment		4 1 5 4 25		(f) 3 4 1 0 00				7 5 6 4 25
11 Store Equipment	42 1 5 8 15						42 1 5 8 15	
12 Acc. Depr.—Store Equipment		8 4 8 0 00		(g) 6 4 2 0 00				14 9 0 0 00
13 Accounts Payable		12 4 5 8 51						12 4 5 8 51
14 Federal Income Tax Payable				(h) 3 9 4 8 91				3 9 4 8 91
15 Emp. Income Tax Pay.		4 6 5 00						4 6 5 00
16 Social Security Tax Payable		4 9 6 00						4 9 6 00
17 Medicare Tax Payable		1 1 6 00						1 1 6 00
18 Sales Tax Payable		1 5 4 8 00						1 5 4 8 00
19 Unemployment Tax Pay.—Fed.		8 00						8 00
20 Unemployment Tax Pay.—State		5 4 00						5 4 00
21 Health Ins. Premiums Pay.		5 0 0 00						5 0 0 00
22 U.S. Savings Bonds Payable		5 0 00						5 0 00
23 United Way Donations Pay.		6 0 00						6 0 00
24 Dividends Payable		4 0 0 0 00						4 0 0 0 00
25 Capital Stock		24 0 0 0 00						24 0 0 0 00
26 Retained Earnings		34 9 4 2 87						34 9 4 2 87

(Note: Work sheet is continued on next page.)

Discount Books, Inc.

Work Sheet

For Year Ended December 31, 20 – –

	ACCOUNT TITLE	TRIAL BALANCE DEBIT	TRIAL BALANCE CREDIT	ADJUSTMENTS DEBIT	ADJUSTMENTS CREDIT	INCOME STATEMENT DEBIT	INCOME STATEMENT CREDIT	BALANCE SHEET DEBIT	BALANCE SHEET CREDIT	
27	Dividends	16 000 00						16 000 00		27
28	Income Summary				(d) 1 848 25		1 848 25			28
29	Sales		430 521 58				430 521 58			29
30	Sales Discount	2 150 0				2 150 0				30
31	Sales Returns and Allowances	4 153 28				4 153 28				31
32	Purchases	174 481 20				174 481 20				32
33	Purchases Discount		3 452 5				3 452 5			33
34	Purch. Returns and Allowances		5 548 74				5 548 74			34
35	Advertising Expense	6 000 00				6 000 00				35
36	Cash Short and Over	4 84				4 84				36
37	Credit Card Fee Expense	5 148 25				5 148 25				37
38	Depr. Exp.—Office Equipment			(f) 3 410 00		3 410 00				38
39	Depr. Exp.—Store Equipment			(g) 6 420 00		6 420 00				39
40	Insurance Expense			(c) 11 000 00		11 000 00				40
41	Miscellaneous Expense	4 150 00				4 150 00				41
42	Payroll Taxes Expense	8 745 25				8 745 25				42
43	Rent Expense	12 000 00				12 000 00				43
44	Salary Expense	97 458 84				97 458 84				44
45	Supplies Expense—Office			(a) 1 448 55		1 448 55				45
46	Supplies Expense—Store			(b) 3 248 11		3 248 11				46
47	Uncollectible Accounts Exp.			(e) 1 500 00		1 500 00				47
48	Utilities Expense	5 648 40				5 648 40				48
49	Fed. Income Tax Expense	16 000 00		(h) 3 948 91		19 948 91				49
50		527 769 40	527 769 40	32 823 82	32 823 82	364 980 63	438 263 82	179 915 93	106 632 74	50
51	Net Income after Fed. Income Tax					73 283 19			73 283 19	51
52						438 263 82	438 263 82	179 915 93	179 915 93	52

16-1 WORK TOGETHER (concluded)

1.

GENERAL JOURNAL

	DATE	ACCOUNT TITLE	DOC. NO.	POST. REF.	DEBIT	CREDIT	
1							1
2							2
3							3
4							4
5							5
6							6
7							7
8							8
9							9
10							10
11							11
12							12
13							13
14							14
15							15
16							16
17							17
18							18
19							19
20							20
21							21
22							22
23							23
24							24
25							25
26							26
27							27
28							28
29							29
30							30
31							31
32							32
33							33

Journalizing adjusting entries

Sturgis Supply, Inc.

Work Sheet

For Year Ended December 31, 20 – –

	ACCOUNT TITLE	TRIAL BALANCE DEBIT	TRIAL BALANCE CREDIT	ADJUSTMENTS DEBIT	ADJUSTMENTS CREDIT	INCOME STATEMENT DEBIT	INCOME STATEMENT CREDIT	BALANCE SHEET DEBIT	BALANCE SHEET CREDIT	
1	Cash	20 158 25						20 158 25		1
2	Petty Cash	5 00 00						5 00 00		2
3	Accounts Receivable	42 488 25						42 488 25		3
4	Allow. for Uncoll. Accts.		1 088 18		(e) 3 250 00				4 338 18	4
5	Merchandise Inventory	315 418 25			(d) 1 648 22			313 770 03		5
6	Supplies—Office	7 148 48			(a) 6 847 15			301 33		6
7	Supplies—Store	6 154 88			(b) 5 548 11			606 77		7
8	Prepaid Insurance	18 000 00			(c) 16 000 00			2 000 00		8
9	Office Equipment	41 484 89						41 484 89		9
10	Acc. Depr.—Office Equipment		16 180 00		(f) 8 450 00				24 630 00	10
11	Store Equipment	90 184 11						90 184 11		11
12	Acc. Depr.—Store Equipment		22 180 00		(g) 8 600 00				30 780 00	12
13	Accounts Payable		22 154 17						22 154 17	13
14	Federal Income Tax Payable				(h) 24 163 72				24 163 72	14
15	Emp. Income Tax Pay.		3 210 00						3 210 00	15
16	Social Security Tax Payable		945 50						945 50	16
17	Medicare Tax Payable		221 13						221 13	17
18	Sales Tax Payable		4 215 02						4 215 02	18
19	Unemployment Tax Pay.—Fed.		32 00						32 00	19
20	Unemployment Tax Pay.—State		216 00						216 00	20
21	Health Ins. Premiums Pay.		1 200 00						1 200 00	21
22	U.S. Savings Bonds Payable		120 00						120 00	22
23	United Way Donations Pay.		140 00						140 00	23
24	Dividends Payable		9 000 00						9 000 00	24
25	Capital Stock		225 000 00						225 000 00	25
26	Retained Earnings		38 179 53						38 179 53	26

(Note: Work sheet is continued on next page.)

16-1 ON YOUR OWN (continued)

Sturgis Supply, Inc.
Work Sheet
For Year Ended December 31, 20 – –

	TRIAL BALANCE		ADJUSTMENTS		INCOME STATEMENT		BALANCE SHEET		
ACCOUNT TITLE	DEBIT	CREDIT	DEBIT	CREDIT	DEBIT	CREDIT	DEBIT	CREDIT	
27 Dividends	36 000 00						36 000 00		27
28 Income Summary			(d) 1 648 22		1 648 22				28
29 Sales		998 148 15				998 148 15			29
30 Sales Discount	1 248 22				1 248 22				30
31 Sales Returns and Allowances	6 488 95				6 488 95				31
32 Purchases	442 518 25				442 518 25				32
33 Purchases Discount		7 154 25				7 154 25			33
34 Purch. Returns and Allowances		6 448 94				6 448 94			34
35 Advertising Expense	15 000 00				15 000 00				35
36 Cash Short and Over	5 25				5 25				36
37 Credit Card Fee Expense	18 487 15				18 487 15				37
38 Depr. Exp.—Office Equipment			(f) 8 450 00		8 450 00				38
39 Depr. Exp.—Store Equipment			(g) 8 600 00		8 600 00				39
40 Insurance Expense			(c) 16 000 00		16 000 00				40
41 Miscellaneous Expense	9 480 00				9 480 00				41
42 Payroll Taxes Expense	18 486 69				18 486 69				42
43 Rent Expense	24 000 00				24 000 00				43
44 Salary Expense	183 000 00				183 000 00				44
45 Supplies Expense—Office			(a) 6 847 15		6 847 15				45
46 Supplies Expense—Store			(b) 5 548 11		5 548 11				46
47 Uncollectible Accounts Exp.			(e) 3 250 00		3 250 00				47
48 Utilities Expense	9 581 25				9 581 25				48
49 Fed. Income Tax Expense	50 000 00		(h) 24 163 72		74 163 72				49
50	1,355 832 87	1,355 832 87	74 507 20	74 507 20	852 802 96	1,011 751 34	547 493 63	388 545 25	50
51 Net Income after Fed. Income Tax					158 948 38			158 948 38	51
52					1,011 751 34	1,011 751 34	547 493 63	547 493 63	52

1.

GENERAL JOURNAL   PAGE 24

	DATE	ACCOUNT TITLE	DOC. NO.	POST. REF.	DEBIT	CREDIT	
1							1
2							2
3							3
4							4
5							5
6							6
7							7
8							8
9							9
10							10
11							11
12							12
13							13
14							14
15							15
16							16
17							17
18							18
19							19
20							20
21							21
22							22
23							23
24							24
25							25
26							26
27							27
28							28
29							29
30							30
31							31
32							32
33							33

16-2 WORK TOGETHER, p. 493

Journalizing closing entries

1.

GENERAL JOURNAL

PAGE 19

	DATE	ACCOUNT TITLE	DOC. NO.	POST. REF.	DEBIT	CREDIT	
1							1
2							2
3							3
4							4
5							5
6							6
7							7
8							8
9							9
10							10
11							11
12							12
13							13
14							14
15							15
16							16
17							17
18							18
19							19
20							20
21							21
22							22
23							23
24							24
25							25
26							26
27							27
28							28
29							29
30							30
31							31
32							32

Journalizing closing entries

1.

GENERAL JOURNAL   PAGE 25

	DATE	ACCOUNT TITLE	DOC. NO.	POST. REF.	DEBIT	CREDIT	
1							1
2							2
3							3
4							4
5							5
6							6
7							7
8							8
9							9
10							10
11							11
12							12
13							13
14							14
15							15
16							16
17							17
18							18
19							19
20							20
21							21
22							22
23							23
24							24
25							25
26							26
27							27
28							28
29							29
30							30
31							31
32							32

16-3 WORK TOGETHER, p. 498

Preparing a post-closing trial balance

1.

ACCOUNT TITLE	DEBIT	CREDIT

1.

ACCOUNT TITLE	DEBIT	CREDIT

16-1 APPLICATION PROBLEM, p. 500

Journalizing adjusting entries

Cellar Books, Inc.

Work Sheet

For Year Ended December 31, 20 – –

	ACCOUNT TITLE	TRIAL BALANCE DEBIT	TRIAL BALANCE CREDIT	ADJUSTMENTS DEBIT	ADJUSTMENTS CREDIT	INCOME STATEMENT DEBIT	INCOME STATEMENT CREDIT	BALANCE SHEET DEBIT	BALANCE SHEET CREDIT
1	Cash	16485 00						16485 00	
2	Petty Cash	400 00						400 00	
3	Accounts Receivable	41483 15						41483 15	
4	Allow. for Uncoll. Accts.		948 15		(e) 1458 00				2406 15
5	Merchandise Inventory	248752 30			(d) 2154 25			246598 05	
6	Supplies—Office	6148 28			(a) 5818 66			329 62	
7	Supplies—Store	5174 85			(b) 4848 04			326 81	
8	Prepaid Insurance	14000 00			(c) 12000 00			2000 00	
9	Office Equipment	38458 25						38458 25	
10	Acc. Depr.—Office Equipment		17480 00		(f) 6480 00				23960 00
11	Store Equipment	41478 50						41478 50	
12	Acc. Depr.—Store Equipment		23450 00		(g) 7650 00				31100 00
13	Accounts Payable		19948 80						19948 80
14	Federal Income Tax Payable				(h) 3660 23				3660 23
26	Retained Earnings		170024 63						170024 63
27	Dividends	12000 00						12000 00	
28	Income Summary			(d) 2154 25		2154 25			
29	Sales		668742 20				668742 20		
30	Sales Discount	1454 85				1454 85			
31	Sales Returns and Allow.	4215 48				4215 48			
32	Purchases	284835 25				284835 25			

(Note: Work sheet is continued on next page.)

Cellar Books, Inc.

Work Sheet

For Year Ended December 31, 20 – –

	ACCOUNT TITLE	TRIAL BALANCE		ADJUSTMENTS		INCOME STATEMENT		BALANCE SHEET	
		DEBIT	CREDIT	DEBIT	CREDIT	DEBIT	CREDIT	DEBIT	CREDIT
33	Purchases Discount		2 41 8 81				2 41 8 81		
34	Purch. Returns and Allow.		4 15 8 41				4 15 8 41		
35	Advertising Expense	12 54 0 00				12 54 0 00			
36	Cash Short and Over	8 08				8 08			
37	Credit Card Fee Expense	9 48 1 10				9 48 1 10			
38	Depr. Exp. —Office Equip.			(f) 6 48 0 00		6 48 0 00			
39	Depr. Exp. —Store Equip.			(g) 7 65 0 00		7 65 0 00			
40	Insurance Expense			(c) 12 00 0 00		12 00 0 00			
41	Miscellaneous Expense	5 41 0 00				5 41 0 00			
42	Payroll Taxes Expense	15 84 1 20				15 84 1 20			
43	Rent Expense	18 00 0 00				18 00 0 00			
44	Salary Expense	174 96 0 33				174 96 0 33			
45	Supplies Expense—Office			(a) 5 81 8 66		5 81 8 66			
46	Supplies Expense—Store			(b) 4 84 8 04		4 84 8 04			
47	Uncollectible Accounts Exp.			(e) 1 45 8 00		1 45 8 00			
48	Utilities Expense	4 54 8 20				4 54 8 20			
49	Fed. Income Tax Expense	20 00 0 00		(h) 3 66 0 23		23 66 0 23			
50		975 67 4 82	975 67 4 82	44 06 9 18	44 06 9 18	595 36 3 67	675 31 9 42	399 55 9 38	319 60 3 63
51	Net Income after Fed. Income Tax					79 95 5 75			79 95 5 75
52						675 31 9 42	675 31 9 42	399 55 9 38	399 55 9 38

16-1 APPLICATION PROBLEM (concluded)

1.

GENERAL JOURNAL   PAGE 22

	DATE		ACCOUNT TITLE	DOC. NO.	POST. REF.	DEBIT	CREDIT	
1								1
2								2
3								3
4								4
5								5
6								6
7								7
8								8
9								9
10								10
11								11
12								12
13								13
14								14
15								15
16								16
17								17
18								18
19								19
20								20
21								21
22								22
23								23
24								24
25								25
26								26
27								27
28								28
29								29
30								30
31								31
32								32

Journalizing closing entries

1., 2., 3., 4.

GENERAL JOURNAL   PAGE 23

	DATE	ACCOUNT TITLE	DOC. NO.	POST. REF.	DEBIT	CREDIT	
1							1
2							2
3							3
4							4
5							5
6							6
7							7
8							8
9							9
10							10
11							11
12							12
13							13
14							14
15							15
16							16
17							17
18							18
19							19
20							20
21							21
22							22
23							23
24							24
25							25
26							26
27							27
28							28
29							29
30							30
31							31
32							32

16-3 APPLICATION PROBLEM, p. 500

Preparing a post-closing trial balance

1.

ACCOUNT TITLE	DEBIT	CREDIT

Journalizing and posting adjusting and closing entries; preparing a post-closing trial balance

1., 2.

GENERAL JOURNAL

PAGE 22

	DATE	ACCOUNT TITLE	DOC. NO.	POST. REF.	DEBIT	CREDIT	
1							1
2							2
3							3
4							4
5							5
6							6
7							7
8							8
9							9
10							10
11							11
12							12
13							13
14							14
15							15
16							16
17							17
18							18
19							19
20							20
21							21
22							22
23							23
24							24
25							25
26							26
27							27
28							28
29							29
30							30
31							31

16-4 APPLICATION PROBLEM (continued)

3., 4.

GENERAL JOURNAL

	DATE		ACCOUNT TITLE	DOC. NO.	POST. REF.	DEBIT	CREDIT	
1								1
2								2
3								3
4								4
5								5
6								6
7								7
8								8
9								9
10								10
11								11
12								12
13								13
14								14
15								15
16								16
17								17
18								18
19								19
20								20
21								21
22								22
23								23
24								24
25								25
26								26
27								27
28								28
29								29
30								30
31								31
32								32
33								33

2., 4.   **GENERAL LEDGER**

ACCOUNT Cash   ACCOUNT NO. 1110

DATE	ITEM	POST. REF.	DEBIT	CREDIT	BALANCE DEBIT	BALANCE CREDIT
20-- Dec. 31	Balance	✔			15 4 8 2 00	

ACCOUNT Petty Cash   ACCOUNT NO. 1120

DATE	ITEM	POST. REF.	DEBIT	CREDIT	BALANCE DEBIT	BALANCE CREDIT
20-- Dec. 31	Balance	✔			5 0 0 00	

ACCOUNT Accounts Receivable   ACCOUNT NO. 1130

DATE	ITEM	POST. REF.	DEBIT	CREDIT	BALANCE DEBIT	BALANCE CREDIT
20-- Dec. 31	Balance	✔			42 1 5 8 80	

ACCOUNT Allow. for Uncoll. Accts.   ACCOUNT NO. 1135

DATE	ITEM	POST. REF.	DEBIT	CREDIT	BALANCE DEBIT	BALANCE CREDIT
20-- Dec. 31	Balance	✔				6 8 4 20

ACCOUNT Merchandise Inventory   ACCOUNT NO. 1140

DATE	ITEM	POST. REF.	DEBIT	CREDIT	BALANCE DEBIT	BALANCE CREDIT
20-- Dec. 31	Balance	✔			274 5 3 5 33	

16-4 APPLICATION PROBLEM (continued)

ACCOUNT Supplies—Office   ACCOUNT NO. 1145

DATE		ITEM	POST. REF.	DEBIT	CREDIT	BALANCE	
						DEBIT	CREDIT
Dec.	31	Balance	✔			6 1 5 8 84	

ACCOUNT Supplies—Store   ACCOUNT NO. 1150

DATE		ITEM	POST. REF.	DEBIT	CREDIT	BALANCE	
						DEBIT	CREDIT
Dec.	31	Balance	✔			5 5 4 8 55	

ACCOUNT Prepaid Insurance   ACCOUNT NO. 1160

DATE		ITEM	POST. REF.	DEBIT	CREDIT	BALANCE	
						DEBIT	CREDIT
Dec.	31	Balance	✔			8 0 0 0 00	

ACCOUNT Office Equipment   ACCOUNT NO. 1205

DATE		ITEM	POST. REF.	DEBIT	CREDIT	BALANCE	
						DEBIT	CREDIT
Dec.	31	Balance	✔			22 1 5 8 66	

ACCOUNT Acc. Depr. —Office Equipment   ACCOUNT NO. 1210

DATE		ITEM	POST. REF.	DEBIT	CREDIT	BALANCE	
						DEBIT	CREDIT
Dec.	31	Balance	✔				4 8 4 8 00

ACCOUNT Store Equipment   ACCOUNT NO. 1215

DATE		ITEM	POST. REF.	DEBIT	CREDIT	BALANCE	
						DEBIT	CREDIT
Dec.	31	Balance	✔			34 1 5 8 11	

ACCOUNT Acc. Depr. —Store Equipment ACCOUNT NO. 1220

DATE	ITEM	POST. REF.	DEBIT	CREDIT	BALANCE DEBIT	BALANCE CREDIT
20-- Dec. 31	Balance	✔				12 4 8 0 00

ACCOUNT Accounts Payable ACCOUNT NO. 2110

DATE	ITEM	POST. REF.	DEBIT	CREDIT	BALANCE DEBIT	BALANCE CREDIT
20-- Dec. 31	Balance	✔				15 4 8 7 99

ACCOUNT Federal Income Tax Payable ACCOUNT NO. 2120

DATE	ITEM	POST. REF.	DEBIT	CREDIT	BALANCE DEBIT	BALANCE CREDIT

ACCOUNT Employee Income Tax Payable ACCOUNT NO. 2130

DATE	ITEM	POST. REF.	DEBIT	CREDIT	BALANCE DEBIT	BALANCE CREDIT
20-- Dec. 31	Balance	✔				1 1 2 5 58

ACCOUNT Social Security Tax Payable ACCOUNT NO. 2135

DATE	ITEM	POST. REF.	DEBIT	CREDIT	BALANCE DEBIT	BALANCE CREDIT
20-- Dec. 31	Balance	✔				9 0 3 96

ACCOUNT Medicare Tax Payable ACCOUNT NO. 2140

DATE	ITEM	POST. REF.	DEBIT	CREDIT	BALANCE DEBIT	BALANCE CREDIT
20-- Dec. 31	Balance	✔				2 1 1 41

16-4 APPLICATION PROBLEM (continued)

ACCOUNT Sales Tax Payable   ACCOUNT NO. 2145

DATE		ITEM	POST. REF.	DEBIT	CREDIT	BALANCE DEBIT	BALANCE CREDIT
20-- Dec.	31	Balance	✔				2 3 4 5 99

ACCOUNT Unemployment Tax Payable—Federal   ACCOUNT NO. 2150

DATE		ITEM	POST. REF.	DEBIT	CREDIT	BALANCE DEBIT	BALANCE CREDIT
20-- Dec.	31	Balance	✔				2 5 60

ACCOUNT Unemployment Tax Payable—State   ACCOUNT NO. 2155

DATE		ITEM	POST. REF.	DEBIT	CREDIT	BALANCE DEBIT	BALANCE CREDIT
20-- Dec.	31	Balance	✔				1 7 2 80

ACCOUNT Health Insurance Premiums Payable   ACCOUNT NO. 2160

DATE		ITEM	POST. REF.	DEBIT	CREDIT	BALANCE DEBIT	BALANCE CREDIT
20-- Dec.	31	Balance	✔				3 5 0 00

ACCOUNT U.S. Savings Bonds Payable   ACCOUNT NO. 2165

DATE		ITEM	POST. REF.	DEBIT	CREDIT	BALANCE DEBIT	BALANCE CREDIT
20-- Dec.	31	Balance	✔				5 0 00

ACCOUNT United Way Donations Payable   ACCOUNT NO. 2170

DATE		ITEM	POST. REF.	DEBIT	CREDIT	BALANCE DEBIT	BALANCE CREDIT
20-- Dec.	31	Balance	✔				6 0 00

ACCOUNT Dividends Payable   ACCOUNT NO. 2180

DATE		ITEM	POST. REF.	DEBIT	CREDIT	BALANCE	
						DEBIT	CREDIT
20-- Dec.	31	Balance	✔				5 0 0 0 00

ACCOUNT Capital Stock   ACCOUNT NO. 3110

DATE		ITEM	POST. REF.	DEBIT	CREDIT	BALANCE	
						DEBIT	CREDIT
20-- Dec.	31	Balance	✔				125 0 0 0 00

ACCOUNT Retained Earnings   ACCOUNT NO. 3120

DATE		ITEM	POST. REF.	DEBIT	CREDIT	BALANCE	
						DEBIT	CREDIT
20-- Dec.	1	Balance	✔				136 8 4 3 68

ACCOUNT Dividends   ACCOUNT NO. 3130

DATE		ITEM	POST. REF.	DEBIT	CREDIT	BALANCE	
						DEBIT	CREDIT
20-- Dec.	31	Balance	✔			20 0 0 0 00	

ACCOUNT Income Summary   ACCOUNT NO. 3140

DATE	ITEM	POST. REF.	DEBIT	CREDIT	BALANCE	
					DEBIT	CREDIT

16-4 APPLICATION PROBLEM (continued)

ACCOUNT Sales   ACCOUNT NO. 4110

DATE		ITEM	POST. REF.	DEBIT	CREDIT	BALANCE	
						DEBIT	CREDIT
20-- Dec.	31	Balance	✔				724 18 3 99

ACCOUNT Sales Discount   ACCOUNT NO. 4120

DATE		ITEM	POST. REF.	DEBIT	CREDIT	BALANCE	
						DEBIT	CREDIT
20-- Dec.	31	Balance	✔			1 6 9 4 48	

ACCOUNT Sales Returns and Allowances   ACCOUNT NO. 4130

DATE		ITEM	POST. REF.	DEBIT	CREDIT	BALANCE	
						DEBIT	CREDIT
20-- Dec.	31	Balance	✔			4 1 8 9 64	

ACCOUNT Purchases   ACCOUNT NO. 5110

DATE		ITEM	POST. REF.	DEBIT	CREDIT	BALANCE	
						DEBIT	CREDIT
20-- Dec.	31	Balance	✔			331 80 5 18	

ACCOUNT Purchases Discount   ACCOUNT NO. 5120

DATE		ITEM	POST. REF.	DEBIT	CREDIT	BALANCE	
						DEBIT	CREDIT
20-- Dec.	31	Balance	✔				3 4 1 8 47

ACCOUNT Purch. Returns and Allowances   ACCOUNT NO. 5130

DATE	ITEM	POST. REF.	DEBIT	CREDIT	BALANCE DEBIT	BALANCE CREDIT
20-- Dec. 31	Balance	✔				4 6 8 4 69

ACCOUNT Advertising Expense   ACCOUNT NO. 6105

DATE	ITEM	POST. REF.	DEBIT	CREDIT	BALANCE DEBIT	BALANCE CREDIT
20-- Dec. 31	Balance	✔			14 5 1 8 00	

ACCOUNT Cash Short and Over   ACCOUNT NO. 6110

DATE	ITEM	POST. REF.	DEBIT	CREDIT	BALANCE DEBIT	BALANCE CREDIT
20-- Dec. 31	Balance	✔			4 60	

ACCOUNT Credit Card Fee Expense   ACCOUNT NO. 6115

DATE	ITEM	POST. REF.	DEBIT	CREDIT	BALANCE DEBIT	BALANCE CREDIT
20-- Dec. 31	Balance	✔			12 1 8 0 00	

ACCOUNT Depr. Exp. —Office Equipment   ACCOUNT NO. 6120

DATE	ITEM	POST. REF.	DEBIT	CREDIT	BALANCE DEBIT	BALANCE CREDIT

ACCOUNT Depr. Exp. —Store Equipment   ACCOUNT NO. 6125

DATE	ITEM	POST. REF.	DEBIT	CREDIT	BALANCE DEBIT	BALANCE CREDIT

16-4 APPLICATION PROBLEM (continued)

ACCOUNT Insurance Expense   ACCOUNT NO. 6130

DATE		ITEM	POST. REF.	DEBIT	CREDIT	BALANCE DEBIT	BALANCE CREDIT

ACCOUNT Miscellaneous Expense   ACCOUNT NO. 6135

DATE		ITEM	POST. REF.	DEBIT	CREDIT	BALANCE DEBIT	BALANCE CREDIT
20-- Dec.	31	Balance	✔			6 4 8 1 00	

ACCOUNT Payroll Taxes Expense   ACCOUNT NO. 6140

DATE		ITEM	POST. REF.	DEBIT	CREDIT	BALANCE DEBIT	BALANCE CREDIT
20-- Dec.	31	Balance	✔			14 1 8 4 60	

ACCOUNT Rent Expense   ACCOUNT NO. 6145

DATE		ITEM	POST. REF.	DEBIT	CREDIT	BALANCE DEBIT	BALANCE CREDIT
20-- Dec.	31	Balance	✔			20 1 5 0 00	

ACCOUNT Salary Expense   ACCOUNT NO. 6150

DATE		ITEM	POST. REF.	DEBIT	CREDIT	BALANCE DEBIT	BALANCE CREDIT
20-- Dec.	31	Balance	✔			168 4 8 3 60	

ACCOUNT Supplies Expense—Office   ACCOUNT NO. 6155

DATE		ITEM	POST. REF.	DEBIT	CREDIT	BALANCE DEBIT	BALANCE CREDIT

ACCOUNT Supplies Expense—Store · · · · · · · · · · · · ACCOUNT NO. 6160

DATE	ITEM	POST. REF.	DEBIT	CREDIT	BALANCE DEBIT	BALANCE CREDIT

ACCOUNT Uncollectible Accounts Expense · · · · · · · · · · · · ACCOUNT NO. 6165

DATE	ITEM	POST. REF.	DEBIT	CREDIT	BALANCE DEBIT	BALANCE CREDIT

ACCOUNT Utilities Expense · · · · · · · · · · · · ACCOUNT NO. 6170

DATE	ITEM	POST. REF.	DEBIT	CREDIT	BALANCE DEBIT	BALANCE CREDIT
20-- Dec. 31	Balance	✔			5 4 8 4 97	

ACCOUNT Federal Income Tax Expense · · · · · · · · · · · · ACCOUNT NO. 7105

DATE	ITEM	POST. REF.	DEBIT	CREDIT	BALANCE DEBIT	BALANCE CREDIT
20-- Dec. 31	Balance	✔			30 0 0 0 00	

16-4 **APPLICATION PROBLEM (concluded)**

5.

ACCOUNT TITLE	DEBIT	CREDIT

Journalizing and posting adjusting and closing entries; preparing a post-closing trial balance

1., 2.

	GENERAL JOURNAL					PAGE 18

	DATE	ACCOUNT TITLE	DOC. NO.	POST. REF.	DEBIT	CREDIT	
1							1
2							2
3							3
4							4
5							5
6							6
7							7
8							8
9							9
10							10
11							11
12							12
13							13
14							14
15							15
16							16
17							17
18							18
19							19
20							20
21							21
22							22
23							23
24							24
25							25
26							26
27							27
28							28
29							29
30							30
31							31

16-5 **MASTERY PROBLEM (continued)**

3., 4.

GENERAL JOURNAL PAGE 19

	DATE	ACCOUNT TITLE	DOC. NO.	POST. REF.	DEBIT	CREDIT	
1							1
2							2
3							3
4							4
5							5
6							6
7							7
8							8
9							9
10							10
11							11
12							12
13							13
14							14
15							15
16							16
17							17
18							18
19							19
20							20
21							21
22							22
23							23
24							24
25							25
26							26
27							27
28							28
29							29
30							30
31							31
32							32
33							33

2., 4.
GENERAL LEDGER

ACCOUNT Cash   ACCOUNT NO. 1110

DATE		ITEM	POST. REF.	DEBIT	CREDIT	BALANCE	
						DEBIT	CREDIT
20-- Dec.	31	Balance	✔			5 1 2 4 12	

ACCOUNT Petty Cash   ACCOUNT NO. 1120

DATE		ITEM	POST. REF.	DEBIT	CREDIT	BALANCE	
						DEBIT	CREDIT
20-- Dec.	31	Balance	✔			2 5 0 00	

ACCOUNT Accounts Receivable   ACCOUNT NO. 1130

DATE		ITEM	POST. REF.	DEBIT	CREDIT	BALANCE	
						DEBIT	CREDIT
20-- Dec.	31	Balance	✔			14 8 4 3 30	

ACCOUNT Allow. for Uncoll. Accts.   ACCOUNT NO. 1135

DATE		ITEM	POST. REF.	DEBIT	CREDIT	BALANCE	
						DEBIT	CREDIT
20-- Dec.	31	Balance	✔				1 2 4 55

ACCOUNT Merchandise Inventory   ACCOUNT NO. 1140

DATE		ITEM	POST. REF.	DEBIT	CREDIT	BALANCE	
						DEBIT	CREDIT
20-- Dec.	31	Balance	✔			154 3 1 8 22	

16-5 MASTERY PROBLEM (continued)

ACCOUNT Supplies—Office   ACCOUNT NO. 1145

DATE		ITEM	POST. REF.	DEBIT	CREDIT	BALANCE DEBIT	BALANCE CREDIT
20-- Dec.	31	Balance	✔			3 4 1 5 58	

ACCOUNT Supplies—Store   ACCOUNT NO. 1150

DATE		ITEM	POST. REF.	DEBIT	CREDIT	BALANCE DEBIT	BALANCE CREDIT
20-- Dec.	31	Balance	✔			6 1 8 4 56	

ACCOUNT Prepaid Insurance   ACCOUNT NO. 1160

DATE		ITEM	POST. REF.	DEBIT	CREDIT	BALANCE DEBIT	BALANCE CREDIT
20-- Dec.	31	Balance	✔			7 0 0 0 00	

ACCOUNT Office Equipment   ACCOUNT NO. 1205

DATE		ITEM	POST. REF.	DEBIT	CREDIT	BALANCE DEBIT	BALANCE CREDIT
20-- Dec.	31	Balance	✔			21 4 8 2 66	

ACCOUNT Acc. Depr. —Office Equipment   ACCOUNT NO. 1210

DATE		ITEM	POST. REF.	DEBIT	CREDIT	BALANCE DEBIT	BALANCE CREDIT
20-- Dec.	31	Balance	✔				6 4 8 0 00

ACCOUNT Store Equipment   ACCOUNT NO. 1215

DATE		ITEM	POST. REF.	DEBIT	CREDIT	BALANCE DEBIT	BALANCE CREDIT
20-- Dec.	31	Balance	✔			40 4 8 1 66	

ACCOUNT Acc. Depr. —Store Equipment   ACCOUNT NO. 1220

DATE	ITEM	POST. REF.	DEBIT	CREDIT	BALANCE DEBIT	BALANCE CREDIT
20-- Dec. 31	Balance	✔				18 4 8 0 00

ACCOUNT Accounts Payable   ACCOUNT NO. 2110

DATE	ITEM	POST. REF.	DEBIT	CREDIT	BALANCE DEBIT	BALANCE CREDIT
20-- Dec. 31	Balance	✔				8 4 1 8 36

ACCOUNT Federal Income Tax Payable   ACCOUNT NO. 2120

DATE	ITEM	POST. REF.	DEBIT	CREDIT	BALANCE DEBIT	BALANCE CREDIT

ACCOUNT Employee Income Tax Payable   ACCOUNT NO. 2130

DATE	ITEM	POST. REF.	DEBIT	CREDIT	BALANCE DEBIT	BALANCE CREDIT
20-- Dec. 31	Balance	✔				4 5 8 00

ACCOUNT Social Security Tax Payable   ACCOUNT NO. 2135

DATE	ITEM	POST. REF.	DEBIT	CREDIT	BALANCE DEBIT	BALANCE CREDIT
20-- Dec. 31	Balance	✔				5 2 8 24

ACCOUNT Medicare Tax Payable   ACCOUNT NO. 2140

DATE	ITEM	POST. REF.	DEBIT	CREDIT	BALANCE DEBIT	BALANCE CREDIT
20-- Dec. 31	Balance	✔				1 2 3 54

16-5 MASTERY PROBLEM (continued)

ACCOUNT Sales Tax Payable   ACCOUNT NO. 2145

DATE		ITEM	POST. REF.	DEBIT	CREDIT	BALANCE DEBIT	BALANCE CREDIT
20-- Dec.	31	Balance	✔				1 4 1 5 30

ACCOUNT Unemployment Tax Payable—Federal   ACCOUNT NO. 2150

DATE		ITEM	POST. REF.	DEBIT	CREDIT	BALANCE DEBIT	BALANCE CREDIT
20-- Dec.	31	Balance	✔				4 00

ACCOUNT Unemployment Tax Payable—State   ACCOUNT NO. 2155

DATE		ITEM	POST. REF.	DEBIT	CREDIT	BALANCE DEBIT	BALANCE CREDIT
20-- Dec.	31	Balance	✔				2 7 00

ACCOUNT Health Insurance Premiums Payable   ACCOUNT NO. 2160

DATE		ITEM	POST. REF.	DEBIT	CREDIT	BALANCE DEBIT	BALANCE CREDIT
20-- Dec.	31	Balance	✔				2 5 0 00

ACCOUNT U.S. Savings Bonds Payable   ACCOUNT NO. 2165

DATE		ITEM	POST. REF.	DEBIT	CREDIT	BALANCE DEBIT	BALANCE CREDIT
20-- Dec.	31	Balance	✔				4 0 00

ACCOUNT United Way Donations Payable   ACCOUNT NO. 2170

DATE		ITEM	POST. REF.	DEBIT	CREDIT	BALANCE DEBIT	BALANCE CREDIT
20-- Dec.	31	Balance	✔				6 0 00

ACCOUNT Dividends Payable   ACCOUNT NO. 2180

DATE		ITEM	POST. REF.	DEBIT	CREDIT	BALANCE	
						DEBIT	CREDIT
20-- Dec.	31	Balance	✔				4 0 0 0 00

ACCOUNT Capital Stock   ACCOUNT NO. 3110

DATE		ITEM	POST. REF.	DEBIT	CREDIT	BALANCE	
						DEBIT	CREDIT
20-- Dec.	31	Balance	✔				80 0 0 0 00

ACCOUNT Retained Earnings   ACCOUNT NO. 3120

DATE		ITEM	POST. REF.	DEBIT	CREDIT	BALANCE	
						DEBIT	CREDIT
20-- Dec.	31	Balance	✔				89 7 6 1 21

ACCOUNT Dividends   ACCOUNT NO. 3130

DATE		ITEM	POST. REF.	DEBIT	CREDIT	BALANCE	
						DEBIT	CREDIT
20-- Dec.	31	Balance	✔			16 0 0 0 00	

ACCOUNT Income Summary   ACCOUNT NO. 3140

DATE		ITEM	POST. REF.	DEBIT	CREDIT	BALANCE	
						DEBIT	CREDIT

ACCOUNT Sales   ACCOUNT NO. 4110

DATE		ITEM	POST. REF.	DEBIT	CREDIT	BALANCE	
						DEBIT	CREDIT
20-- Dec.	31	Balance	✔				514 8 15 35

ACCOUNT Sales Discount   ACCOUNT NO. 4120

DATE		ITEM	POST. REF.	DEBIT	CREDIT	BALANCE	
						DEBIT	CREDIT
20-- Dec.	31	Balance	✔			2 15 4 94	

ACCOUNT Sales Returns and Allowances   ACCOUNT NO. 4130

DATE		ITEM	POST. REF.	DEBIT	CREDIT	BALANCE	
						DEBIT	CREDIT
20-- Dec.	31	Balance	✔			6 18 4 74	

ACCOUNT Purchases   ACCOUNT NO. 5110

DATE		ITEM	POST. REF.	DEBIT	CREDIT	BALANCE	
						DEBIT	CREDIT
20-- Dec.	31	Balance	✔			301 5 48 60	

ACCOUNT Purchases Discount   ACCOUNT NO. 5120

DATE		ITEM	POST. REF.	DEBIT	CREDIT	BALANCE	
						DEBIT	CREDIT
20-- Dec.	31	Balance	✔				2 15 4 65

ACCOUNT Purch. Returns and Allowances   ACCOUNT NO. 5130

DATE	ITEM	POST. REF.	DEBIT	CREDIT	BALANCE DEBIT	BALANCE CREDIT
20-- Dec. 31	Balance	✔				2 8 8 9 41

ACCOUNT Advertising Expense   ACCOUNT NO. 6105

DATE	ITEM	POST. REF.	DEBIT	CREDIT	BALANCE DEBIT	BALANCE CREDIT
20-- Dec. 31	Balance	✔			2 4 9 1 95	

ACCOUNT Cash Short and Over   ACCOUNT NO. 6110

DATE	ITEM	POST. REF.	DEBIT	CREDIT	BALANCE DEBIT	BALANCE CREDIT
20-- Dec. 31	Balance	✔			5 25	

ACCOUNT Credit Card Fee Expense   ACCOUNT NO. 6115

DATE	ITEM	POST. REF.	DEBIT	CREDIT	BALANCE DEBIT	BALANCE CREDIT
20-- Dec. 31	Balance	✔			8 1 5 4 62	

ACCOUNT Depr. Exp. —Office Equipment   ACCOUNT NO. 6120

DATE	ITEM	POST. REF.	DEBIT	CREDIT	BALANCE DEBIT	BALANCE CREDIT

ACCOUNT Depr. Exp. —Store Equipment   ACCOUNT NO. 6125

DATE	ITEM	POST. REF.	DEBIT	CREDIT	BALANCE DEBIT	BALANCE CREDIT

16-5 MASTERY PROBLEM (continued)

ACCOUNT Insurance Expense   ACCOUNT NO. 6130

DATE	ITEM	POST. REF.	DEBIT	CREDIT	BALANCE DEBIT	BALANCE CREDIT

ACCOUNT Miscellaneous Expense   ACCOUNT NO. 6135

DATE	ITEM	POST. REF.	DEBIT	CREDIT	BALANCE DEBIT	BALANCE CREDIT
20-- Dec. 31	Balance	✔			4 1 0 00	

ACCOUNT Payroll Taxes Expense   ACCOUNT NO. 6140

DATE	ITEM	POST. REF.	DEBIT	CREDIT	BALANCE DEBIT	BALANCE CREDIT
20-- Dec. 31	Balance	✔			14 1 8 4 60	

ACCOUNT Rent Expense   ACCOUNT NO. 6145

DATE	ITEM	POST. REF.	DEBIT	CREDIT	BALANCE DEBIT	BALANCE CREDIT
20-- Dec. 31	Balance	✔			15 4 0 0 00	

ACCOUNT Salary Expense   ACCOUNT NO. 6150

DATE	ITEM	POST. REF.	DEBIT	CREDIT	BALANCE DEBIT	BALANCE CREDIT
20-- Dec. 31	Balance	✔			102 2 4 0 30	

ACCOUNT Supplies Expense—Office   ACCOUNT NO. 6155

DATE	ITEM	POST. REF.	DEBIT	CREDIT	BALANCE DEBIT	BALANCE CREDIT

ACCOUNT Supplies Expense—Store   ACCOUNT NO. 6160

DATE	ITEM	POST. REF.	DEBIT	CREDIT	BALANCE DEBIT	BALANCE CREDIT

ACCOUNT Uncollectible Accounts Expense   ACCOUNT NO. 6165

DATE	ITEM	POST. REF.	DEBIT	CREDIT	BALANCE DEBIT	BALANCE CREDIT

ACCOUNT Utilities Expense   ACCOUNT NO. 6170

DATE	ITEM	POST. REF.	DEBIT	CREDIT	BALANCE DEBIT	BALANCE CREDIT
Dec. 31	Balance	✔			4 15 4 51	

ACCOUNT Federal Income Tax Expense   ACCOUNT NO. 7105

DATE	ITEM	POST. REF.	DEBIT	CREDIT	BALANCE DEBIT	BALANCE CREDIT
Dec. 31	Balance	✔			4 00 0 00	

16-5 **MASTERY PROBLEM (concluded)**

5.

ACCOUNT TITLE	DEBIT	CREDIT

16-6 CHALLENGE PROBLEM, p. 504

Inventory auditing challenges

1. Grain in a grain elevator:

2. Lumber in a lumber yard:

3. Diamond rings in a jewelry store:

4. Nails in a home improvement store:

An accounting cycle for a corporation: end-of-fiscal-period work

12., 13., 14.

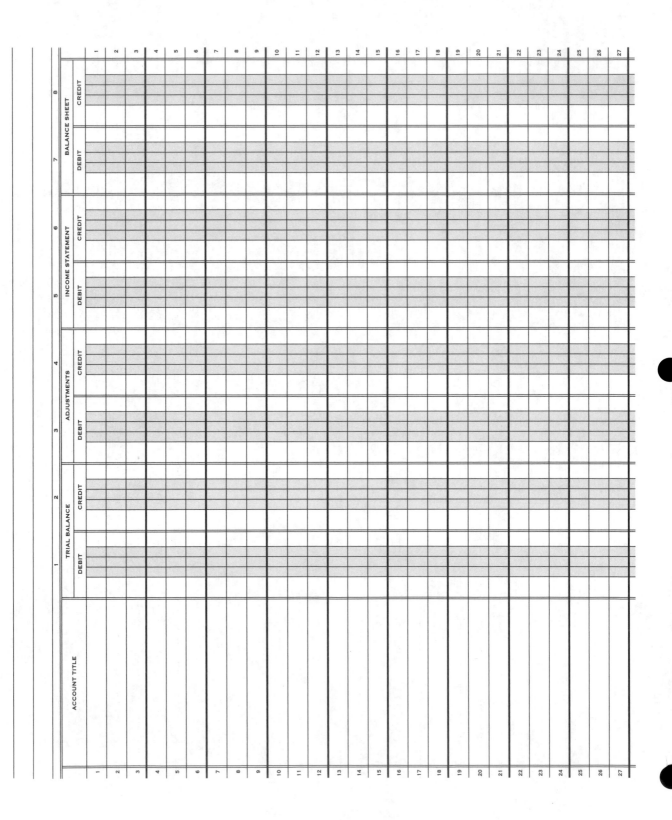

REINFORCEMENT ACTIVITY 2

PART B (continued)

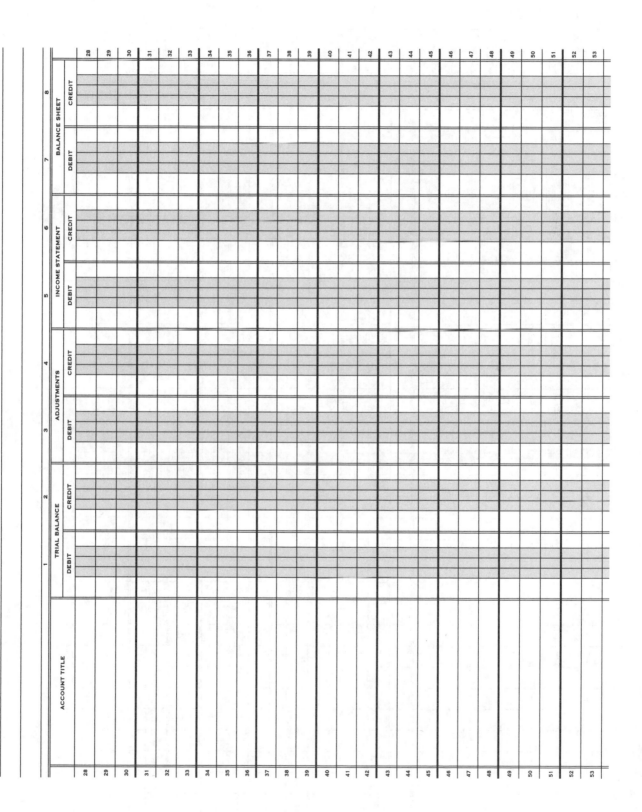

15.

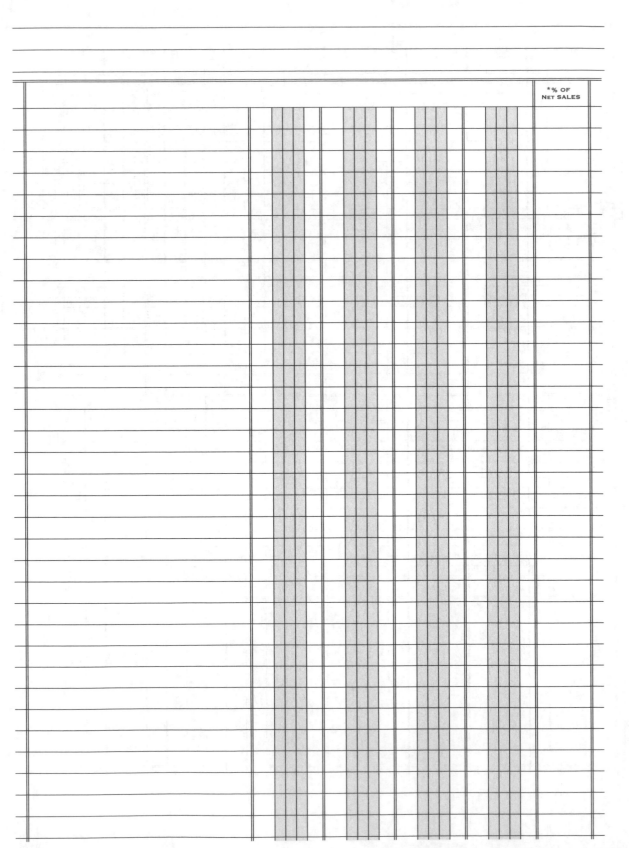

REINFORCEMENT ACTIVITY 2

PART B (continued)

16.

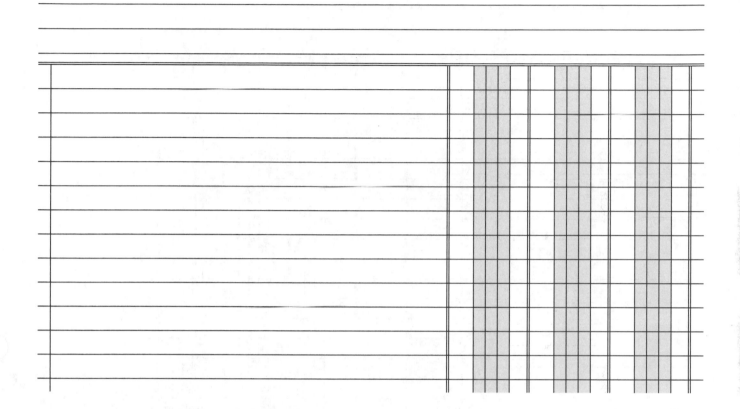

17.

REINFORCEMENT ACTIVITY 2

PART B (continued)

18.

Earnings per share:

Price-earnings ratio:

19.

GENERAL JOURNAL PAGE 13

	DATE	ACCOUNT TITLE	DOC. NO.	POST. REF.	DEBIT	CREDIT	
1							1
2							2
3							3
4							4
5							5
6							6
7							7
8							8
9							9
10							10
11							11
12							12
13							13
14							14
15							15
16							16
17							17

REINFORCEMENT ACTIVITY 2

PART B (continued)

20.

<table>
<tr><td colspan="2" align="center">GENERAL JOURNAL</td><td align="right">PAGE 14</td></tr>
</table>

	DATE	ACCOUNT TITLE	DOC. NO.	POST. REF.	DEBIT	CREDIT	
1							1
2							2
3							3
4							4
5							5
6							6
7							7
8							8
9							9
10							10
11							11
12							12
13							13
14							14
15							15
16							16
17							17
18							18
19							19
20							20
21							21
22							22
23							23
24							24
25							25
26							26
27							27
28							28
29							29
30							30
31							31
32							32

REINFORCEMENT ACTIVITY 2

PART B (continued)

21.

ACCOUNT TITLE	DEBIT	CREDIT

VOLUME 1
Student Activities Manual

Megan Echevarría
University of Rhode Island

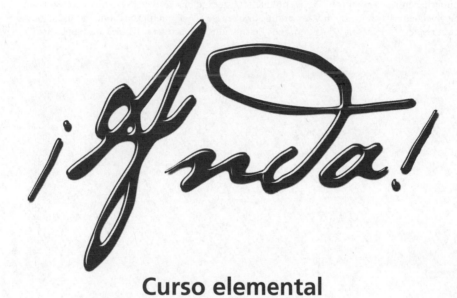

Curso elemental

SECOND EDITION

Audrey L. Heining-Boynton
Glynis S. Cowell
The University of North Carolina at Chapel Hill

PEARSON

Boston   Columbus   Indianapolis   New York   San Francisco   Upper Saddle River
Amsterdam   Cape Town   Dubai   London   Madrid   Milan   Munich   Paris   Montréal   Toronto
Delhi   Mexico City   São Paulo   Sydney   Hong Kong   Seoul   Singapore   Taipei   Tokyo

...aldi

Development Editor, Elementary Spanish: Celia Meana
Development Editor, Spanish: Meriel Martínez
Senior Managing Editor for Product Development:
  Mary Rottino
Associate Managing Editor (Production): Janice Stangel
Senior Production Project Manager: Nancy Stevenson
Executive Editor, MyLanguageLabs: Bob Hemmer

Senior Media Editor: Samantha Alducin
Development Editor, MyLanguageLabs: Bill Bliss
Editorial Coordinator, World Languages: Regina Rivera
Senior Art Director: Maria Lange
Operations Manager: Mary Fischer
Operations Specialist: Alan Fischer
Full-Service Project Management: Melissa Sacco,
  PreMediaGlobal
Composition: PreMediaGlobal
Printer/Binder: Bind-Rite Graphics
Cover Printer: Bind-Rite Graphics
Publisher: Phil Miller

This book was set in 10/12 Janson Roman.

10 9 8 7 6 5 4 3 2 1

ISBN-10: 0-205-23978-1
ISBN-13: 978-0-205-23978-8